W9-BYY-876

THE

Dimensions

of

Engaged

Teaching

A
PRACTICAL
GUIDE *for*
EDUCATORS

Foreword by ARI GERZON-KESSLER

LAURA WEAVER & MARK WILDING

Solution Tree | Press

a division of

Solution Tree

Copyright © 2013 by Solution Tree Press

Materials appearing here are copyrighted. With one exception, all rights are reserved. Readers may reproduce only those pages marked "Reproducible." Otherwise, no part of this book may be reproduced or transmitted in any form or by any means (electronic, photocopying, recording, or otherwise) without prior written permission of the publisher.

555 North Morton Street
Bloomington, IN 47404

800.733.6786 (toll free) / 812.336.7700
FAX: 812.336.7790

email: info@solution-tree.com
solution-tree.com

Visit **go.solution-tree.com/instruction** to download the reproducibles in this book.

Printed in the United States of America

17 16 15 14 13   2 3 4 5

Library of Congress Cataloging-in-Publication Data

Weaver, Laura.
  The five dimensions of engaged teaching : a practical guide for educators / Laura Weaver and Mark Wilding.
       pages cm
  Includes bibliographical references and index.
     ISBN 978-1-936764-48-8 (perfect bound : alk. paper) 1. Teaching. 2. Effective teaching. 3. Teacher-student relationships. 4. Classroom environment. I. Title.
     LB1025.3.W388 2013
     371.102--dc23
                                      2013008439

Solution Tree
Jeffrey C. Jones, CEO
Edmund M. Ackerman, President

Solution Tree Press
President: Douglas M. Rife
Publisher: Robert D. Clouse
Editorial Director: Lesley Bolton
Managing Production Editor: Caroline Wise
Senior Production Editor: Suzanne Kraszewski
Proofreader: Elisabeth Abrams
Text and Cover Designers: Amy Shock and Jenn Taylor

Praise for *The 5 Dimensions of Engaged Teaching*

"It is time for us to recognize that any positive changes will come from us, not the greater system. This book provides a compelling road map for how we navigate the difficult terrain of this time, persevere, and create educational experiences that are meaningful to kids and to us as professionals. I am grateful for this map, and also delighted by the levels of joyful collaboration that gave rise to it."—Margaret J. Wheatley, Author

"This book is critical to the future of education because it honors teachers and their deep commitment to being fully engaged in their work. Every teacher in America can learn deeply from the wisdom of this resource to nurture their own development and that of their students."—Mark T. Greenberg, Bennett Chair of Prevention Research, Penn State University

"This book offers wisdom, inspiration, and practical strategies for being an effective and connected teacher. I wish every teacher would read this book, discuss it with his or her colleagues and loved ones, and then implement some of the powerful ideas and practices the authors share. The impact on students worldwide would be very positive."—Roger P. Weissberg, President and CEO, Collaborative for Academic, Social, and Emotional Learning

"We know from both science and practice that our children do better in school and in life when they have teachers who understand and care about them in a meaningful way. Laura Weaver and Mark Wilding show us how to become that kind of teacher. Newcomers and veterans alike will delight in seeing a pathway to a more fulfilling teaching practice and the skills to attain it."—Timothy P. Shriver, Chairman and CEO, Special Olympics, and Board Chair of Collaborative for Academic, Social, and Emotional Learning

"This essential book has the power to reform educational practice in a significant way. I can open to any two pages and find much to think about and much to try with students or with myself. It can—and should—redefine teaching."—Maurice J. Elias, Rutgers University, Co-developer of the *Social Decision Making/Social Problem Solving* curricula and Coauthor of *Talking Treasure*

"We often forget to pay attention to how emotional engagement drives the learning of students and adults alike. I witnessed firsthand the profound positive impact of such an approach on our teachers, school culture, and students' success. A must-read for anyone who is deeply committed to urban school reform."—Pat Sánchez , Superintendent, Adams County School District 14, Colorado

"This is the most comprehensive book yet to emerge from the mindfulness in social-emotional learning movement. It is a storehouse of personalized activities for supporting teachers and students to deepen learning."—Richard C. Brown, Founder of Naropa University's Contemplative Education Department, and Coauthor of the Garrison Institute's CARE for Teachers Program

"The wisdom and advice contained within this book are a must-have for any teacher genuinely interested in educating the whole student and creating the kind of classroom in which all of us would like to be students." —Scott Troy, Science Teacher, Westminster High School, Colorado

"This book is a thoughtful, comprehensive, and user-friendly guide for all educators. In secular and approachable terms, Weaver and Wilding underscore the core competencies of the Engaged Teaching Approach with clear sequence and practicality. Rare is the text that speaks with equal candor and kindness to the lives of both teachers and students, and rarer still is the text that does so with practicality and purpose. The 5 Dimensions of Engaged Teaching is such a text, and I look forward to using it with my preservice teachers." —David Lee Keiser, Associate Professor, Montclair State University, New Jersey, and Facilitator, CARE for Teachers Program

"The 5 Dimensions of Engaged Teaching is a treasure trove of valuable information and practical tools for supporting teachers' joy and commitment to teaching. It is unique in that it addresses important foundational capacities such as presence, self-observation, and social and emotional competencies that have been long overlooked in teacher preparation and professional development. This book is a must-have for teachers!" —Patricia A. Jennings, Research Assistant Professor, Department of Human Development and Family Studies, Penn State University

"What is so special about this book is that it not only draws attention to, and provides suggestions for how educators can develop these universal human qualities, but it also proposes ways that educators might bring them into the classroom in the service of culturally responsive teaching—those classroom teaching practices that celebrate diversity and equity, eschew discrimination, and recognize our shared humanity simultaneously." —Robert W. Roeser, Professor of Psychology and Human Development, Portland State University

"This book provides venerable and vital ideas and practices that will offer a North Star for educators on their own journey to identity, purpose, and authenticity. Herein is a guide to becoming a reflective, mindful, and emotionally intelligent mentor." —Len Fleischer, Professor of Education, Keene State College, New Hampshire

"This remarkable collaborative effort offers a potentially healing blend of five remedies that could bring American education back to life. From preventing school violence to promoting sustainable academic excellence, this book is an elixir that truly nourishes the soul of education." — Mark Gerzon, Author of Leading Through Conflict and Global Citizens

"The 5 Dimensions of Engaged Teaching offers a wealth of wisdom that articulates sensible and applicable practices of social, emotional, and academic learning. With the increased demands in the educational arena, it is refreshing, inviting, and exciting to have a resource that supports a nurturing and meaningful culture for the learner and educator." —Sam Jilka, Teacher, Lexington High School, Nebraska

"The authors have offered a clear guide that will enrich the effectiveness of teachers and the experience of students at all levels of development. Highly recommended!" —Jack Zimmerman and Virginia Coyle, Educators and Trainers, Center for Council Practice, The Ojai Foundation, and Authors of The Way of Council

"Relationship is the foundation on which emotional intelligence and healthy brain architecture are built. It is also the field in which both humanity and creativity flower. These are the innate gifts that the practical wisdom in this fine book nurture in our children and our teachers." —Joan Borysenko, Author of Minding the Body, Mending the Mind

We dedicate this book to the educators who work every day to support the learning, growth, and development of their students.

We also dedicate this book to Rachael Kessler (1946–2010) and Mary Utne O'Brien (1952–2010), who devoted their lives to empowering and supporting teachers and students, and to creating meaningful and engaging classrooms.

Acknowledgments

This book is the result of rich collaboration with many brilliant educators, field experts, advisors, and editors. We would not have been able to develop and offer this book without the support and input of this wide circle of partners. We offer our deepest gratitude to all who participated in this project. In particular, we'd like to thank the writing and development team, our focus group participants, our reviewers, our publisher Robb Clouse, our editor Sue Kraszewski, and the whole Solution Tree team. We also honor the life and contributions of Barbara Cushing (1947–2012) from the Kalliopeia foundation, and give thanks for the many ways she touched our hearts and supported this work.

We also extend our gratitude to the following individuals and organizations:

To Maurice Elias for his support of this book and wise guidance along the way. To Roger Weissberg, Mark Greenberg, Linda Lantieri, and the Collaborative for Academic, Social, and Emotional Learning (CASEL) team for their encouragement and assistance.

To Mark Gerzon for his generous counsel and friendship. To Tish Jennings, Laura Simms, Rob Roeser, and Shelley Zion for brilliant written contributions, many important conversations, and ongoing input. To Richard Brown, Susan Skjei, Anne Parker, and Naropa University for many years of ongoing collegial support and encouragement. To Parker Palmer, Pamela Seigle, Terry Chadsey, Margaret Golden, and Dan Liston for many years of collaboration and for their wisdom, skill, and devotion in support of the inner and outer lives of educators. To Jack Zimmerman, Gigi Coyle, and Joe Provisor and the Ojai Foundation's Council in Schools Initiative. To Karen Wilding for her incredible patience, generosity, and keen editorial eye.

To PassageWorks faculty members and facilitators John McCluskey, Batya Greenwald, Ari Gerzon-Kessler, Cathy Fink, Carrie Simpson, Dana Knox, Ron Lamb, Chuck Fisher, and Francisco Garcia-Quezada for all the ways they have brought this work into the world with authenticity, creativity, and heart and for their devotion to transforming the field of education. To Jim Marsden for his presence and skillful guidance. To George Lopez for supporting every aspect of this project with attention to detail, humor, and good dark chocolate. To Dayna Schueth and Ben Levi for web and systems support.

To Helene and Robert Hanson of NPR for their belief in this book and for their generous offer of experience and help. To Kim Schonert-Reichl, Adele Diamond, David Rome, Arthur Zajonc, Tobin Hart, Jerry Murphy, Peggy McCardle, Liz Robertson, Robin Stern, Laura Rendon, Christa Turksma, Trish Broderick, Susan Fountain, and Adi

Fleischer, Diana and Jonathan Rose, and the Garrison Institute team for their encouragement and many inspiring and provocative dialogues about contemplative teaching and learning. To Michael Fullan and Peter Senge for their vision and assistance.

To Aaron Claman, Tova Jacober, Judy and Jim Warner, Randy Compton, Julie Dolin, Brad Armstrong, John Esterle, John Steiner, Mary Willis, Margaret Thompson, Elizabeth Weinstein, Pamela and Marty Krasney, Lynnaea Lumbard, Mark and Terry Retzloff, Michael and Michelle Osterman, Martha Records, Mark Carson, Jenny and Robert Charthoff, and Ulco Visser for supporting the evolution of this work over the last decade.

To Fred Bay for his steadfast loyalty and inspiring dedication to supporting educators. To the profoundly wise and compassionate team at Kalliopeia foundation—Barbara Sargent, Barbara Cushing, Alan Zulch, and Cynthia Loebig—we would not have been able to bring this book to the world without their support and belief in the importance of this work. To Ron Miller for his suggestions and early encouragement. To Tom Callanan for a magical meeting about the movement in education and for his unwavering support and kindness. To Scott Kriens, and Dinabandhu and Ila Sarley of 1440 Foundation for their critical analysis and guidance. To Whitman Institute, New Visions, Bay and Paul, Compton, Israel, Trio, Pajwell, and the many family foundations and individuals who supported this project.

To Angeles Arrien for a catalytic meeting at the beginning of the project and her heartfelt endorsement. To Gordon Dveirin and Joan Borsenko for their wisdom and insights about the writing and publishing journey. To Melissa Michaels and Tom Hast for their support and friendship.

To Pat Sanchez, Andra Brill, Barb Catbagan, Stevan Kalmon, Diana Bamford, Scott Troy, Sam Jilka, Jenelle Peterson, Derek Peterson, Trish Alley, Len Fleischer, Donna Turnbo-Smith, Mellisa Heath, Margaret Dodd, Sabine Smead, Scott Bain, Sara Hiris, Lorri Acott-Fowler, Bob Kenny, Jeff Weissglass, Chris Foster, Karla Reiss, Scott Nine, and Charles Elbot for your stories, thoughtful comments, and feedback along the way.

To PassageWorks board members—David Brand, Lyn Ciocca, Gordon Dveirin, John Lainson, KJ McCorry, Rona Wilensky, Ari Gerzon-Kessler, and Erica Shafroth—for their countless hours of service and for their guidance, good questions, and devotion to the project.

To all the teachers, administrators, and schools who have creatively and courageously integrated the principles and practices of this book into their professional practice and brought their own unique contributions to this approach.

To all the young people in classrooms across the nation whose brilliance, dreams, hopes, questions, laughter, and creativity remind us every day why we do what we do and how essential it is to offer meaningful and engaging educational approaches.

So many people have contributed to this book. It was not possible to list every name here. Please visit engagedteaching.org for a more complete list.

Solution Tree Press would like to thank the following reviewers:

McKinley Broome
Fourth-Grade Teacher
Woodholme Elementary School
Pikesville, Maryland

Morgan Cuthbert
Seventh-Grade Teacher
Milken Award Winner
Frank Harrison Middle School
Yarmouth, Maine

Maurice J. Elias
Professor of Psychology and Internship
    Coordinator
Director of Clinical Training
    PhD Program in Psychology
Rutgers University
Piscataway, New Jersey

H. Lynn Erickson
International Consultant on Concept-
    Based Curriculum and Instruction
National Writer, Author, and Presenter
    on Curriculum and Instruction
Mill Creek, Washington

Michael Fullan
Professor Emeritus
Ontario Institute for Studies in
    Education of the University of
    Toronto
Toronto, Ontario, Canada

Greg Lineweaver, NBCT
Assistant Head of School
Dean of Faculty
Herron High School
Indianapolis, Indiana

Ryan Mahoney
Social Studies Teacher
Lincoln Southwest High School
Lincoln, Nebraska

Richard Mayer
Professor of Psychology
University of California, Santa Barbara

Visit **go.solution-tree.com/instruction** to download the reproducibles in this book.

Table of Contents

Reproducible pages are in italics.

About the Authors

Laura Weaver, MA, is the coexecutive director of the PassageWorks Institute, an educational nonprofit providing innovative principles and practices that support educators in developing a reflective and authentic teaching approach; integrating social, emotional, and academic learning into classrooms; and building meaningful and effective learning communities and school cultures. PassageWorks offers courses, onsite professional development, curricula for the transitions years, and a variety of publications. Additionally, PassageWorks collaborates with educators and organizations across the United States on field-building initiatives and programs. The PassageWorks Institute was founded in 2001 by author and educator Rachael Kessler (1946–2010) and her colleagues after Kessler published the groundbreaking book *The Soul of Education: Helping Students Find Connection, Compassion, and Character at School* in 2000.

Laura joined the institute in 2003. In addition to her role as coexecutive director, she has served as a lead faculty member, taught courses and workshops, offered presentations at schools and conferences, led all-faculty professional development, consulted with school leadership, developed resources for educators and parents, and facilitated transitions programs for young people. She is the coauthor (with Rachael Kessler) of two PassageWorks curricula for the transitions years: *Journey Into High School* (for incoming high school students) and *Newcomers' Passage* (for students who have recently immigrated to the United States) and the chapters "Six Passages of Childhood" from the book *Educating From the Heart* and "Nourishing the Souls of Students in Jewish Education" from the book *Growing Jewish Minds, Growing Jewish Souls*. She is also a primary editor and contributor to three other curricula: *First Steps* (for the kindergarten years), *Making Healthy Transitions Into Middle School*, and *Senior Passages*. Laura's articles, chapters, essays, and poems have been published in numerous journals, magazines, and books.

Before joining PassageWorks, Laura taught English and creative writing at the University of Colorado. She was also the cofounder and director of Bridges, a nonprofit dedicated to serving the needs of people living with hunger and poverty in the greater Philadelphia region. Laura earned her master's degree at the University of Colorado

Boulder and her bachelor's degree from Trinity College in Hartford, Connecticut. Laura lives in Colorado and is the parent of two young adults who inspire her every day.

You can Follow Laura on Facebook, www.facebook.com/engagedteaching.

Mark Wilding, MA, is the coexecutive director of PassageWorks Institute, a nonprofit organization that offers publications, curricula, and professional development for K–12 educators. Mark is also a member of the core faculty of PassageWorks and teaches courses and workshops, facilitates conferences and dialogues, and presents keynotes and lectures. Mark works closely with institute staff and faculty to create and deliver programs that support educators in developing their personal and professional capacities.

Mark has been teaching and facilitating professional development programs and graduate courses for over seventeen years. Before joining PassageWorks in 2008, Mark was a staff and faculty member of Naropa University, where he continues to teach graduate courses in leadership and systems thinking. Mark joined Naropa in 1994 and served as director of environmental studies and helped launch a new graduate degree program. Mark also served as director of advancement for the university and established and directed the human resources department. In 2001, Mark founded Naropa's professional development center for leadership and business, and served as its director until he left to become an executive director of PassageWorks. Before his tenure at Naropa, Mark helped found a public computer software company and served on its board and in several other roles until he left as president and CEO. Mark also served as vice president of the board of CORE, Colorado's Education Fund for Corporate Social Responsibility. He is currently a member of the national Leadership Council for Contemplative Teaching and Learning at the Garrison Institute. Mark earned a BS from Syracuse University and State University of New York (SUNY) and an MA in environmental leadership from Naropa University.

You can follow Mark on Twitter @mwilding and Google+ at gplus.to/Engaged Teaching.

To book Mark or Laura for professional development, contact pd@solution-tree.com.

The Writing and Development Team

This book contains the wisdom and experience of thousands of educators. The writing and development team includes K–12 teachers, assistant principals, principals, researchers, curriculum designers, and university faculty who have integrated the principles and practices of engaged teaching in their own learning communities. In writing and developing this book, the team drew upon our own action research and personal experiences, as well as the experiences of thousands of educators we have worked with in courses, professional development, interviews, focus groups, and research projects.

Vivian Elliott, PhD, is a senior consultant with Learning Forward and with ESSI Solutions, Inc. She provides professional development and leadership coaching to teachers, school administrators, and managers in organizations throughout the United States. Vivian earned her PhD at the University of Colorado Boulder, studying organizational change, equity, and leadership. For more than thirty years, she has conducted educational research, designed and facilitated workshops, and published educational writings to promote cultural responsiveness and bias elimination. Vivian is known in school districts, universities, and nonprofit organizations for skillful facilitation, excellent team leadership, and quality project management. She co-created the Colorado Coalition for Equity in Education, and served in leadership roles for the National Coalition for Equity in Education and the Colorado Partnership for Educational Renewal.

Catherine Fink is a Los Angeles–based educator and writer who has taught language arts and human development at three independent schools for grades 7 and 9–12 and at Los Angeles Community College. She also taught three PassageWorks transitions curricula in school advisory programs. Catherine was a student of a PassageWorks transitions program in Colorado in 1997, was a founding board member of the PassageWorks Institute in 2001, and has been a faculty member with the institute since its inception. She helped to revise and edit several PassageWorks curricula and coauthored a chapter on social and emotional learning in *Handbook of Moral and Character Education*. Her creative writing has been published in print and online.

Susan Keister is an author, speaker, workshop facilitator, and educational leader with more than thirty years of experience in leading the research, development, and training of international programs and professional development in comprehensive school reform, social and emotional learning, positive prevention of drug use and bullying, character development, conflict management, and service learning. As president of Integral Vision Consulting, Susan provides international consulting and professional development services to the Collaborative for Academic, Social, and Emotional Learning (CASEL), Lions Clubs International Foundation, and PassageWorks Institute.

Ari Gerzon-Kessler, MA, is the principal at Arapahoe Ridge Elementary School in Westminster, Colorado. Before his current position at Arapahoe Ridge, Ari served as an assistant principal at four other elementary schools. He has also taught third, fourth, and fifth grades, as well as high school Spanish, and worked as an educational consultant, journalist, and oral historian. In addition to completing extensive research on best practices in education within the United States (particularly in the area of social and emotional learning), Ari also traveled as a Fulbright recipient to visit schools in Japan and taught briefly in Mexico and Thailand. Ari is the author of two books, and his writings on education have been featured in a variety of publications.

Carrie Simpson has taught kindergarten and first grade at Friends' School in Boulder, Colorado, and Stanley British Primary School in Denver. Carrie has also taught adults in a variety of ways: mentoring intern teachers, presenting on child development and social and emotional topics, and facilitating PassageWorks courses. She co-authored, with Rachael Kessler, the PassageWorks kindergarten transitions curriculum and served as an editor on the fifth-grade transitions curriculum. Carrie is currently enjoying being at home as a new mom, while she continues to write and teach for PassageWorks.

Rona Wilensky is an educational consultant and social entrepreneur working in the areas of leadership development, contemplative teaching and learning, and the transformation of K–12 education toward an emphasis on relationships, relevance, and rigor. Rona is founder of New Vista High School in Boulder, Colorado, and was principal from 1992 to 2009. Prior to that, she worked as an education policy analyst for the governor of Colorado, the Education Commission of the States, and various education reform initiatives in Colorado. During the 2009–2010 academic year, Rona was a resident fellow at the Spencer Foundation in Chicago. A contributor to state and national conversations on high school reform, her essays have appeared in *Education Week*, the *Chronicle of Higher Education*, *Phi Delta Kappan*, and *Education News Colorado*. Rona is currently a board member of PassageWorks Institute and SOAR Charter School (Denver). She is also cochair of the Leadership Council for Contemplative Teaching and Learning at the Garrison Institute. Rona holds a BA and PhD in economics from Yale University.

Foreword

By Ari Gerzon-Kessler

I started my teaching career in 2001 at an elementary school in Colorado that was on state watch because it had the lowest test scores in the district. At the time, reading proficiency for third graders was a dismal 7 percent. During my early teaching years, I relied almost solely on my own experiences as a student and the classroom practices I had learned from my mother, Rachael Kessler (1946–2010). As the founder of the PassageWorks Institute and author of the groundbreaking book *The Soul of Education* (2000a), my mother collaborated with hundreds of educators and colleagues in the field of social and emotional learning to develop many of the elements of the Engaged Teaching Approach.

As I integrated engaged teaching practices in my classroom in that first year of teaching, I saw my bilingual students' rate of reading proficiency on the Colorado Student Assessment Program leap from 7 to 60 percent. In the second year, my third graders averaged more than two years of growth in their reading level. In my third year, on the state writing exam, 92 percent of my students were proficient compared to 9 percent in the other third-grade classrooms at my school, and 46 percent were advanced proficient compared to 10 percent statewide. I attribute much of this success to the inclusion of simple and effective social and emotional practices that deepened students' motivation and increased their joy of learning.

The principles and practices of the Engaged Teaching Approach were also part of my family and school life—I grew up with them. As a seventh-grade student, I was blessed with the opportunity to participate in a school-based transitions program that my mother initiated at my school. This once-a-week class embedded many aspects of the Engaged Teaching Approach presented in this book. Before beginning the program, I felt incredibly disconnected from my peers and lacked self-confidence. However, practices such as community circles, council, and focusing activities revealed the more substantive connections that linked me to my classmates and allowed me to honor the strengths and possibilities within me. In that class we had the opportunity to experience authentic community with peers, talk about the challenges we faced, explore what we looked for in friendships, and share what we wondered about and yearned for in our lives. This experience dramatically increased my motivation to learn and enhanced the quality of my relationships with peers, teachers, and my family.

Later, as a senior in high school, I longed to experience a true sense of community with my classmates and gain greater clarity about my future. At that point, much of my high school experience was characterized by shallow interactions and school work that lacked meaning or joy. As I participated in our year-long Senior Passages class, I discovered that when I risked authenticity, there were many rewards. This class helped me build strong relationships with others, gain confidence that I could succeed in future endeavors, and recognize gifts I was previously unaware of. These potent early experiences continue to inform my teaching practice and leadership approach today.

During my career, I have served as an elementary and high school teacher, assistant principal, and principal in eight diverse schools. Throughout this time, I have noticed consistent themes in education that colleagues across the United States are also witnessing in their schools. Whether serving impoverished communities or highly affluent ones, educators are experiencing an all-too-familiar litany of woes:

- We are caught in a web of systemic tensions that has driven teacher morale to an all-time low—including high-stakes testing, new evaluation systems, financially strapped school districts, and politically driven attacks on educators.

- No matter how hard we try to pace ourselves as educators to avoid burnout, many of us feel overextended and overwhelmed.

- Students are arriving in our classrooms with shorter attention spans and a host of distractions.

- Many students do not have the skills they need to successfully forge relationships, self-regulate, and successfully problem solve.

Looking at these trends, we see that there is a profound need to find or rediscover approaches that engage students and teachers in more effective ways.

In my teaching career, I have implemented many of the engaged teaching principles, practices, and frameworks in this book in my classrooms and schools. Here are the outcomes I have noticed:

- Student engagement increases dramatically.

- Teachers feel more empowered, effective, and able to reconnect to the original spark that drew them to education.

- Students and staff develop a deeper sense of trust and improved collaboration.

- Students and teachers experience a more engaging, meaningful, and inclusive classroom and school culture.

- Student learning becomes more joyful and personally relevant.

- Students thrive as their social and emotional intelligence grow.

- Academic achievement rises to new and often unprecedented levels.

In today's schools, educators have fewer resources, greater pressures, and more content to teach in less time. Although many of us believe in the importance of developing the whole child, we do not always know how or when to address our students' social and emotional development. *The 5 Dimensions of Engaged Teaching* makes a powerful case that it is possible and critical to integrate these different dimensions of learning and growth. The book is designed to support both our day-to-day teaching practice and nurture our teaching souls so that we can more effectively meet the diverse needs of our students.

The 5 Dimensions of Engaged Teaching draws on the experience of hundreds of educators and a strong research base. It makes a unique contribution by offering proven tools, compelling evidence, concrete tips, and inspiring stories that will help you renew your passion for teaching, cultivate your joy, and become a more effective educator. The approach of this book has transformed my experience as a teacher and school leader. I am confident that it will also enrich your work and impact your students profoundly.

Introduction

Teaching is at a crossroads: a crossroads at the top of the world. Never before have teachers, teaching, and the future of teaching had such elevated importance. There is widespread agreement now that of all the factors inside the school that affect children's learning and achievement, the most important is the teacher—not standards, assessments, resources, or even the school's leadership, but the quality of the teacher. Teachers really matter.

—Andy Hargreaves and Michael Fullan

When we think of what's right with education, we think of teachers. Since 2001, we have met and talked with thousands of educators and witnessed their dedication, creativity, courage, and intelligence firsthand. As we listened to their experiences, we heard time and time again that they are facing a very real dilemma: they have become overloaded and overwhelmed with new policies and standards, and it has become difficult to find the time and energy to engage in anything beyond what is absolutely required by schools or districts. In the current educational climate, where test scores serve as the primary indicator of student success and teacher quality, many teachers feel they have to teach to the test and give up some of the essential elements of teaching that positively impact learning. In this data-driven system, they see their students losing their capacity to focus and think creatively and critically. And, at times, they feel powerless to make a difference in the lives of the students they teach.

Many current educational paradigms separate social and emotional learning from academic learning, leading us to believe we must choose between these very important dimensions. However, recent discoveries about the nature of the brain and learning invite us to consider a different approach. Neuroscience, learning theory, and teaching experience all illustrate that the social and emotional dimensions of learning are not only inextricably linked to academic success, but are indeed its very foundation. In this way, even if all we cared about was raising test scores, we would need to address the social and emotional lives of our students. In fact, most teachers and educators *do* care about the multiple dimensions of learning and want to develop educational approaches that support students to become resilient, creative, and productive human beings who can live meaningful and purposeful lives.

The pressure of current mandates has also challenged teachers to find creative solutions to complex problems and to reexamine the conditions that impact student learning. This inquiry has led to approaches that focus not only on instruction, but also on how we can engage students in new ways so they are available and able to learn. As individual teachers and schools have implemented these approaches and seen powerful results, a new movement in education has begun to take shape. This movement, in which we can all take part, invites us each to participate in transforming education from the inside out—through our own individual teaching practice, classroom methodologies, and professional relationships with colleagues. From our perspective, this emerging movement acknowledges the powerful impact of teachers' presence in the classroom; the importance of student engagement and participation in learning; the critical role of relationships and cultural contexts within a classroom and school; and the ways in which social, emotional, and academic learning are inextricably connected.

The Engaged Teaching Approach we describe is designed to empower and inspire teachers and engage and enliven students. The principles and practices in the chapters ahead connect and integrate social and emotional learning with academics, heart with mind, inner life with outer life, and content with contexts, and offer a path to reconcile these essential aspects of learning and human development.

At the core of the Engaged Teaching Approach are the Five Dimensions of Engaged Teaching.

Five Dimensions of Engaged Teaching

1. Cultivating an open heart
2. Engaging the self-observer
3. Being present
4. Establishing respectful boundaries
5. Developing emotional capacity

Each of the dimensions of engaged teaching includes principles and practices that support educators in developing a more intentional, rewarding, and effective teaching practice and support students in thinking creatively and critically, excelling academically, managing their emotions, communicating effectively, and working with people who are different from themselves. These are the 21st century skills and capacities that young people need to survive and thrive in our complex world.

A note on engaged teaching: we realize that the term *engagement* in education may be used in different ways in various settings. By engagement, we refer to the integration of the inner and outer capacities, practices, and skills that lead to effective teaching and student achievement. We recognize that there are countless books that address instructional methods that are specific to content and grade level. This book emphasizes more general instructional strategies and the vital connection between capacity building and effective teaching practice.

Why We Wrote This Book

According to a MetLife survey (MetLife, 2012):

> Teacher job satisfaction has fallen by 15 percentage points since 2009 . . .
> from 59 percent to 44 percent responding they are very satisfied. This rapid
> decline in job satisfaction is coupled with a large increase in the number of
> teachers reporting that they are likely to leave teaching for another occupa-
> tion (17 percent in 2009 vs. 29 percent today). (p. 1)

We wrote this book because we wanted to offer immediate and practical support to
teachers—the kind of support that is empowering and useful because it acknowledges and
builds on the wisdom and experience of educators themselves. Across the United States,
we have seen the predictable failure of school reform when teachers are not included in
the process. We spent a great deal of time listening to educators from a variety of K–12
classrooms. We asked educators about their challenges and their inspirations. We asked
them to share what was working and what was not. We asked them what got them up in
the morning to teach in such challenging situations. We asked them, "With all that is
happening in education right now, what would be helpful for you?" A summary of their
answers follows.

What Teachers Need

- Strategies to help them stay inspired and energized
- Practical classroom-ready tools to help them teach content, meet learning goals, engage stu-
  dents, and manage behavior issues
- Support from and collaboration with colleagues in the field and school community
- Ideas, practices, and tools to effectively and equitably meet the diverse needs of the students
  they teach
- Approaches to help them connect or reconnect with their passion for teaching

---

Using This Book

We invite you to use this book actively—to engage with the text, mark up and dog-ear
the pages, ask yourself questions, and bring your questions and ideas to colleagues. We
invite you to try out the approaches presented here and to be curious about what works
for you and what doesn't. And we invite you to consider finding an engaged teaching partner or small group to explore the approach in this book and to offer each other support
along the way.

This book and the online community launched with it (engagedteaching.org) are
designed to be interactive platforms for discussion and learning—allowing you to share
your experiences and best practices with colleagues in your school and other schools. Your
wisdom and knowledge—along with that of millions of other educators—are critical to
the evolution of the field of teaching.

Ways to Use This Book

- As an individual teacher (K–12, veteran, or new to the field)
- As teachers in pairs, small groups, or learning communities
- With a group of educators in a faculty study group
- As a visioning and planning tool, among a group of teacher leaders
- As a principal or assistant principal as a resource for schoolwide culture change
- As a text for a pre-service or in-service course for educators

This book will explore the Five Dimensions of Engaged Teaching, the roots of the Engaged Teaching Approach, and the outcomes of this approach as they relate to teachers, students, and school communities. Figure I.1 shows how these topics break down by chapter.

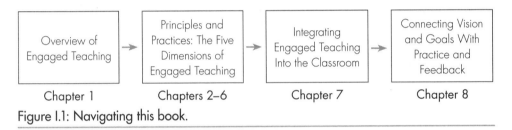

| Overview of Engaged Teaching | Principles and Practices: The Five Dimensions of Engaged Teaching | Integrating Engaged Teaching Into the Classroom | Connecting Vision and Goals With Practice and Feedback |
| Chapter 1 | Chapters 2–6 | Chapter 7 | Chapter 8 |

Figure I.1: Navigating this book.

Chapter 1 introduces the Five Dimensions of Engaged Teaching, presents the roots of the approach, and makes the case for engaged teaching.

Chapters 2 through 6 explore each of the five dimensions of the Engaged Teaching Approach and the principles and practices associated with each dimension. The dimensions support teachers in:

1. Creating and sustaining an authentic teaching practice

2. Employing meaningful classroom practices related to the five dimensions

3. Engaging and collaborating with colleagues with increased skillfulness and heart

Chapter 7 offers ways to integrate and apply the five dimensions in the classroom across the arc of a school term or year (what we later refer to as the "Learning Journey"). The classroom principles and practices in chapter 7 foster learning readiness and academic excellence, build trusting learning communities, support students in navigating transitions, contribute to a proactive approach to classroom management, and create productive and meaningful learning environments.

Chapter 8 lays out a step-by-step process for educators to create an engaged teaching action plan that involves: developing a vision, identifying long-term and intermediate outcomes, and charting an action path for reaching those goals. Finally, it includes examples of formative assessment tools for teachers to give and receive feedback.

The appendix includes reproducible samples of activities and a list of tools and resources. Visit **go.solution-tree.com/instruction** to download reproducible materials.

The Engaged Teaching Approach

The Engaged Teaching Approach is a practical approach to teaching and learning that improves social, emotional, and academic outcomes and fosters a lifelong sense of meaning, purpose, and relevance, along with motivation in the classroom. The principles and practices are designed to be integrated into any classroom and to transform and improve how we teach and how we engage with our students and colleagues.

The Engaged Teaching Approach can be depicted using the metaphor of a tree (figure I.2, page 6). The roots are the foundations that support and inform the principles and practices of engaged teaching (the trunk of the tree). These principles and practices, in turn, build capacities and skills in educators and students. These capacities and skills, when applied to teaching and learning, bring about and sustain long-term outcomes (the branches).

The principles and practices of this approach create immediate results in classrooms and school communities. In addition, working with allies within organized learning communities to engage in these principles and practices over an extended period will help produce longer-term, collective outcomes that come from consistent collaborative effort.

In chapter 1, we will explore the foundational roots of the Engaged Teaching Approach, define each of its five dimensions, and examine the research that supports the approach.

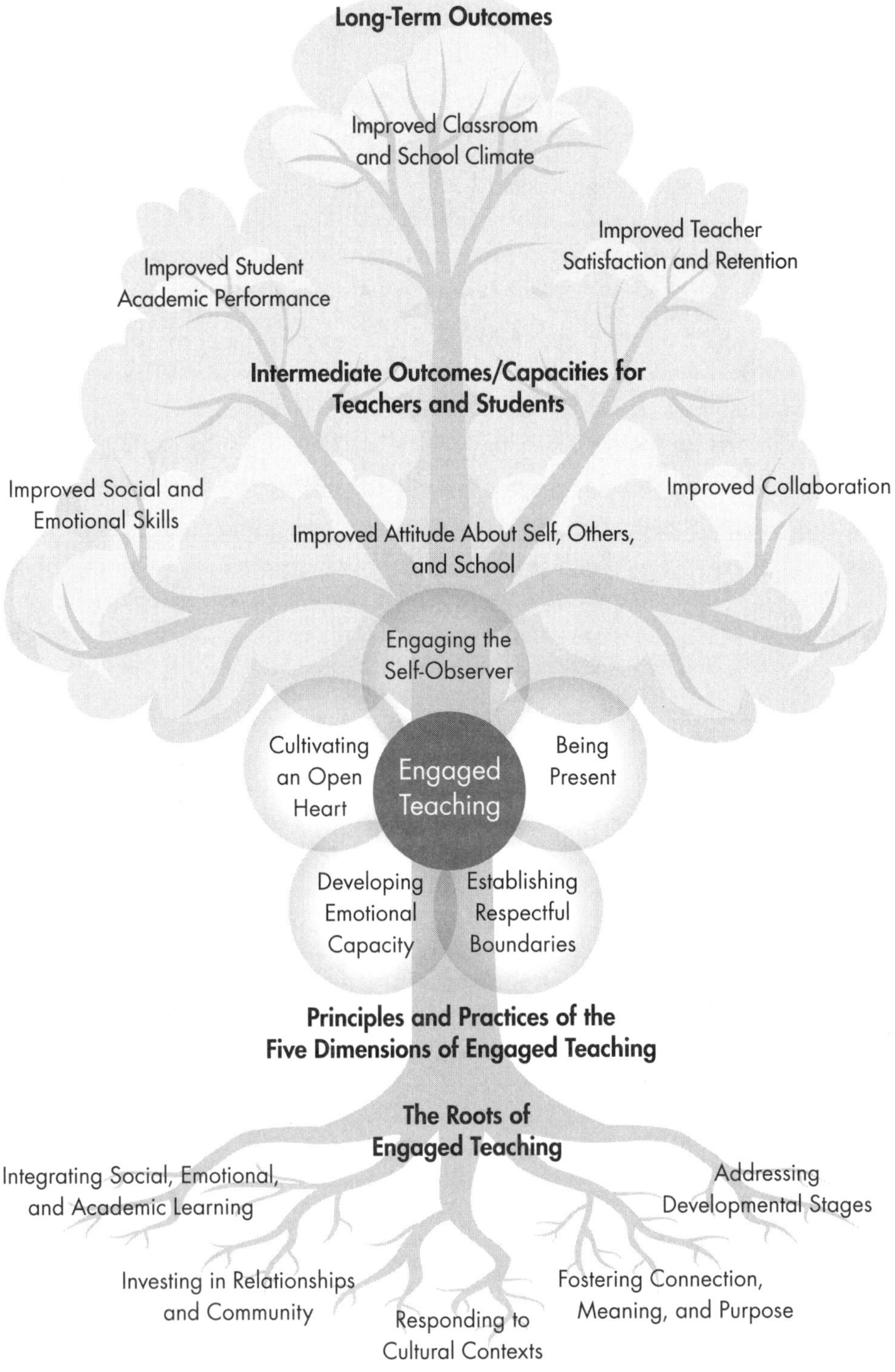

Long-Term Outcomes

Improved Classroom
and School Climate

Improved Teacher
Satisfaction and Retention

Improved Student
Academic Performance

**Intermediate Outcomes/Capacities for
Teachers and Students**

Improved Social and
Emotional Skills

Improved Collaboration

Improved Attitude About Self, Others,
and School

Engaging the
Self-Observer

Cultivating
an Open
Heart

Engaged
Teaching

Being
Present

Developing
Emotional
Capacity

Establishing
Respectful
Boundaries

**Principles and Practices of the
Five Dimensions of Engaged Teaching**

**The Roots of
Engaged Teaching**

Integrating Social, Emotional,
and Academic Learning

Addressing
Developmental Stages

Investing in Relationships
and Community

Fostering Connection,
Meaning, and Purpose

Responding to
Cultural Contexts

Figure I.2: The Engaged Teaching Approach.

1 Engaged Teaching

> Excellent teachers don't develop full-blown at graduation; nor are they just "born teachers." Instead, teachers are always in the process of "becoming." They continually discover who they are and what they stand for, through their dialogue with peers, through ongoing and consistent study, and through deep reflection about their craft.
>
> —Sonia Nieto

Self-Reflection

Who were the teachers who inspired you? How did they inspire you? What specific qualities, behaviors, and dispositions did they possess? Now think of your own students. How would they describe you? What kind of teacher do you aspire to be?

Our society often focuses on the idealized teachers—like the ones characterized in the feature films *Freedom Writers*, *Stand and Deliver*, and *Dead Poets Society*—the teachers who go to extraordinary lengths or give up their health or well-being to meet their students' needs. These messages give us the impression that great teachers are born, not made, that we must have a particular kind of charisma to inspire young people, or that exemplary teachers must make enormous sacrifices against impossible odds to reach their students.

Think about the teachers who inspired you. Perhaps these teachers taught you something important, changed your perspective about school or life, recognized your gifts, sparked a love for a subject, or inspired you to push past self-limiting beliefs. Perhaps they had a great sense of humor or exuded a contagious passion for their subject matter. Perhaps they were thoughtful and took your ideas seriously. Maybe they had a firm but caring attitude that kept you afloat when you experienced difficulty.

The premise of this book is that effective, authentic teaching *can* be learned, developed, and practiced over time in ways that positively impact students and dramatically enhance our own experience as educators. To do this, we do not have to be "super teachers" or adopt a persona or charismatic style that might not be our own. Nor do we have to drain ourselves. Instead, sustaining an authentic teaching practice is about each of us discovering our own unique gifts, building on our strengths, learning from others, and engaging in lifelong learning. It is about cultivating our best qualities, nurturing ourselves as teachers, raising our level of self-awareness, managing our stress, fostering meaningful relationships with students, and connecting or reconnecting with our passion for teaching.

The Roots of the Engaged Teaching Approach

The Engaged Teaching Approach is not a prescriptive or linear process, but rather a lifelong learning journey. This approach involves becoming a reflective practitioner, studying our own experiences, learning from successes and mistakes, cultivating social and emotional intelligence, and developing a deep understanding of what effective teaching looks and feels like. Whether we are veteran teachers or have just entered the field, in the Engaged Teaching Approach, we simply start where we are.

> "Of all the professional forms of work I have seen, teaching is the most difficult. . . . Doctors are prepared for thirteen years for the work they do. We try to prepare teachers in one year, in many cases, and then drop them into very difficult challenges, give them little sustained development and then we wonder why teaching is so difficult."
>
> —Lee S. Shulman

In the introduction of this book, we used the metaphor of a tree to describe the Engaged Teaching Approach. In this chapter, we will continue with this metaphor and delve deeper into the view that underlies it. We have identified five major roots of the Engaged Teaching Approach—each represents a fundamental aspect of the approach (see figure I.2, page 6). Together, these roots support a holistic view of teaching and learning that empowers and sustains teachers and effectively prepares students for the complexities of the 21st century. These roots also directly support and inform the trunk (the principles and practices) and branches (the intermediate and long-term outcomes) of the Engaged Teaching Approach.

These five foundational roots are:

1. Integrating social, emotional, and academic learning

2. Investing in relationships and community

3. Responding to cultural contexts

4. Fostering connection, meaning, and purpose

5. Addressing developmental stages

Integrating Social, Emotional, and Academic Learning

Brain research and learning theory illustrate that social, emotional, and academic learning are inseparable and that integrating these aspects of learning helps students succeed in school and life (Durlak et al., 2011). Professor Emeritus and author Robert Sylwester (1995) writes, "We know that emotion is very important to the educative process because it drives attention, which drives learning and memory" (p. 72). Figure 1.1 shows this progression. Even if our only focus is on meeting academic goals, we still need to foster social and emotional skills and capacities in ourselves and our students to achieve the academic results we desire.

> "Addressing young people's social, emotional, and ethical lives is an immediate, pressing, and urgent need. . . . The definition of a well-educated person is one who possesses an education of the heart and spirit as well as the mind."
>
> —Linda Lantieri

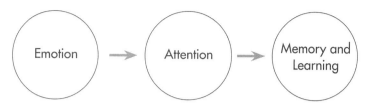

Figure 1.1: Robert Sylwester's progression of emotions and learning.

Investing in Relationships and Community

Learning does not happen in a vacuum, but rather in a very particular context. When we work conscientiously to build trusting relationships and to acknowledge and respond to cultural contexts, we foster our students' capacity to learn and grow. When we invest in community building and create a healthy "container" for learning, we simultaneously foster student safety and resilience. Academic excellence is inextricably tied to the development of caring relationships (teacher-student and student-student). For this reason, taking the time and space to cultivate an intentional and positive learning environment is essential to achieving academic outcomes and school safety (Eccles & Roeser, 2011). When we invest in relationships and utilize effective strategies to engage students, staff, families, and community members, we directly impact students' learning and well-being.

> "Our ability to learn has deep roots in relationships. Our learning performance may be deeply affected by the emotional environment in which the learning takes place."
>
> —Nancy Frey, Douglas Fisher, and Sandi Everlove

Responding to Cultural Contexts

Culture is the water we swim in, the air we breathe, the lens we see through. Students and teachers come into the classroom with a particular understanding based on their cultural context and background. When we acknowledge the role of culture (including access to resources and other issues related to equity), we are better able to identify, value, and respond to the multiple identities and cultures present in our schools. As Gloria Ladson-Billings writes:

> "Recognizing that everyone has unique traditions, values, and beliefs that are important to them helps us see how we are connected."
>
> —Kim Kennedy White

> Culture is central to learning. It plays a role not only in communicating and receiving information, but also in shaping the thinking process of groups and individuals. A pedagogy that acknowledges, responds to, and celebrates fundamental cultures offers full, equitable access to education for students from all cultures. (as cited in Benitez et al., 2009, p. 324–325)

Fostering cultural responsiveness—in ourselves and our students—is key to meeting academic goals, addressing inequities, and creating inclusive, engaged learning communities. Teachers who recognize the importance of culture often discover powerful opportunities to engage students. But teachers also must be aware of how they unconsciously express culture and how this impacts their students. The authors of *Cultural Identity and Teaching* assert that "coming to an understanding of the ways in which one's beliefs, experiences, values, and assumptions are linked to culture is an essential feature of culturally responsive practice" (White, Zion, Kozleski, & Equity Alliance at ASU, 2005, p. 2). As we become more aware of our own cultural lens, we are better able to respond to the multiplicity of cultures present in our classroom. As research shows, teachers who include culturally responsive practice and cultivate safety, belonging, inclusion, and equitable treatment among their students more readily engage and motivate students (Roeser, Eccles, & Sameroff, 2000).

Fostering Connection, Meaning, and Purpose

> As teachers, we can honor our students' search for what they believe gives meaning and integrity to their lives, and how they can connect to what is most precious for them. In the search itself, in loving the questions, in the deep yearning they let themselves feel, young people can discover what is essential in their own lives and in life itself, and what allows them to bring their own gifts to the world.
>
> —Rachael Kessler

According to a report by the Commission on Children at Risk (Kline, 2003), the brain is hardwired to connect. *Connectedness* not only refers to connections to other people, but also to deep connections to values and meaning. Fostering a sense of meaning, purpose, and connection in the classroom is directly related to teaching and learning outcomes. When students have a sense of purpose and feel connected to themselves, their teachers, their peers, and the larger community, they are more resilient, compassionate, and motivated. They are more likely to care about their schoolwork and make healthy choices in school and in their personal lives.

Students are yearning for more connection at school—to feel seen, known, and understood. Without this sense of connection, students are much more likely to disengage, check out, become apathetic, or turn to risky behaviors. When the level of connection is shallow and the majority of learning does not feel relevant, students are unmotivated, and as a result often do not excel academically. Studies show that "approximately 40 to 60 percent of high school students become chronically disengaged from school" (Payton et al., 2008, p. 3). Connection is fundamental to academic excellence, academic success, and *resilience*—the capacity for students to work with challenge and manage adversity. As Kessler notes in a 1999 article in *Educational Leadership*:

> Students who feel deeply connected don't need danger to feel fully alive. They don't need guns to feel powerful. They don't want to hurt others or themselves. Out of connection grows compassion and passion—passion for people, for students' goals and dreams, for life itself. (p. 53)

One key way we can help students connect is with activities that specifically address the inner lives of students. In this book, we define *inner life* as the essential aspect of human nature that yearns for deep connection (to self, others, the community, and the world), grapples with questions of meaning and purpose, seeks genuine forms of self-expression, and longs to learn and grow. The inner life includes our thoughts, beliefs, emotions, questions, wonder, intuition, hopes, dreams, visions, creative impulses, ethical and moral leanings, and deepest longings for connection. The inner life also includes our innate curiosity that, when activated and engaged, naturally leads to a willingness and desire to learn and contribute. It is essential to support the inner life in school and to connect the inner life with the outer life. The Engaged Teaching Approach supports the inner and outer lives of both students and teachers.

Addressing Developmental Stages

Individuals and groups of students naturally progress through stages of development that directly relate to and impact learning. One aspect of addressing the developmental stages of individuals and groups involves paying attention to students' changing developmental needs (individually and as a group) throughout the arc of the school term or year. Bringing this awareness to our teaching practice can help us identify the activities and practices that are effective for students during particular stages of development. An activity that might build trust halfway through the school year might be too risky in September.

A second aspect of addressing students' developmental needs involves providing support and guidance for students during the "transition years" into and out of elementary, middle, and high school (National Council for Accreditation of Teacher Education, 2008). If students are experiencing a significant transition that is not directly addressed (such as the shift from elementary to middle school), they may be left to grapple with the complex feelings and issues associated with this shift on their own, and this may interfere with their capacity to learn. When we directly and intentionally address developmental stages and transitions (through curriculum, scaffolding, differentiated instruction, and transitions or SEL programs), we support student learning and help them make healthy choices, avoid risky behaviors, experience the relevance of their academic work, and stay in school (Eccles & Roeser, 2011).

> "At an absolute minimum, adults need a high school diploma if they are to have any reasonable opportunities to earn a living wage . . . . Yet, with little notice, the United States is allowing a dangerously high percentage of students to disappear from the educational pipeline before they graduate from high school."
>
> —Gary Orfield, Daniel Losen, Johanna Wald, and Christopher Swanson

The Origins of Engaged Teaching

The Engaged Teaching Approach includes the wisdom, knowledge, and experience of many educators and field experts. The seed of this approach first originated with the collaborative work of Rachael Kessler (1946–2010)—visionary educator, author, and founder of the PassageWorks Institute. Over the course of twenty-five years, Kessler worked with colleagues and K–12 educators across the United States to develop an approach that welcomed the inner life of students and teachers into schools. Kessler's groundbreaking book *The Soul of Education: Helping Students Find Connection, Compassion, and Character at School* (2000a) offers a unique and powerful perspective on the purpose and practice of education and has been used as a text in universities throughout the United States since its publication.

> "We can have the best curricula available, train teachers in technique and theory, but our students will be unsafe and our programs hollow if we do not provide opportunities for teachers to develop their own souls, their hearts, their own social and emotional intelligence."
>
> —Rachael Kessler

As Kessler and her colleagues worked in schools across the United States, they saw a marked difference in the quality of different classroom environments. As they observed these differences, they wondered why the same lesson plan could engage students, build trust, and encourage academic rigor in one class, while creating a sense of chaos, disconnection, and lack of productivity in another. Of course, they understood that each class of students has its own unique chemistry and conditions. However, they also saw that *who* the teacher is as a human being and how he or she expresses this unique presence in the classroom have a profound impact on students' learning and engagement. They called this aspect of teaching "teaching presence."

Kessler and colleagues used the term *teaching presence* to describe the aspects of teaching that go beyond curriculum, strategy, and technique and emphasize the importance of who we are, how we express ourselves, and how we connect with our students (see also Palmer, 1998). This authentic presence relates to how we express and embody our authentic selves in our teaching. In her article "The Teaching Presence," Kessler (2000b) identifies three dimensions of teaching presence: (1) open heart, (2) respectful discipline, and (3) being present. Later, she and her colleagues added two other dimensions: (4) engaging the self-observer and (5) developing emotional range. Subsequently, colleagues renamed and expanded these dimensions so that they would relate more directly to both personal teacher practice and classroom practice.

The Engaged Teaching Approach has evolved over time, with the input of many colleagues and educators. The approach supports the development of meaningful and authentic connections: teacher to teacher, teacher to student, student to student, student to community, and student to self. And it acknowledges how essential it is that we as educators cultivate and develop the social, emotional, and cognitive aspects of ourselves so that we can embody and express these capacities in our own classrooms and schools. One middle school teacher shared the following about the impact of developing her own teaching presence with students over the course of a school year. She notes: "Over time, I have become more human in their eyes, so that now, I am building stronger bonds with a larger percentage of my students." When this bond is in place, we can inspire and encourage students in ways we never thought possible.

The Five Dimensions of Engaged Teaching

The Five Dimensions of Engaged Teaching form the core of the Engaged Teaching Approach. They support our capacity to express and embody our authenticity, develop productive relationships with students and colleagues, and bring innovative principles and practices to the classroom. These dimensions are not sequential, but instead are *interrelated capacities* that we cultivate simultaneously. Each of the five dimensions supports the development of the other, and together they create a whole that is more than the sum of its parts. Figure 1.2 shows the five dimensions, and the feature box on page 13 sums up each dimension.

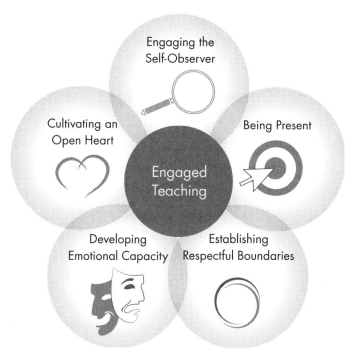

Figure 1.2: The Five Dimensions of Engaged Teaching.

The Five Dimensions of Engaged Teaching

 Cultivating an open heart: Expressing warmth, kindness, care, compassion; cultivating connection (teacher-student and student-student); and intentionally engaging in practices that build trusting, inclusive learning communities

 Engaging the self-observer: Cultivating the aspect of ourselves that can notice, observe, and then reflect on our thoughts, beliefs, biases, emotions, and behaviors to make more conscious choices about our actions; includes fostering self-observation or "self-science" in students as well

 Being present: Engaging in the ongoing process of bringing attention to the present moment and learning to manage distractions so we can be responsive, aware, focused, and creative in the classroom; includes supporting students to develop *learning readiness*—the capacity to pay attention, focus, and engage

 Establishing respectful boundaries: Respectfully establishing clear and compassionate boundaries for ourselves (self-discipline) and with others—in the classroom and in our school communities; includes supporting students and the learning community with a proactive approach to classroom management

 Developing emotional capacity: Developing emotional intelligence, expanding our emotional range, and cultivating emotional boundaries so we can effectively address a range of feelings in ourselves and others; includes supporting students in developing their capacity to express and manage emotions

We use five icons to symbolize the five dimensions. In later chapters, these icons identify activities and information that are particularly relevant to developing a certain dimension.

Engaged Teaching Capacities and Skills

In the upcoming chapters, we will discuss how educators can learn and apply the principles and practices of engaged teaching to develop their capacity and skills in three domains:

1. In their own teaching pedagogy and practice

2. In their classrooms (to cultivate these dimensions in students)

3. With colleagues and school communities

Developing these capacities and skills helps educators achieve the intermediate and long-term educational outcomes we strive for. The diagram in figure 1.3 includes examples of these capacities and skills in each of the three domains of the work of teachers.

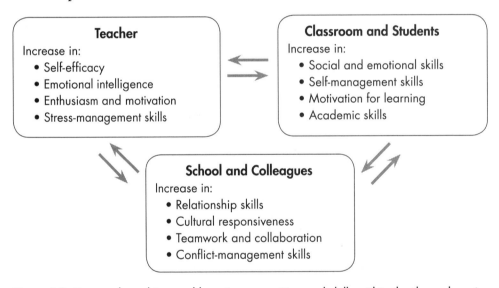

Figure 1.3: Engaged teaching and learning capacities and skills within the three domains of teaching.

A Map for the Journey

Throughout this book, we will explore how the Engaged Teaching Approach helps make the connection between daily work in the classroom and long-term vision and goals. The principles and practices within the Five Dimensions of Engaged Teaching serve as the action paths that connect the foundational roots of this approach with the desired outcomes. Figure 1.4 provides a detailed map of the Engaged Teaching Approach.

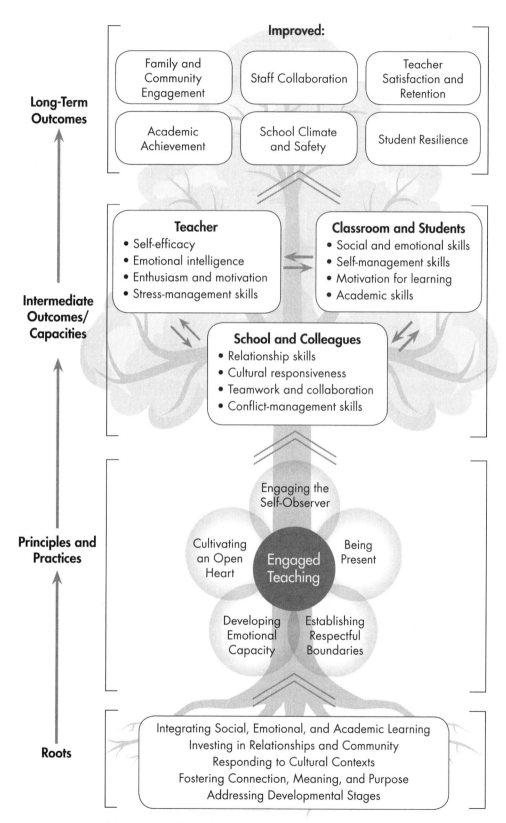

Figure 1.4: Map of the Engaged Teaching Approach.

The Case for Engaged Teaching

There is growing evidence that suggests that cultivating an engaged teaching approach can positively affect students' social, emotional, and academic learning and improve our own experience of teaching (Darling-Hammond & Bransford, 2005; Jennings & Greenberg, 2009; Roeser, Skinner, Beers, & Jennings, 2012). Educator experience, research, and learning theory corroborate that the intermediate outcomes and capacities for both teachers and students described in figure 1.4 (page 15) lead to many of the desired long-term outcomes that educators seek to achieve, including goals related to academic performance and school climate. Following is a brief summary of research related to a few of the key skills and capacities in the Engaged Teaching Approach.

Teacher Emotional Intelligence and Relationship Skills

- Positive relationships are central to creating learning environments that are conducive to student engagement, motivation, and learning (Roeser, Peck, & Nasir, 2009). When teachers foster a sense of community in their classrooms, students exhibit more helpful, cooperative behavior and more concern for others. Such teacher practices may create a classroom atmosphere that is protective despite the negative effects of poverty on academic performance (Battistich et al., 1997; Battistic, Schaps, Watson, Soloman, & Lewis 2000).

- Supportive student-teacher relationships are the keystone to effective classroom management. A meta-analysis of over 100 studies found that teachers who had high-quality relationships with their students had 31 percent fewer behavior problems over the course of a school year than teachers who did not (Marzano & Pickering, 2003). Supportive teacher-student relationships play a critical role in healthy school and classroom climate, students' connection to school, and both academic and social-emotional outcomes (Abbott et al., 1998; Darling-Hammond, Ancess, & Ort, 2002; Gambone, Klem, & Connell, 2002; McNeely, Nonnemaker, & Blum, 2002; Osher et al., 2008).

- Warm and supportive teachers provide students with a sense of connectedness to the school social environment and the safety and security to explore new ideas and take risks. Both of these elements are essential to learning (Mitchell-Copeland, Denham, & DeMulder, 1997; Murray & Greenberg, 2000; Watson & Ecken, 2003). A teacher's support and sensitive responses to students' challenging behaviors may have lasting positive effects on their social and emotional development, especially in the early grades (Lynch & Cicchetti, 1992). Bridget Hamre and Robert Pianta (2001) found that kindergarten teachers' reports of negative feelings toward a particular student predicted problematic social and academic outcomes for that student through at least fourth grade. In addition, researchers (Hughes, Cavell, & Willson, 2001) found that students take cues from their teacher in determining whether a peer is likable or not. If a teacher dislikes a student, peers are more likely to dislike that student as well.

Teacher Self-Efficacy, Enthusiasm, and Motivation

- We teach who we are. Teachers who generate enthusiasm and passion for the curriculum encourage student learning (Fried, 2001).

- Teachers who experience mastery feel more efficacious, and teaching becomes more enjoyable. Teachers who overcome personal challenges help students overcome their social and emotional challenges (Goddard, Hoy, & Hoy, 2004; Roeser, Midgley, & Urdan, 1996).

Teacher Stress Management and Habits of Mind

- Teachers who remain cool under pressure, addressing disciplinary issues in a matter-of-fact way without taking behaviors personally, are the most effective classroom managers. "Mental set" has the largest effect on reductions in disruptive behavior (Marzano et al., 2003). The idea of *mental set* is similar to Langer's (1997) construct of *mindfulness* involving "a heightened sense of situational awareness and a conscious control over one's thoughts and behavior relative to that situation" (Marzano et al., 2003, p. 65). Regular mindfulness practice increases the ability to regulate emotion, reduces stress and distress, and enhances subjective well-being (Holzel et al., 2011). Mindfulness is associated with greater emotional self-awareness (Brown & Ryan, 2003) and may contribute to *psychological presence*, defined as "feeling open to oneself and others, connected to work and others, complete rather than fragmented, and within rather than without the boundaries of a given role" (Kahn, 1992, p. 322).

- Mindful awareness can support cognitive and emotional regulation. Reflecting on and broadening one's perspective allows a broader array of interpretations of and responses to stressful situations (Zelazo & Cunningham, 2007). Mindfulness training for teachers can "foster teachers' habits of mind and thereby help them to meet and succeed in the context of the demands of teaching in the 21st century" (Roeser et al., 2012, p. 172).

Student Motivation for Learning

- Teaching that supports autonomy and intrinsic motivation is more effective than teaching that relies on rewards and teacher control. In one study, Maarten Vansteenkiste and colleagues found that students who had an intrinsic goal rather than an extrinsic goal were more autonomously motivated, demonstrated better performance, and were more persistent (Vansteenkiste, Simons, Lens, Sheldon, & Deci, 2004).

- Students' sense of belonging and motivation influence classroom achievement. In a study of middle school students (Goodenow, 1993), researchers found that belonging and teacher support were related to motivation and that both belonging and motivation affected achievement. Teacher support explained over a third of students' assessment of the interest, importance, and value of the academic work in the class. Teacher and school connectedness is a significant contributor to adolescent emotional health, lower levels of violence, and less use of alcohol, cigarettes, and marijuana. Even among adolescents, school and teacher connectedness is a protective factor (Resnick et al., 1997).

- Connection is an antidote to disengagement. Research reveals that motivation and dropout rate go hand in hand—"Poor basic skills in reading, writing, and computation were not the main reason for the high dropout rate: It turns out that will, not skill, is the single most important factor" (Wagner, 2010, p. 149). According to the National Center for Education Statistics, among the major reasons cited for dropping out of school, several involve social and emotional factors: not getting along with teachers or peers (35 percent and 20 percent, respectively), feeling left out (23 percent), and not feeling safe (12 percent) (Zins & Elias, 2006).

Student Social, Emotional, and Self-Management Skills

- Social and emotional learning (SEL) programs support academic achievement. The Collaborative for Academic, Social, and Emotional Learning (CASEL) describes SEL as "a process for helping children and adults develop the fundamental skills for life effectiveness. SEL teaches the skills we all need to handle ourselves, our relationships, and our work, effectively and ethically" (see CASEL, n.d., and figure 1.5). The results of a 2011 meta-analysis of 213 K–12 SEL studies provide significant support for this claim. The meta-analysis, which involved 270,034 kindergarten through high school students, found that students in SEL programs demonstrated significantly improved social and emotional skills, attitudes, behavior, and an 11-percentile-point gain in academic achievement (Durlak et al., 2011). Researchers Shelley Hymel, Kimberly Schonert-Reichl, and Lynn Miller concluded their 2006 article with this statement: "Supporting the social-emotional development of children and youth not only provides a foundation for academic growth, but also for creating a safe, caring and inclusive community of learners that fosters universal human qualities (compassion, fairness, respect) that underlie socially responsible citizenship" (p. 27).

School and Colleagues Capacity Building: Teamwork and Collaboration

- Evidence-based programs are necessary but not sufficient for successful program implementations. An extensive body of research from the field of implementation science has shown that a deliberate focus on the implementation process determines whether reform efforts will achieve the intended effects. Quality implementation of teaching strategies and school-based prevention and intervention programs is thus an essential component of realizing positive and sustainable outcomes. Successful implementation involves a number of specific factors, including staff training and organizational support (Durlak & DuPre, 2008; Fixsen, Naoom, Blase, Friedman, & Wallace, 2005; Odom et al., 2010).

- Staff and organizational capacity have been found to be key components of successful implementation. This is true in a variety of prevention and intervention contexts, including school-based interventions (Halgunseth et al., 2012; Meyers, Durlak, & Wandersman, 2012). One study (Flaspohler, Duffy, Wandersman, Stillman, & Maras, 2008) found that staff capability, staff background, and staff openness were characteristics of individual staff that impacted dissemination and implementation. In another study (Han & Weiss, 2005), researchers found that teachers with higher self-efficacy tended to invest greater effort into program implementation, which in turn increased the likelihood of program success and fostered positive student outcomes.

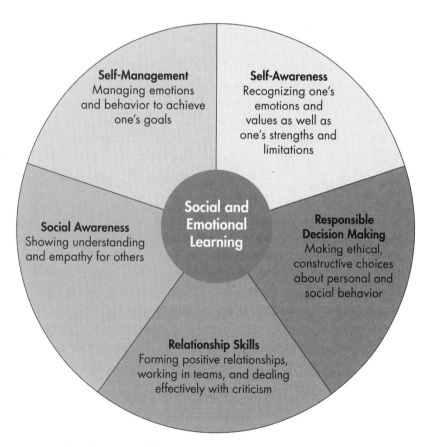

Figure 1.5: Social and emotional learning competencies.

Source: Adapted with permission from the Collaborative for Academic, Social, and Emotional Learning (CASEL) (n.d.b).

- Mentoring supports practice. Mentoring can help support teachers in sustaining quality practice over time. Good mentors are encouraging, supportive, committed, sensitive, flexible, respectful, enthusiastic, diplomatic, patient, and willing to share information, credit, and recognition (McCormick & Brennan, 2001).

- Coaching and support of teachers in the classroom improve interventions. In a meta-analysis of school-based interventions involving teacher training (Joyce & Showers, 2002), researchers found that the combination of training and ongoing and individualized coaching resulted in documented implementation of the school-based intervention about 95 percent of the time as opposed to only 5 percent with demonstration in the training alone.

Studies like these illustrate the interconnection and interactions between the social, emotional, and academic dimensions of teaching and learning. Throughout this book, we will refer to current studies that support the principles and practices presented. Go to engagedteaching.org for more research on these and other skills and capacities.

Conclusion

In this chapter, we have explored the roots of the Engaged Teaching Approach and looked at how they support the principles and practices offered in this book. We also provided a sampling of the research underlying this approach to teaching and learning. In the chapters that follow, we delve into each of the five dimensions of engaged teaching, offering principles and practices that support the development of each dimension. The next chapter explores the dimension of cultivating an open heart as it relates to teacher practice, the classroom community, and our professional relationships with our colleagues.

2 Cultivating an Open Heart

My teaching philosophy was born from my own negative experience. When I was in school I was treated as if I were not intelligent, as if I were less than. The islands in the sea of public education were the teachers who cared—who shared not only emotion but authentic belief in my ability. Those teachers who made a difference saw intelligence and believed I was intelligent, and then their behavior matched that belief.

—Principal, Colorado High School

Self-Reflection

When you are in the classroom, what behaviors and experiences tend to open your heart? Which ones tend to close your heart?

Cultivating an open heart refers to the capacity to express warmth, compassion, care, authenticity, and, at times, vulnerability with students and colleagues. It also refers to the ways we intentionally foster meaningful connections with and amongst our students and create culturally responsive classrooms where all students feel welcome and included. These are the kinds of learning environments where students can safely open their hearts and minds to learning and growth.

As we consider the dimension of the open heart, it is important to note that at times this aspect of teaching and learning is disregarded, or spoken of pejoratively. For example, at a webinar on engaged teaching, a participant commented that the webinar "was much more touchy-feely than [she] had expected, but it was really positive, powerful, and effective." What exactly do people mean when they use the term *touchy-feely*, and why is this term used at times to diminish the importance of community building or social and emotional work? Many people have participated in professional development or group work that felt unfocused, forced, sappy, frivolous, or ineffective. Perhaps a facilitator asked educators to share in an overly personal way or to take risks in a group that had not yet established much trust. Or, perhaps this work was obligatory instead of invitational, and people felt forced to share things they did not feel comfortable sharing. These kinds of poorly designed workshops or experiences can lead us to avoid any professional development that involves our emotions. However, there are rigorous and appropriate methods and practices that can help us engage our hearts as well as minds and develop our emotional capacities. Learning to effectively work with our emotions and to risk caring about students is some of the most challenging and rewarding work we can do as educators, and it is at the core of meeting our teaching and learning goals.

We can cut ourselves off from tremendous learning opportunities if we choose to dismiss any professional development or curricula that work with emotional intelligence and the heart because we consider them touchy-feely. Remaining open to methods of teaching and learning that are experiential and not solely cognitive, that engage our hearts as well as our minds, and that support self-regulation of emotions can be very beneficial for us as professionals and for our students.

Teaching With an Open Heart

In the following sections, we will explore a number of principles and practices related to cultivating an open heart. These are designed to inform our own teaching practice and to support our capacity to create connections and positive relationships with our students and colleagues.

Principle: Sustaining an Open Heart

Teaching with an open heart is not just about being warm and caring with our colleagues and students. It also includes having clear emotional boundaries that allow us to safely and wisely open our heart (more on this in chapter 5 on respectful boundaries, page 69). Boundaries and an open heart are like the two wings of a bird—without both, we cannot fly straight or for sustained periods of time. Boundaries involve our capacity to identify when we are taking on too much, when we are consciously or unconsciously trying to "fix" a student or colleague, and when we need to step in and draw a clear limit.

It is difficult to safely open our hearts in school settings if:

- The overall culture lacks respect and trust

- We do not have a sense of where our students' lives end and where ours begin—and therefore feel overwhelmed by the personal problems of our students and our desire to fix these problems

- We haven't begun to identify how to stop "taking it home"

- We have not established trust, boundaries, and respect in the classroom

One of the most challenging aspects of teaching is learning how to leave our work life at school so our personal life is not consumed by the complexities of our profession. Many teachers struggle with the emotional burden of their teaching lives—especially because teaching involves so many personal relationships and interactions with students, colleagues, and families. When we develop healthy habits to help leave the concerns of the workday behind, we foster clearer boundaries between our work and personal life. This can take the form of a five-minute period of silence or a five-minute debriefing conversation with a colleague at the end of the day to review what we have experienced and then intentionally leave it behind. Or, we might take a daily walk after school or participate in some kind of vigorous exercise or reflective practice to create that sense of a boundary. Having clear boundaries helps us to replenish ourselves so that we can be more present in school and express care and compassion with our students. The practices described in the following sections support us in sustaining an open heart over time.

Practice: Overcoming Obstacles to Caring

When cultivating an open heart, it is essential to understand what tends to get in the way of our capacity to express care for our students and others. To do this, it can be helpful to ask ourselves on an ongoing basis, "When is my heart open in the classroom?" and "When is it closed?" This simple inquiry can help us understand more about our own internal state and how this impacts our capacity to feel empathy and compassion and create connection and positive relationships. When our hearts are closed, we may feel constricted, alone, tight, defensive, inflexible, numb, irritable, or uncaring. Our breathing may be shallow, our chest tight, our attention narrow. Our hearts may be closed because of some difficulties at home or a difficult interaction with a colleague. Or perhaps we are simply exhausted from the speed and pace of life. Whatever the obstacle, once we have more awareness about the state of our heart, we can make more conscious choices. For example, if we have just had a difficult conversation with a colleague and notice our heart is closed, we may realize we need to remain extra attentive to a tendency to overreact to student behavior that would not otherwise trigger us.

Some common reasons we close our hearts may include:

- Fear of being hurt or criticized

- Attachment to a specific agenda or to a particular outcome and concern that opening our heart may compromise that agenda or outcome

- Feeling overwhelmed, overloaded—that it's not possible to take on "one more thing"

- Fear of making a mistake

- Believing that a challenge or difficulty is ours alone to figure out

- Experiencing emotional intensity, numbing, or grief in one's personal or professional life

- Noticing that others do not share our values or feeling that our perspective is not being valued

- Believing there is not enough time or space for an open-hearted approach

Inquiring into the state of our heart can help us identify our own personal obstacles to caring so that we can recognize what kinds of support and resources we need to take action and open our heart again. For example, if we feel our perspective is consistently not valued in a school setting, we may need to set up a personal meeting with the principal or find a colleague who is supportive. If we have a student whose behavior or attitude triggers us to close our heart, we may need to find a way to create a different kind of relationship with that student, shift our own attitude, or set up a one-on-one meeting with that student to find out what is beneath the behavior. If our heart is closing because we feel constantly overwhelmed, we may need to practice saying no to requests or commitments or to carve out more space and time for rest and rejuvenation. Following is a list of practices that educators have used to overcome these obstacles to caring.

Activities for Overcoming the Obstacles to Caring

- This week, note when your heart is opened and when it is closed. Notice if there is a particular reason why your heart is opened or closed.
- Notice what tends to open your heart when it has been closed.
- Try engaging daily for a week in an activity that opens your heart, and note the difference for you personally and for your students.
- Before class, think of one thing you appreciate about each of your students or about the class as a whole.
- Consider sharing a compliment with each of your students about his or her work or behavior.
- Engage in some kind of activity at the end of the day that helps you let go of any heaviness or sense of burden as you intentionally make the shift from your professional to your personal life.
- Ask for help from colleagues, family, and friends.

Practice: Including Vulnerability

As Brené Brown (2010) points out, "Staying vulnerable is a risk we have to take if we want to experience connection." *Vulnerability* refers to our willingness to share aspects of ourselves that don't feel polished and perfected. It includes the willingness to be our authentic selves, to share what is true for us, and to allow ourselves to be seen in our wholeness. It may mean admitting we don't know an answer or asking a colleague for support. It may mean sharing a story from our lives that holds an important lesson for our students. It may mean sharing with our students that we are going through a personal issue and need to take some time off to take care of ourselves. Expressing vulnerability might also mean engaging in "truth telling," in which we take the risk to speak up at a faculty meeting about an issue that is challenging, or talking to a colleague we have had a conflict with. Being vulnerable may require offering an apology, admitting a mistake, or presenting an opposing point of view. And finally, vulnerability might include offering our experience and expertise, as sometimes it is much easier to share our imperfections, doubts, and shortcomings than our strengths.

In the simplest sense, vulnerability means that we welcome and express the full range of our humanness—with all of our gifts and quirks and foibles. As Brown (2010) also notes, our attempts to avoid our own vulnerability cut off other rich experiences in our lives as well:

> We live in a vulnerable world. And one of the ways we deal with it is we numb vulnerability. . . . I learned this from the research—that you cannot selectively numb emotion. You can't say, here's the bad stuff. Here's vulnerability, here's grief, here's shame, here's fear, here's disappointment . . . I don't want to feel these. . . . You can't numb those hard feelings without numbing all our emotions. You cannot selectively numb. So when we numb those, we numb joy, we numb gratitude, we numb happiness.

In this way, our vulnerability is a gateway to our authenticity and to the joy, purpose, and meaning that come from engaging our whole selves. As part of acknowledging and welcoming our vulnerability, it is also helpful to learn to practice compassion with ourselves. Self-compassion invites us to relax our perfectionism and judgment and to accept and forgive ourselves when we have an off day, make a mistake, don't have the answer to a problem, or when we simply need help or support. Of course, it's necessary to use our own internal compass about when and how to express our vulnerability in ways that take into consideration our own communities and contexts. Our school communities may not provide the safe or appropriate place for personal issues that might be better explored in therapeutic contexts. And, just as we can teach our students how to be authentic without being overly confessional, we can take a similar approach with adult learning communities. However, when we do appropriately share our personal stories, flaws, strengths, and joys, we help to create a more compassionate and rewarding professional community.

The following activities can support us in including our own vulnerability.

Activities for Including Vulnerability

- Acknowledge a mistake that you make this week—whether it is to yourself or another person. Notice the impact of this sharing.
- Identify the situations and moments when you tend to feel most vulnerable. (Note: sometimes the expression of joy, play, and spontaneity can feel vulnerable.) See if you can recognize any gifts that come from your vulnerability.
- Consider how self-judgment and perfectionism impact your life. What do you tend to be hard on yourself about? Why? Try engaging in one act of self-compassion this week.
- Notice how you tend to respond to your own feelings of vulnerability. Do you recoil or suppress? Do you isolate? Do you seek support or connection with others?
- Consider how you react or respond to others when they are vulnerable. How do you react to your colleagues? Students?
- Think about how vulnerability might be a birthplace of innovation, creativity, or change in your life.

Practice: Considering Forgiveness

The word *forgive* means to give up resentments or to pardon an offense. As Desmond Tutu (2004) remarked, "Because we are not infallible, because we will hurt especially the ones we love, we will always need a process of forgiveness to deal with those all too human breaches in relationships. They are an inescapable characteristic of the human condition." Every day, students and teachers will make mistakes—this is a natural and necessary aspect of teaching and learning. The willingness to forgive ourselves and others is an important and powerful aspect of teaching with an open heart.

When we feel that someone has offended or hurt us or made a mistake at our expense, we can harden our hearts and allow each error to solidify our views about ourselves or a student or colleague—or we can intentionally choose to consider forgiveness. Forgiveness invites a fresh, open way of seeing ourselves and others, and it allows us to acknowledge both the suffering in the situation and the possibility for moving into new ways of relating in the future. When a violation of a boundary has occurred, conscious forgiveness requires naming what has happened and speaking about the ways it affected us. Forgiveness does not mean that we excuse the behavior in any way, but rather acknowledge it and consider letting go of the pain and resentment in ourselves. It also invites us to consider the ways we have hurt others—intentionally or unintentionally—and how we may wish to be forgiven.

Think back to your school experiences. Did a teacher ever give you a second chance when you had crossed a boundary, broken a rule, or hurt someone? How did you feel about this? How did you respond? So many times, when a student violates a boundary, our tendency can be to either ignore the situation or make light of it, to exile or label the student in some way, or to close our heart to that student. However, we can draw clear boundaries, ask students to take responsibility, and offer forgiveness and a fresh start in a way that invites students to stay present and involved in the community rather than checking out.

Studies show that people who forgive are happier and healthier than those who hold resentments (McCullough, Pargament, & Thoresen, 2001). One study examined how forgiving an offender led to improved functioning in cardiovascular and nervous systems (Witvliet, Ludwig, & Laan, 2001). However, forgiveness can be an extremely difficult practice, especially in highly volatile situations. For example, if one student has bullied another student, how can we find it in our hearts to forgive the bully while addressing the behavior? In this situation, to forgive is not to deny or condone what has happened. Instead, we can take the time to listen to the students involved, see what is behind the behavior, and create clear consequences for the destructive behavior. We can then consider that something new may happen in the future and once again open our hearts and minds to this student who has bullied another. As one teacher remarked, "I let my students know that every day is a new day and they can change the course of their behavior and experience at school at any time." By giving her students this invitation, this teacher lets them know that she is always holding the possibility for their best selves to show up at school and that what they have done in the past does not have to shape who they are.

Note: When forgiveness is coupled with reconciliation, it also requires that the offender make a commitment to repair the harm and not repeat the behavior in the future. When considering forgiveness, the following activities can be helpful.

Activities for Considering Forgiveness

- Consider one thing you might forgive in yourself this week.
- Reflect on how you might use forgiveness with a colleague or student this week.
- Initiate a discussion with students on forgiveness and trustworthiness. We may be willing to forgive someone for a boundary crossed, but it often takes time to build trust again after such a situation.
- Brainstorm with students or colleagues how we can show our trustworthiness in a relationship. Trusting relationships involve both the act of trusting and the act of being trustworthy.

In the first part of the chapter, we looked at ways to work with an open heart in our own teaching practice. Next, we will look at how to foster safe, trusting, inclusive classrooms where students can cultivate an open heart and a sense of connection with self and others.

Cultivating an Open Heart in the Classroom

As research shows, fostering positive relationships and classroom climates is critical to students' learning, development, growth, and attachment to school. The following principles and practices will offer a variety of ways to create safe, engaging, inclusive learning environments that welcome both the hearts and minds of students (Roeser et al., 2006).

Principle: Investing in Relationships and Community Building

Investing time and energy in creating safe, inclusive, respectful learning communities is an essential aspect of fostering social, emotional, and academic learning. If we want students to engage both their hearts and minds, we need to create conditions of safety in which this can occur. When thinking about the interrelationship between physical, intellectual, and emotional safety, Cathy O'Neill-Grace's observations are helpful. She notes, "You can't learn effectively if you are scared of being beaten up after school or if you are getting dirty looks all day from the in crowd" (O'Neill-Grace & Thompson, 2002, p. 213). Not only are students distracted when they feel anxious or threatened, but studies have shown that their emotions directly impact the parts of their brain that are available for learning (Durlak et al., 2011).

Investing in the learning community does take some time, *and* it yields tremendous benefits—from a more efficient and less disruptive learning environment, to increased student engagement and academic achievement, to greater joy in learning and a deepening sense of meaning and purpose in the classroom.

One seventh-grade teacher shared a story about a student he struggled with every day. She would talk back to him, put down other students, and crack hurtful jokes. As soon as the teacher saw her walk in the door, his heart would close and his whole body would tighten. He realized he was fortifying himself against her "assaults." One day, she made a wisecrack, and the teacher lost his temper and sent her into the hall. When the other students went to recess, he asked her to stay in and talk. Her eyes welled up as she asked, "Why do you hate me?" In that moment, he realized that he was contributing to the standoff between them. Later that day, a colleague told him about a practice she had been doing for years with particularly troubling students: she made time before every class to picture their faces and think of one thing she appreciated about each of them, focusing on the great potential she saw in them. The teacher tried this practice and made a concerted effort to warmly greet the student as she came in, something he naturally did with other students, but because his heart had felt so closed to her, he hadn't been able to show her this same caring. Over time, her behavior changed significantly, they developed a close, trusting relationship, and the whole tenor of the classroom changed because this student was now engaged in the class in a new way.

Practice: Modeling and Encouraging Authentic Self-Expression

Modeling authentic self-expression includes sharing our interests, background, sense of humor, and personal stories. As teachers, it is important to model how to share aspects of our personality and personal experiences in appropriate and relevant ways. For example, when introducing our content area, we might share a story about how we first came to discover our passion for the subject. When introducing a unit on heroes, we could talk about our own childhood heroes and who our heroes are now. Many students may not have considered who their teachers are outside of their school-defined roles, and yet this information is often riveting to students when shared in ways that relate to the content and learning goals of the class.

In service of this personal connection, we can bring a variety of activities into our classrooms that allow students to know more about us in appropriate ways. One Denver high school began its school year by having students play "teacher bingo." Students were asked to find the teachers who met certain descriptions such as, "the teacher who has climbed three mountains in Colorado" or "the teacher who grew up in a village outside of Mexico City" or "the teacher who was a semi-professional baseball player." Students were often pleasantly surprised by which teachers matched the descriptions, and they began to see their teachers as more complex human beings with rich lives and histories.

Of course, these same activities can be used to support students to share authentically about themselves and learn more about each other. As we create the learning community, it is helpful to regularly integrate activities that allow students to bring their personal interests, experiences, and stories into the room to foster a deeper sense of meaning, purpose, and relevance. The following activities can support authentic self-expression in the classroom.

Activities for Modeling and Encouraging Authentic Self-Expression

- At the beginning of the school year, introduce an activity that helps you get to know students and helps them get to know you, such as teacher bingo. (See the appendix, page 159, for additional activities.)
- Share a story about yourself from a time when you were your students' age. What kind of student were you? What motivated you? What challenged you? What was school like then? Students are often captivated by these stories.
- At the beginning of the year, ask students to write short biographies or share stories about their summer or last school year. If possible, ask each student to share a part of the story. Begin with a story of your own.
- Ask students to bring in a "people bag" in which they include five important artifacts from their life and explain why each matters to them. Make sure to bring in a people bag of your own to share as well.

Practice: Cultivating Gratitude

Consciously choosing to practice gratitude, personally and in a learning community, can dramatically improve the experience of our work, students, and classroom. Practicing gratitude helps us to open our hearts to our students, reframe, and successfully meet challenging situations, and notice and appreciate unexpected gifts in our teaching life. When we bring gratitude practices to the classroom, we are also fostering students' resilience and capacity to learn. Research has shown that incorporating gratitude practices with students leads to "higher reported levels of the positive states of alertness, enthusiasm, determination, attentiveness and energy" (Emmons & McCullough, 2013b, p. 1).

For example, one teacher begins each Monday morning with a five-minute period dedicated to celebrations. In this short period of time, students are asked to share what they are celebrating in their week or in their lives. Another teacher asks students to begin class by journaling about what they are grateful for and then gathers the students together and invites them to share one thing from their list—small or large. For some students, this might be a moment in the hallway with a friend or walking to school with a parent. For other students, their gratitude sharing might be that they won a big soccer game. Other students may simply feel grateful that the sun is shining today. In a world rife with complex problems and rampant cynicism, practicing gratitude can draw attention to our inner and outer resources, help us build on the positive aspects of life, and support us in finding the strength to meet the challenges we may face in the future. However, cultivating and practicing gratitude is necessarily invitational rather than obligatory. There may be days or times when any one of us may not feel we can authentically take part in such a practice, and that is important to recognize too.

The following activities can support us in cultivating gratitude.

Activities for Cultivating Gratitude

- At the beginning or end of the day, ask each student to share one thing for which he or she is grateful for right now or from earlier in the day. Or, end the day or class with a gratitude note card or a quick sharing circle in which each person offers one word about something he or she is grateful for.

- Consider starting gratitude journals in which students consistently note what they are grateful for. This practice immediately and effectively opens our hearts to ourselves and to each other.

- Cultivate gratitude for your students. Note, on a daily basis, what you are grateful for in relation to your classroom, students, colleagues, and professional life.

- For a week, greet your students at the door authentically and with kindness as they come in. Feel your appreciation for them. See how this impacts your teaching and relationships.

Practice: Helping Students Develop Compassion

How can we directly help students develop compassion for themselves and each other? When we give them opportunities to know each other beyond their roles in the classroom, this naturally opens a doorway to new ways of seeing each other. There are many strategies for engaging students in this way—from personal storytelling in community circles to clearly defined group projects. Consider the following activities to help students develop warmth and compassion for their classmates.

Activities for Helping Students Develop Compassion

- As the school year progresses, develop an occasional appreciation practice during which students write appreciations to three other students in the classroom. Each student then receives three written or spoken appreciations from other students.

- Engage in some kind of service project as a class. Discover what students care about in the community. Encourage them to take action as part of your class and support their efforts.

- Create a classroom mural in which each person contributes an image, phrase, their handprint—whatever is appropriate—but that represents and illustrates the diversity and beauty of the community. Display this mural in the classroom.

Practice: Supporting Students to Develop Trust and Discernment

When sequencing community-building activities, it is essential that we do not push our students to go too deep too fast and that we support them to safely share personally in a public context. When students are asked to share personally, it is essential that we also offer them the option to pass or participate by simply listening. The following story illustrates the potency of trusting students to decide when they are ready to share something personal.

A ninth-grade teacher shared that she was concerned about one of her students who seemed disconnected from her classmates. The teacher respected the student's privacy, knew that she was shy, and understood that culturally the girl had been taught to be a more private person. As trust was built within the group, the teacher and students addressed the issue of body image. For the first time, the student spoke when it was her turn and shared her fears about recently being diagnosed with a medical condition that could cause her to gain weight. She shared that though she was scared, she knew she could count on the group to support her. The group was surprised that the girl who had never shared would open up about something so personal. One by one, her peers responded by saying how much they admired her strength and found her to be a beautiful person inside and out. By the end of class, the girl was beaming, and there was a very strong sense of connection in the room. Had the teacher insisted that the student share before she was ready, it is likely that she would not have felt safe enough to eventually talk about something that really mattered to her.

We can support the development of classroom safety by trusting our students to know when it's the right time to speak up. We can also help our students discern what stories and experiences are appropriate to share in class and which might be better shared in a counselor's office. Learning how to share authentically and appropriately is an essential skill for young people, both in school and life. It is helpful to remind students that though class may involve some personal sharing, they are not being asked to share secrets. Instead, everyone shares personally in the service of learning more about ourselves and each other and to support the group's social, emotional, and academic development.

With older students, it is also important to share that teachers are legally required to report situations where they feel concerned about a student's safety and well-being—including times when there is concern that students may hurt themselves or others. Please see page 114 on confidentiality agreements for more on this important topic.

As we discuss the parameters of personal sharing, we may also wish to include a conversation about social media. These technologies, along with many popular reality television shows, have contributed to fostering a particular kind of confessional culture that has influenced the way students communicate their own personal stories and feelings. Imitating the media, students might choose to reveal dramatic or inappropriate things about themselves that create negative consequences for them in their peer community or school lives. The following activities support students in developing trust *and* discernment.

Activities for Helping Students Develop Trust and Discernment

- Have a conversation with students in which you talk about personal sharing in the context of academic learning. How does it help them learn, remember, make connections, and feel engaged?

- With older students, distinguish between personal sharing and counseling or therapy and give examples of personal sharing that is appropriate and inappropriate for the classroom.
- Explicitly spend time discussing how personal sharing is invitational and not obligatory. With older students, discuss why.
- Have a conversation about trust and trustworthiness as they relate to personal sharing.
- Discuss the role of technology. How has the Internet and media such as Facebook, texting, and even reality television impacted how we express ourselves and what we share?

Principle: Developing Cultural Responsiveness

Cultivating an open heart also means fostering and demonstrating a deep appreciation of diversity in all of its forms. The United States has one of the most heterogeneous societies in the world. According to the 2010 U.S. Census, non-Hispanic whites make up 63.4 percent of the population—while 36.6 percent (more than a third) of the U.S. population consists of people of color from different ethnic, racial, and cultural backgrounds. Every year, our school system becomes more ethnically, religiously, culturally, and socially diverse.

Our individual cultural orientations are evident in all of our interactions. According to Shelley Zion, Elizabeth Kozleski, and Mary Lou Fulton (2005):

> Cultural identity development is an ongoing process, as we are exposed to more and different sets of beliefs and values, and may choose to adopt ones that were not part of our original upbringing. Cultural identity is constructed within the individual, but continually influenced by the interactions among and between people in society. (p. 3)

Part of our job as educators is to help students better understand their diverse identities and communities and become more comfortable and confident interacting with others—especially those people they perceive as being different from themselves. In this way, an open heart is necessary but not sufficient—as we also need the commitment and discipline to engage in this work and to facilitate it with our students.

When we make conscious choices to help students break down stereotypes and divisions, we foster an inclusive learning community. Here, students learn to value their own perspective, as well as the perspectives of others. They begin to understand themselves in the context of the larger, complex community of which they are a part. To create such a classroom, we can take specific steps to promote inclusion, foster the valuing of diversity, and create genuine connections that support students in going beyond mere tolerance to a place of real understanding and care.

Geneva Gay (2000), in her book *Culturally Responsive Teaching*, states that culturally responsive teaching has the following characteristics:

- It acknowledges the legitimacy of the cultural heritages of different ethnic groups, both as legacies that affect students' dispositions, attitudes, and approaches to learning and as worthy content to be taught in the formal curriculum.

- It builds bridges of meaning between home and school experiences, as well as between academic abstractions and lived sociocultural realities.
- It uses a wide variety of instructional strategies that are connected to different learning styles.
- It teaches students to know and praise their own and each other's cultural heritages.
- It incorporates multicultural information, resources, and materials in all the subjects and skills routinely taught in schools. (p. 29)

Modeling and teaching cultural responsiveness is an essential ingredient in creating an inclusive, relationship-based classroom in which all students thrive. With every student demographic, this approach develops critical skills and awareness that relate directly to learning outcomes and students' capacity for success in a global culture and workplace.

Developing our own capacity for cultural responsiveness gives us the foundation to cultivate this with our students. Taking a deep look at our own worldviews and beliefs and biases allows us to see when we might be hindering the sense of inclusivity in our classroom. What did we learn from our families and communities about other cultures? What messages do society and the media give us about race, class, culture, ethnicity, gender, and sexual orientation? Which of those messages do we believe, and how does that affect our behavior? What aspects of difference scare us or trigger us, and why? Self-inquiry can be an important first step, as it raises our awareness about ourselves and about our own perspectives and worldview. The next steps along this path call us to have the courage and discipline to act on this awareness—to speak up, take risks, and reach out even when we are uncomfortable.

When teachers integrate social and emotional learning activities into the curriculum, students get to know each other personally in meaningful contexts, allowing social masks and conditioned roles to more easily drop away. From this place of authenticity, students are better able to see each other with openness and relate to each other with compassion. One high school student noted his experience after a year-long advisory class:

> At the beginning of the year, I never talked to any of the native Spanish speakers at our school. But being in this class with a number of Spanish speakers, we began to talk more and hang out at lunch and after school. We started playing pick-up soccer. We began to see we had things in common despite our language difference.

A native Spanish-speaking student in this same class shared his experience:

> At first I didn't want to talk much. I wasn't sure how other students would react to me. But then we had the time to hear from each other—to talk about things that were important to us—and things began to change.

A classroom community will grow stronger as teachers expect and support students to move beyond assumptions and stereotypes. In this process, we are not striving for "sameness," but for an environment that acknowledges difference, welcomes diverse experiences and perspectives, and acknowledges our common humanity. There is no magic formula for working with the complex issues of difference, but educators can take an intentional and proactive approach to create a community that feels safe and values diversity of backgrounds, perspectives, and experiences.

Creating a culturally responsive classroom also involves raising our own awareness as teachers about how certain activities and norms might impact students differently because of culture. As with all learning endeavors, we will not always be able to see beyond our own conditioning or foresee what issues might emerge in the classroom. We *will* make mistakes, and we can be *responsive*—that is, we can have the humility, curiosity, and willingness to learn from our experiences and seek the help we need. We can listen to and learn from colleagues and community members who might have very different perspectives from our own.

One team of teachers working in an urban high school was preparing for a social-emotional learning lesson in which students would share stories about their names. Students were invited to speak about their names: that is, the meaning of their names, who they were named after (if anyone), why their parents chose their name, and any nicknames they had that they wanted to share. One teacher of European ancestry suggested that the class extend the activity and create a unit in which students researched the origins of their name and how it connected them back to their ancestors. She shared that this kind of activity had been very meaningful and powerful for her earlier in her own life. Through that process, she had discovered her Swedish ancestry and the stories of her people as they had immigrated to the United States.

The students in the class, who were mostly African American and Latino, engaged in this name research activity with enthusiasm. Their research unearthed some difficult truths that many of these students were encountering for the first time. Some of the African American students discovered that their last names were connected to the slaveholders. Some Latino students discovered how their names were connected to the complex history of Mexico and Latin America (including the devastating impact of the conquistadors on the native peoples of the Americas). Many of the students experienced anger, grief, and confusion at learning these stories. While this information was critical for the students' understanding of their identities and our global histories, the teachers later reflected that it would have been wise to have a larger context for these stories and a way to process the emerging emotions.

The name stories, which were initially intended to help students simply remember each other's names, catalyzed a much larger field of inquiry and feeling. In debriefing this experience, teachers decided that in the future, they would connect this name research to a larger social studies unit exploring various cultural histories. They would bring in community members to share some of their name stories and to support students with any questions that might arise, and they would schedule the activity later in the year when there was more trust and emotional capacity. Though initially the students' feelings and realizations were a lot to handle, the teachers felt good about the way they worked with the issues and developed a plan for the future. In this way, the name story experience became a rich learning opportunity for both students and teachers.

Cultural responsiveness does not mean we will always be able to anticipate or see all the complex issues that may emerge in a situation in the classroom. The simplest of inquiries can evoke confusing, conflicting, and sometimes painful emotions. It is always helpful to engage in professional development or training that explicitly supports cultural awareness. It is essential to commit to working to expand our own views, actively value the rich cultural histories of our students, and be thoughtful about our strategies and approaches. When we make mistakes, it is also important to have the courage to take responsibility for these mistakes, make amends, and get the support we need to shift our practices.

Cultivating an open heart supports us in more compassionately and effectively engaging with issues of cultural difference. Cultural responsiveness requires self-inquiry and reflection *and* commitment and action. An open heart helps us work from a foundation of caring, as we dive into this complex territory that involves painful histories of oppression, as well as current-day realities of unequal access to resources. An open heart can also help us look at our own personal worldview and history and to do the work of recognizing and dismantling assumptions we might have about our students or parent community. Finally, an open heart can help us to remember that there is no single or universal cultural orientation and that we must continue to work to broaden our worldview so that we do not act or react from a limited or narrow place.

As we grow and develop as lifelong learners and practitioners of cultural responsiveness, it is important to remember that there are no quick fixes or easy formulas. However, engaging in this work is richly rewarding and essential to fostering social, emotional, and academic learning in our students. See engagedteaching.org for other books and organizations that support a culturally responsive school.

The following activities can support us in building cultural responsiveness in our own practice and with our students.

Activities for Building Cultural Responsiveness

- Learn more about your own history, heritage, community, family, culture, and traditions, and share this information with your students.
- List some characteristics of your culture. Consider your communication style and other cultural norms. Notice how this impacts your teaching approach, and consciously bring in other approaches.
- Pay attention to the following in your classroom and school: Who is silent, and who participates? Who tends to be reprimanded or disciplined most frequently? What kinds of teacher-student interactions occur? What about student to student? Do you notice any pattern? Over time, see if these correspond with cultural differences.
- Examine disparate discipline data and tracking patterns in schools and see what you discover. Discuss these findings as a faculty.
- Integrate discussions of culture into your classroom. Invite students to share about their own cultural traditions. Use personal cultural history exercises (personal narratives) and affirm cultural identity.

- Survey the resources you use in your classroom—books, texts, posters, illustrations, and magazines. Notice what cultures these resources represent and consciously expand the diversity of resources you offer and work with.

- Teach students about racism, classism, ableism, sexism, and other isms. Teach students to think critically, examine multiple perspectives, and understand historical oppression.

- Be clear about what is acceptable in your classroom—for example, "In this class, I will not tolerate jokes or derogatory comments about skin color, ethnicity, language, gender, or culture."

- Help students and colleagues rethink the stereotypes they express. Provide accurate information that helps them learn new perspectives and rethink learned stereotypes.

- Seek out antibiased and multicultural curricula.

- Read and discuss Peggy McIntosh's (2003a, 2003b) research and writing on white privilege. Invite kids to explore implications and discuss how to change systems.

Note: Adapted from Understanding Culture *(Zion et al., 2005) and personal communication with Dr. Vivian Elliott (September 15, 2012).*

Practice: Using Personal Storytelling

One powerful way that we can help open the hearts of our students and create an inclusive learning community is by including personal storytelling in our class time. As Laura Simms, international storyteller, writer, and educator, notes:

> There is nothing more transformational or deeply beneficial than being able to tell one's story and be heard. . . . In the daily world of schools and curriculum, children's personal histories are a living library or medicine chest of creative energy and meaning. (L. Simms, personal communication, June 16, 2012)

Personal storytelling invites and honors all student voices and expands students' communication skills beyond more conventional approaches such as reports, debate, and dialogue. As students practice sharing stories, they learn to see and experience each other with an openness that fosters an increased sense of belonging and inclusion. The invitation to share personal stories appropriate for the classroom also helps students make connections between their own lives and the content they are studying. When they experience their stories being respectfully heard and honored, students feel that they matter to their teachers and peers. As author Sam Keen notes, "We don't know who we are until we hear ourselves speaking the drama of our lives to someone we trust to listen with an open mind and heart" (Elbot & Fulton, 2008, p. 60).

This practice creates a wonderful and unique opportunity for all students to feel heard and known. Two of the primary formats that support generative personal storytelling are council and community circle (see the appendix and summary of instructional practices, page 159). In these practices, students have an opportunity to tell their stories, uninterrupted and one by one, on a common theme. They are invited to listen to each other without judgment, to see each other anew. They are encouraged to speak spontaneously, with authenticity and without judgment of self or other and to listen and speak from the heart, rather than from the analytical mind. These are essential skills not only for school, but for life. When we know each other's stories, we are less likely to stereotype or label each other and more likely to reach out compassionately and kindly to one another. As one middle school student said, "When I know someone—really know them—I don't want to hurt them." In this way, personal storytelling can be a highly effective and poignant way to bring students together—to see, celebrate, and honor our differences and commonalities. The following activities can support students with personal storytelling.

> ## *Activities for Using Personal Storytelling*
>
> - As part of a unit, invite students to write stories about their cultural background and to share those in class with one another.
> - Initiate a council or community circle in which students share one important tradition from their family or community.
> - Invite one student to volunteer to share at the beginning of class each Friday about a song, poem, book, or movie that connects to a class theme or topic.
> - If developmentally appropriate, read *Seedfolks* by Paul Fleischman and have a discussion about the gifts of culture and different cultures coming together. Or read *The House on Mango Street* by Sandra Cisneros and have students write their own versions, using the vignettes about family, community, and culture as prototypes. Both of these books can be directly connected to activities inviting personal storytelling from students.

Cultivating an Open Heart With Colleagues

Developing an open heart with our colleagues can support us in building positive relationships within the adult learning community, letting go of our entrenched beliefs about each other, and engaging in our work together with a true sense of possibility and collaboration.

Principle: Developing Allies Within the School Community

We often go about our days feeling disconnected from our colleagues. Cultivating an open heart with colleagues involves reaching out and developing more intentionally positive and caring professional relationships. The rich exchange of ideas and feedback in the school community is an appealing idea, but educators frequently feel alone in facing classroom challenges. The pressure of an intense workload can often cause us to withdraw, especially when there are not many opportunities to gather with colleagues in authentic and supportive ways. When we are busy and stressed out, it can simply be difficult to find the time to reach out to others. However, finding allies allows collaboration and connection with others, helps us to work more effectively and efficiently, and develops a positive school culture from the inside out.

> "As school systems developed a greater educator capacity (i.e., as teachers got better), it was peers who became the strongest source of innovaetion."
>
> —The McKinsey report, "How the World's Most Improved School Systems Keep Getting Better"

Following are some of the benefits of having supportive colleagues:

- Changing how we teach and how we interact in our schools is hard work, and we are more likely to stay with an Engaged Teaching Approach if we have the moral support of one or more colleagues. A commitment to do this work with colleagues will help sustain the approach in spite of missteps, failures, and obstacles.

- Even veteran teachers have only one set of experiences to inform their understanding. Exchanging perspectives and knowledge with others will yield a fuller, richer, more nuanced understanding of teaching and of the school culture.

- Other colleagues not only have different views and ideas, but they may have complementary skills that are better suited to address certain challenges.

- Finding supportive colleagues enhances the quality of work life. Being part of even the smallest collaborative network will, at a minimum, help sustain the commitment to changing our own classroom practice and can catalyze change in the larger school culture.

The following activities support us in reaching out to colleagues and engaging our adult learning community.

Activities for Reaching Out to Colleagues and Engaging Your Community

- Invite colleagues to join a faculty group, school team, or committee to work on an issue that matters to you.
- Ask colleagues to join a book discussion group focusing on topics important to your school or community.
- Find one colleague for a weekly lunch check-in during which you share challenges and successes and set goals for the upcoming week. Interview one another to get to know each other's teaching approach and philosophy.
- Explore opportunities to spend time socially with colleagues. Consider initiating a monthly gathering of colleagues who share a common interest.
- Take time during a professional development day or planning time to share about cultural backgrounds and traditions. Consider including celebrations from different cultures throughout the year.
- Notice when your heart opens and closes with colleagues. Who are the colleagues who tend to trigger you to close your heart? Use self-inquiry to understand more about why your heart closes around these individuals. Do you feel a lack of trust? Fear? Judgment? Competition? Take time to focus on seeing something new about that colleague.
- Find a way to approach a colleague you generally avoid. Actively cultivate appreciation for him or her in an authentic way. If you are willing, reach out with a gesture, such as a note of appreciation or an invitation to coffee.

Conclusion

Throughout this chapter we have explored the many facets of cultivating an open heart in our own practice, as well as with and among our students and colleagues. When we foster our capacity to care deeply, act with compassion, develop connection, effectively engage others who are different from ourselves, and practice cultural responsiveness, we directly support the learning environment. And, as we develop and sustain positive professional relationships with our students and colleagues, we are likely to experience increased satisfaction and joy in our workplace. In the next chapter, we will explore how engaging our self-observer can further support our teaching practice.

3

Engaging the Self-Observer

Reflection is one of the greatest contributors to our ability to positively alter our own thinking and behavior.

—Robyn R. Jackson

Self-Reflection

What tools do you currently use in your life to reflect on your teaching practice, build on your strengths, and learn from your challenges?

Engaging the self-observer means tapping into the part of ourselves that has the capacity to notice our own thoughts, behaviors, and triggers; reflect on what we notice; make conscious choices going forward; and shift our course of action when necessary. This dimension includes both developing the self-observer in ourselves and fostering this capacity in our students.

The Teacher as Self-Observer

Cultivating our self-observer helps us develop a lifelong-learning approach to teaching, during which we continually learn from and improve our practice. Engaging this dimension supports us to learn from past situations, reflect on and shift our behaviors in the present, and plan ahead for future situations.

Principle: Becoming a Reflective Practitioner

Becoming a reflective practitioner involves a commitment to regularly looking at how we teach, how we act, what we believe, and the ways these impact our students and colleagues. As John Vitto (2003) says, "We all have certain deeply held beliefs about our profession and how to educate children. These beliefs not only influence our behavior but may also hinder our consideration of new strategies and ideas. If our goal is to prioritize teacher-student relationships

> "Clearly, teaching is a skill, and like any skill, it must be practiced. Just as athletes wanting to improve their skills must identify personal strengths and weaknesses, set goals, and engage in focused practice to meet those goals, teachers must also examine their practices, set growth goals, and use focused practice and feedback to achieve those goals. These reflective processes are essential to the development of expertise in teaching."
>
> —Robert Marzano

41

and other strategies that enhance resiliency, we must carefully examine our own belief systems" (p. 232).

Practice: Observing Ourselves

Practicing regular self-observation supports us to reflect on our practice and manage our emotions. Taking a moment before a class period helps us check in with ourselves and consider which direction the class needs to go. Taking a few minutes at the end of each class period to reflect on what worked and what didn't can help us improve our lessons. Noticing the moments when students are engaged, making intellectual leaps, or connecting with each other allows us to identify and build upon our own successes. And because we all have blind spots, talking regularly with a trusted colleague can support us in seeing things about our teaching we might not otherwise see. The following is a list of strategies that further develop our capacity to observe ourselves and learn from our own experiences.

Activities for Observing Ourselves

- Notice when you are feeling stressed and overwhelmed and consciously make time to take care of yourself in some way.
- Make a list of areas of your professional life that feel particularly challenging right now. Commit to getting help or support from a colleague, friend, mentor, or coach in at least one of those areas.
- Begin a practice in the classroom of noticing what energizes and inspires you, what challenges or depletes you, and what deepens your understanding of yourself and your teaching practices.
- Note what is working and not working in your teaching. Track lessons and approaches that are particularly successful. Build on these successes for future lesson planning.
- Become curious about your own worldview, beliefs, and perspectives (around culture, race, class, personality, style, and so on). This may include joining a training or study group on cultural responsiveness.
- Create a learning community with other educators in which each person gives and receives support, guidance, or feedback. This group could include colleagues from your school or other colleagues in the field.
- Schedule regular time (daily or weekly, if possible) to reflect on your own teaching practice. Consider setting quarterly goals and sharing those with a colleague. If possible, meet to discuss how you are doing with your goals and where you might need support. (See chapter 8 for more on goal setting.)

Practice: Engaging in Mindfulness

Observing ourselves in the heat of the moment can be challenging. However, we can develop practices that support us in slowing down and engaging in this kind of "reflection in action" (Schön, 1983, pp. 49–50). One way of developing this capacity in ourselves is to engage in mindfulness practices. As defined by Jon Kabat-Zinn (1994), "Mindfulness is paying attention in a particular way: on purpose, in the present moment, and nonjudgmentally" (p. 4). There are a growing number of programs and courses for educators that include simple mindfulness practices for teachers and school leaders. The manual of one stress-reduction program describes the benefits of mindfulness:

> An important aspect of mindfulness practice is to meet each experience with open attention. This is simple, but not easy, given the pervasiveness of the self-critical judging mind. By introducing mindfulness into our life, we can open ourselves to opportunities for increased clarity, insight, and relaxation. A variety of institutions have begun to incorporate mindfulness practices into their array of offerings, and mindfulness is now being taught in hospitals, prisons, schools, corporations, sports teams, and other organizations. (Cullen, Wallace, & Hedberg, 2009, pp. 11–12)

Activity for Breath Awareness

The following mindfulness activity is an example of a breath awareness practice. A version of this activity is often the first step in mindfulness courses.

1. Find a quiet place.
2. Sit on a chair so that both feet are flat on the ground. If possible, sit in a relaxed but upright posture in which you are supporting yourself rather than leaning on the back of the chair.
3. You can do this practice with open or closed eyes. If your eyes are open, gaze downward toward the floor in front of you. Relax your gaze so that you are not focused on anything in particular.
4. Take three deep breaths—slowly inhaling and exhaling.
5. Return to your normal relaxed breathing pattern and notice where you feel your breath entering and leaving your body. This could be in your nose, in your chest, or in your belly. Allow your attention to rest on that feeling of your body breathing.
6. At some point, you will notice that your attention has wandered from your breathing, and you are thinking about something. Acknowledge that you are thinking, whatever it might be about, and return your attention to the sensation of your body breathing. This provides the opportunity for you to notice what you are doing and come back to your breath and the present moment.
7. Engage in this breath awareness practice for five or ten minutes several times a week to develop your capacity for reflection.

For more information about mindfulness, see www.mindful.org/resources.

Practice: Cultivating Kindness Toward Ourselves

Consciously engaging our self-observer can help us become more aware of our values and strengths. And, at times, it can also shine a light on aspects of ourselves we are less comfortable with. As we look more closely at our own behaviors and perspectives, we may not like everything we discover. Because of this, one of the most important aspects of developing our self-observer is cultivating kindness toward ourselves. If we are harsh and judgmental toward ourselves when we uncover habits, biases, or belief systems that we don't want to have, then we may avoid any efforts toward further self-discovery. Adopting an attitude of kindness toward ourselves, along with a commitment to continual improvement, helps us to acknowledge our strengths and challenges and to continue to learn and develop our personal and professional capacities. The following activities can support this process.

Activities for Cultivating Kindness Toward Ourselves

- Devote a few minutes on the drive home to celebrate what went well during your day and to acknowledge your own strengths.
- If you find it difficult to offer kindness and compassion toward yourself, imagine you are writing an encouraging letter to a dear friend. What would you say to this friend?
- Because it is often easier to extend kindness to others, we can begin this practice by focusing on developing empathy for family, friends, and colleagues who are hurting, and then extend that same empathic feeling toward ourselves and our own difficulties. Take a few minutes each day to practice kindness toward yourself and others.

Practice: Reflecting on Actions and the Actor

Typically, we take an action, and then we reflect on the outcomes of the action, noticing what worked and what didn't. If we didn't accomplish our goal, we then try a new action. This has been referred to as *single-loop learning,* and it can be effective in solving many simple problems. However, if the actions we try still do not help us meet our goals, we may feel frustrated and disheartened. We could keep trying new actions, looking for the silver-bullet solution, or we could bring in a whole other aspect of observation to our process, in which we reflect on the *actor* (us) as well as the *action* (Senge et al., 2000). This process is called *double-loop learning.* The following story explores the way self-observation and the resulting double-loop learning supported the evolution of a freshman seminar program.

The staff of an urban high school decided to institute a freshman seminar to support their students with the transition to high school. The teachers were given several highly touted activity books to create some relationship-building and leadership lessons. However, within a month of the start of the seminar, most teachers dreaded the class and struggled with making the time productive and enjoyable. At the same time, they all felt they should know how to make this program successful—after all, the class was about connecting with kids, building relationships, and creating mentorship—something they all felt they did well. After that first year of the seminar, many of the teachers were frustrated and demoralized, and many had simply made the shift toward holding a study hall, with an occasional game or activity thrown in. Most everyone agreed it was time to cut the program and move on.

Then, an assistant principal suggested the teachers hold a staff meeting to take a fresh look at the whole situation. She guided the teachers through a process in which they revisited their vision, goals, successes, and challenges. She also asked questions like: What are our assumptions about advisories? Did we spend enough time gaining confidence in the concept before we launched? Did we have clear objectives? Did we invest enough time planning a clear and detailed curriculum?

In the midst of this process, a math teacher spoke up, saying, "You know, we get all kinds of training around teaching content, but I'm realizing I've never had any kind of training to do an advisory. At first, when we met today, I was one of those who thought we should throw this program out, but when I look at why we are doing this, it seems important to stick with it in some way." Another teacher chimed in, "Maybe we need to look at how we can also shift some aspects of our school culture, so this seminar doesn't feel like a token forty-five-minute class once a week." As soon as these two teachers spoke up, the entire faculty engaged in a rich discussion that led them to see the seminar "problem" in a whole new way. They realized that if they were going to create this kind of dedicated time with students, they needed to get the training and resources necessary to make it work well.

We have all had spontaneous "Aha!" moments when we suddenly see a problem from a completely different point of view, so that the solution becomes obvious. Though this happens naturally at times in our lives, self-observation can support us in more regularly cultivating these moments. Self-observation and double-loop learning involve going beyond a simple reflection on "what worked and what didn't" and engage us in deeper inquiry to understand more about how our own perceptions of the situation are affecting the outcome. A double-loop learning approach invites us to make these assumptions explicit so we can understand why we are seeing the situation the way we are. Double-loop learning can then help us discover novel solutions and creative approaches to stubborn challenges.

Principle: Shifting From Reacting to Responding

We all find ourselves in challenging situations in the classroom. Perhaps we have a radically different worldview from a student, and whenever that student speaks, we don't want to listen. Maybe we have developed feelings of resentment toward a student who continually disrupts the class. Perhaps we tend to get angry whenever a particular colleague speaks in a faculty meeting, because that person reminds us of someone else in our lives we struggle to get along with. Maybe we repeatedly end up in tense situations with the principal and can't quite figure out why we rub each other the wrong way. Self-observation gives us the opportunity to uncover what is beneath our reactions, so that we are able to consciously choose our behaviors and shift from reacting to responding.

Practice: Working With Triggers Through Inquiry

One of the first steps in shifting from reacting to responding is to acknowledge and work with our triggers. A *trigger* is a strong, reflexive, and often instantaneous reaction to a situation or behavior. Triggering often happens when we feel a boundary has been crossed or someone is threatening us—one of our students, a colleague, our class. Triggering can also happen when we feel our power, integrity, or authority is being undermined. In fact, at times triggering may signal us to pay attention to a legitimate and important violation of our boundaries. When we know we are in a triggered state, pausing, waiting, and reflecting before acting often open up our vision so that we can consider alternative ways of responding.

The practice of inquiry can also help us interrupt the reactive trigger cycles that leave us feeling disempowered and exhausted. As Robert Marzano (2011) suggests:

> To practice awareness and control over one's interpretations, teachers might ask themselves three questions: How am I interpreting this event? Will this interpretation lead to a positive outcome? If not, what's a more useful interpretation? (p. 90)

By taking a moment to ask one or more of these questions, we are able to choose a more productive approach. The following story illustrates the power of engaging the self-observer in an uncomfortable and tense situation.

After coming down hard on two fifth-grade boys at the end of one particularly long afternoon, an elementary teacher realized that she tended to discipline these two students more often than other students in part because of their assertive and dominating personalities. When she inquired into this situation, she saw a very particular pattern: they would interrupt her or crack a joke, she would snap at them and assign them extra work, and then she would feel guilty about her reaction and avoid those students. She was determined to do a more effective job managing the situation. After some more reflection, she realized that the reason these students triggered her was because their personalities reminded her of her older brother, who, as a child, picked on her mercilessly when he had friends over. In a flash of insight, she remembered that she finally got through to her brother when she spoke to him directly about his bullying when they were alone, instead of yelling at him in front of his friends. Connecting this experience to her classroom, she knew that she could more successfully honor, respect, and guide the students if she could choose not to take their behavior personally and overreact. In fact, she saw that it was her job to remember that this was likely to be a trigger for her and to consciously choose to relate to these students in a compassionate and clear way.

She also got curious about why these two students were acting in this way and decided to have a one-on-one conversation with each of them. In these conversations, the students revealed that they hadn't felt like their behavior was disruptive and were just trying to liven things up and be funny. The teacher discussed classroom dynamics and expectations, as well as appropriate ways for them to bring in their humor. She was then able to appreciate specific qualities they brought to class as well as set boundaries for the future. After their meetings, she was able to build on that foundation and continue the positive connection with each student.

The following activity can support us in interrupting our own trigger cycles.

Activity for Working With Triggers

When we feel triggered, the self-observer aspect of ourselves can help us pause and ask the following questions:

1. What is actually happening right now in this situation?

2. What emotions am I feeling? What am I experiencing in my body?

3. What other situations does this remind me of?

4. What am I really reacting to? How am I interpreting what is happening now? What are the values, beliefs, and assumptions that shape my interpretation?

5. Am I in the present? Or has this situation taken me to a memory of the past?

6. What does this student (or colleague) really want or need? What is underneath this behavior?

7. How might I reframe the situation so that I have more options?

8. How do I want to respond, and when? Now? Later?

Practice: Practicing the Pause

When we find ourselves feeling full-blown anger over a comment at a faculty meeting or a student snickering in class, it is likely that we are experiencing *emotional* or *amygdala hijacking*. Daniel Goleman (1995) coined this term to describe the reactive amygdala response in the brain. The amygdala is an almond-sized part of the temporal lobe of the brain in the limbic system; it is our brain's security alarm system. When the amygdala registers a strong sensory input that could signal potential danger, it triggers a physical response in the body before we have even had the chance to rationally think about the situation. The amygdala then sends urgent messages to every other major part of the brain, initiating the secretion of the body's fight-or-flight response hormones, mobilizing the brain center for movement, and activating the cardiovascular system. When we are hijacked in this way, we literally cannot think rationally or consciously choose a response. However, if we can recognize the signs that our body is moving into a fight-or-flight response pattern, we can engage our neocortex and executive functioning to insert a pause that interrupts this hijacking cycle before it takes us over.

The following story illustrates the way "practicing the pause" and using inquiry can move us from a pattern of reacting to responding and can open up new possibilities in challenging situations.

A facilitator was leading a workshop on social and emotional learning to a group of fifty faculty members at a rural public high school. The group was in the midst of a conversation about brain research and emotional intelligence, when one veteran teacher stood up and protested, "I just don't know about all of this stuff. I've been teaching for twenty years, and I've been doing just fine. This is a waste of our time." The facilitator's heart began to race—she wanted to defend what she was teaching and present the research to back up why this social and emotional work was so core to academic learning. She took a breath, decided to "practice the pause," and calmed her impulse to react. Then, she responded, saying, "Can you say more about why this feels like a waste of time to you?"

The teacher looked at her, surprised, and said, "Sure. Well, it just feels like you're trying to make me into someone I'm not. I mean, I'm sorry, but I'm just never going to be the kind of teacher that walks around the halls hugging kids."

In that moment, the facilitator understood a whole other layer to this teacher's concerns. "Thank you so much for speaking about that. I want to assure you that this work is not about hugging kids. And it's not about doing anything that feels inauthentic to you. This is about every teacher in this room finding their particular way of making a connection with students—that's all."

He nodded. "Well that's a relief to me, because sometimes we get these outside people coming in telling us how to run our classrooms and be with kids, and I get sick of it."

The facilitator stayed with the teacher's concerns for five more minutes, and it led to a rich discussion about the disempowerment that teachers sometimes felt in the school, especially when their own expertise and wisdom weren't being acknowledged or honored. After the session ended, the facilitator saw that both she and the teacher had been given an opportunity to work with their own triggers. And, unexpectedly, their willingness to practice the pause and engage the triggers with curiosity had led the group into important territory that they would not have otherwise explored.

The following sequence can support us to disengage from emotional hijacking and practice the pause in situations where we might otherwise react.

Activity for Practicing the Pause

The following five-step process will help you raise your awareness and capacity to reflect, so that you are able to pause before you act:

1. **Observe what's occurring.** Pay attention to what's happening both within yourself and in the classroom or school. See if you can separate what you are feeling from the situation itself. Often when we are triggered, we are thrown into a feeling state that relates to the past, and so we feel a level of intensity that may not actually be present. So, in this step we might notice things like, "I am in the library with colleagues I trust, and someone is asking a question that is bringing up a reaction in me."

2. **Notice your response or reaction.** As you recognize that you are triggered, notice how you are behaving and what your body is experiencing. Are you calm, focused, poised, and responsive? Or are you frantic, tight, and reactive? What habits, worldviews, or biases might be impacting your feelings, thoughts, and interpretations of other people's behavior? For example, you might notice, "In this moment my heart is racing and my breath is tight. I'm acting calm, but I'm feeling angry. I have the perspective that this colleague of mine is railroading other people and not respecting their views and perspectives. I'm feeling disregarded and unheard."

3. **Acknowledge your choices.** Remember that you always have a choice about how you respond to situations. Are you making a choice in this situation or reacting out of habit? For example, "I could speak up right now, or I could wait until later and talk with this colleague one on one. I might normally just sweep these feelings under the rug and not say a word, but I know I need to address this at some point."

4. **Acknowledge what you don't have control over.** There may be aspects of the situation that you may not be able to change (such as a school policy or a difficult family situation impacting a student's behavior). What *do* you have control over in this situation? What is out of your range of influence? For example, "I realize that this colleague might not like what I have to share, and she may not change how she feels about this school policy."

5. **Make a choice.** Consciously make a choice about how to respond or, alternatively, delay decision making until the strong feelings have subsided and you have the capacity to think more clearly. For example, "I am really feeling too distraught now to speak to this colleague, but I am going to raise my hand and suggest we stick with our proposed agenda so that we can move through our meeting as planned. And, I will talk with my colleague tomorrow after school about this."

Self-Observation in the Classroom

Supporting students to engage their self-observer helps them to deepen their understanding of their own learning process and their social, emotional, and cognitive strengths and challenges. In this way, we can invite our students' curiosity, inquiry, and reflection in ways that engage them more meaningfully in their academic work and in the learning community.

Principle: Supporting Students to Become Self-Scientists

Just as cultivating our self-observer directly impacts our experience of teaching, so can this same capacity support student learning. With students, we often talk about the dimension of self-observation as the invitation to be a "self-scientist"—to observe and understand ourselves with the curiosity of a scientist, and, in this way to learn more about our own behaviors, emotions, learning styles, strengths, and challenges. This approach offers another way for students to become more active, engaged, and thoughtful learners. As self-scientists, students identify what tools support them to focus more effectively, access their own resilience, and navigate challenging situations. We can give students explicit practices that help them to observe themselves and ask them to notice the results. For example, we might introduce silence or a reflective activity and ask students to note how they feel before and after this activity. Or we might ask them to reflect on their progress throughout a project and write more directly about their challenges, struggles, and successes, so they can apply this learning to the future.

Practice: Introducing Silence and Reflection

Silence and reflection allow students to refresh themselves and refocus their attention on school. Teachers can introduce as little as thirty seconds of silence at the beginning of a class simply to allow students to arrive, settle, and quiet down. Teachers can then extend this time in silence with students, as they develop more comfort with this kind of reflection and quiet. Though students may be uncomfortable at first, as time goes by and they experience the benefits, they often ask for longer periods of silence. When we engage in silence and reflection, we can signal the beginning and end of that time with the sound of a chime or bell. We can ask students to simply sit quietly in their seats or play quiet music or give them the option of drawing during this time. The following story illustrates the power of introducing short periods of silence into the classroom to help students focus.

A second-grade teacher decided she wanted to introduce a "golden moment" into her classroom—a brief period of time during which she and her students would sit in silence together. She would ring a chime or bell to indicate when the moment began and when it ended. As they engaged in daily golden moments, the teacher asked her students to be self-scientists and to notice how they felt before, during, and after the moment of quiet. At the beginning of the year, the teacher began with one minute of silence. At first, many students could barely make it through that minute. They would fidget, look around the classroom, tap on their desks, and make distracting sounds. But after about two weeks of the golden moment practice, something began to shift. Gradually, the students were able to fully relax during the minute of silence. And, later in the year, if the teacher forgot to start the morning meeting with a golden moment, students would remind *her* to take a moment of silence. Over the months, the students got more and more comfortable with silence, until by the end of the year, the class started the day with five minutes of silence. If things got crazy and chaotic, one of the students would raise his or her hand and ask for a golden moment. The students, as self-scientists, were able to see when they were getting off track and what they needed to refocus and calm themselves.

Following are some activities for introducing silence and reflection into the classroom.

Activities to Introduce Silence and Reflection

- With younger students, introduce a golden moment during which students sit quietly on the floor or at their desks with eyes closed or open. (See page 163 in the appendix for more on this.)

- At the beginning of a class or in the midst of a particularly chaotic time, ask students to engage in a short period of silence. Strike a chime or bell, and ask students to listen to the sustained sound of the chime until they can no longer hear it anymore. Students can raise their hands as soon as they no longer hear the sound. Simply listening to the sound of the chime or bell can help them to refocus their attention.

- Start the day with reflective journaling during which students write in silence for two to five minutes on an open-ended theme.

- Introduce a short breathing practice in which students gently focus on breathing from their bellies (belly breathing) and learn to increase the length of their inhale and exhale.

Practice: Exploring Students' Learning Edges

Each of our students has a unique set of challenges or "learning edges." In order to meet these learning edges and develop their skills and capacities, students must be willing to take risks and move beyond their comfort zone. For students who tend to speak loudly or act in spirited ways, simply listening to others or reflecting inwardly may feel uncomfortable; they may feel they are risking their own power, personhood, or role in the class. For shy students, speaking in a group or engaging in a kinesthetic activity can make them feel vulnerable. Some students feel challenged by math, others by language arts. By asking students to become self-scientists, to identify their own particular learning edges, and to engage with these challenges intentionally, we give students the confidence and the tools to move into new areas of learning.

The diagram in figure 3.1, adapted from Lev Vygotsky and Michael Cole (1978), depicts the learning zone, and links learning theory and human development. This diagram is a helpful frame to share with students as they identify their social, emotional, and academic learning edges and create goals for the future. Students can identify what activities and subjects are currently in their comfort, learning, and excessive risk zones. They can set goals accordingly and be asked to reflect on their progress toward their goals. Midway through the term or year, students can revisit this diagram, noting how their zones and learning edges may have changed. The learning zone is also a helpful frame for educators as we plan our lessons and scaffold our social and emotional learning activities to build trust and support with our students so they land within the learning zone. And finally, this framework can support us in thinking about our own comfort level with new learning.

Note: Goals can relate to specific academic tasks, such as learning multiplication tables, and also to social and emotional goals, such as communicating effectively with peers.

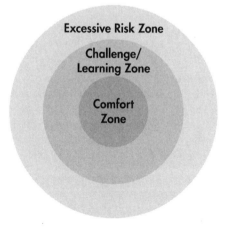

Figure 3.1: The learning zone.

Adapted from Vygotsky & Cole, 1978, pp. 79–91.

In her book *Mindset*, Carol Dweck (2006) discusses another critical aspect of working with learning edges. She points out that when students have fixed ideas about who they are and what their potential is, they tend to take fewer risks, give up on difficult tasks more easily, and disengage quickly. However, we can encourage and help students to hold a *growth mindset*, which she defines as "the belief that your basic qualities are things you can cultivate through your efforts" (p. 7). She goes on to say, "Although people may differ in every which way—in their initial talents and aptitudes, interests, and temperaments— everyone can change and grow through application and experience" (p. 7).

When we encourage students to identify and engage their own learning edges, we fos- ter their capacity to access their inner and outer resources, develop resilience, and move beyond perceived limitations (such as, "I can only get a C in this class" or "I'll never be good at math"). Studies on neuroplasticity show us that our brains are malleable and are deeply impacted by our environment, our own thoughts, and our cultural conditioning (Kitayama & Uskul, 2011). When students understand that their intelligence is not fixed, they can then feel empowered to develop and change their own brains and learning pat- terns. As students learn more about their state of mind, negative self-talk, and limiting expectations, they can be encouraged to develop the capacity for positive self-talk and goal setting. When students adopt this kind of growth mindset, they are much better able to move through initially challenging situations, take healthy risks, and trust their capacity to learn and develop. The following activities support students to explore their learning edges and develop their self-scientist or self-observer.

Activities for Exploring Students' Learning Edges

- Design a process in which students create a map or diagram of their own personal learning edges. This map or diagram could relate directly to content or to a full spectrum of social, emotional, and academic learning.

- If there are activities that fall into the excessive risk zone, ask students to identify where they need support from others—family members, counselors, mentors, teachers—to shift the zone. For example, if a student feels terrified and panicked about speaking in front of a group, what are the steps that can be taken to make this challenge more manageable?

- Introduce a growth-mindset activity to students. First, have them identify what they believe about their own capacities and skills in a particular subject area or class. Help them to excavate their limiting beliefs and expectations. Then, ask students to identify areas for growth. Where can they learn, grow, and push themselves in new ways without judgment or limiting beliefs? A growth mindset welcomes and includes mistakes as part of learning. It recognizes that excellence and learning require effort, practice, and challenge.

Practice: Including Self-Reflection and Goal Setting

Another way of encouraging students to be active self-scientists is to assign them the task of creating social, emotional, and academic learning goals for the semester or school year that they can then use as a navigational tool to measure their growth. Students can be asked to assess their progress in relation to their learning goals three to four times a year and to turn those assessments in to their teacher. This kind of assessment can then serve as a touchstone for both the teacher and student and can be used for conferences or "grade checks." Grade checks offer teachers a time to meet one on one with students to check their progress in school and to discuss areas of strength and challenge.

In one teacher's first-grade classroom, students reflect on their strengths and challenges and set and reflect on goals twice a year. In September, they write and draw about a strength of theirs in each category (social, emotional, and academic)—for example, listening, making friends, and reading. Then, they write and draw about one thing they want to improve on in each category. In January, students revisit their goals and reflect on whether or not they have made progress toward them. Figure 3.2 shows a self-reflection activity for a kindergarten classroom.

Figure 3.2: Kindergarten survey.

Another way of promoting self-reflection in students is to offer them the opportunity to regularly reflect on and assess their assignments and progress over time. One high school English teacher in California asked her students to keep a writing feedback log and a file of returned and graded written work. The log categories included constructive feedback, progress, and goals for the next essay. When the students received written feedback on an essay, they read it and then chose three specific constructive comments to include in their log. They then reviewed previous notes and listed three areas of improvement based on past feedback and goals. Finally, they set goals for their next paper based on the trends they saw in their writing. This process helped students to "see beyond the grade" they received, improve their self-awareness, and make positive changes in their study habits.

When students are given the tools and opportunities to reflect on their own learning goals and mindsets, they become more actively engaged in the learning process and more capable of assessing where and how they need to grow. Additionally, when students engage in this self-reflection and goal setting as a community, they develop greater compassion for themselves and others—as they recognize that all students have challenges and strengths. These tools reinforce lifelong skills as students move beyond school and make critical decisions about their lives and futures (Porter, Gamoran, & Board on International Comparative Studies in Education, 2002). The following is a list of diverse activities that support students in developing their capacity for self-reflection, self-assessment, and goal setting.

> ## Activities for Including Self-Reflection and Goal Setting
>
> To encourage students to engage in self-reflection and goal setting, ask them to:
> - Examine their learning process and understand more about how they learn and what their strengths and challenges are, perhaps including a learning style inventory
> - Identify their learning edges and celebrate risk taking
> - Determine specific strategies that support their learning
> - Notice when they are able to pay attention and when they are distracted, and design strategies to manage distractions
> - Set goals for the future
> - See, acknowledge, and write about changes and development over time
>
> Note: It is most powerful and impactful when students share about their findings in some way with the teacher and their peers. You may wish to have them write or draw about any of these topics.

Self-Observation With Colleagues

This same capacity to reflect and observe ourselves and our own practice can be extended to our work with our colleagues. In an adult learning community, we can learn a great deal by engaging in inquiry and reflection together. Not only do these practices strengthen relationships with our colleagues, but they help us delve into areas of practice that we might not otherwise be able to see.

Principle: Engaging in Peer-to-Peer Learning

When we develop regular opportunities to work with colleagues on our challenges and successes, we expand our thinking, see new possibilities and solutions, and build on our strengths. We can support each other by asking good questions, reflecting on what we hear and see, listening deeply to what our colleagues are sharing, and harvesting our individual and collective learning.

Practice: Using Inquiry With Colleagues

In the section on self-inquiry earlier in this chapter, we presented a process for working with triggers. This same process can be used during inquiry with a colleague. Each partner chooses a challenge to work on, while the other acts as a coach. It is important that neither colleague try to resolve the issue for the other, but rather pose the following questions (adapted for your communication style) and listen wholeheartedly to support the other colleague's mutual self-discovery, learning, and growth.

- What is actually happening with this situation?

- What would you like to have happen?

- What emotions arise?

- What other situations does this remind you of?

- What might be triggering you?

- What is your story about this situation? How are you interpreting what is happening now? What are the values, beliefs, and assumptions that might shape your interpretation?

- What perspectives might you take to help you see the situation in different ways? For instance, what do the students or colleagues involved in this situation really want or need? What might be beneath their external behaviors?

- How might you reframe the situation now?

- How do you want to respond or shift the situation now?

After one person responds to any of these questions, the listener can reflect back or directly mirror what he or she is hearing from the other person without interpretation.

In addition to this inquiry process, the following activities can be used to engage the self-observer.

Activities for Using Inquiry With Colleagues

- Approach a trusted colleague at your school and propose that together you engage in a double-loop learning process about a particularly sticky issue in your own teaching practice. Take turns sharing about the issue. Then use inquiry to support the other person so he or she can understand more about the lens he or she might be using and what the blind spots might be.

- Engage in a success analysis protocol with a colleague as a way of identifying how you can build on your own strengths (National School Reform Faculty, n.d.; see the appendix, page 173). Reflect on a time in the classroom when you felt successful in your teaching, when you used a particularly effective approach, or when you connected well with a student during a challenging time. Identify specifically what you did that worked, how you felt in the moment, what thoughts and assumptions underpinned your choices, and what the outcome or impact was on your student or classroom. With your partner, take time to identify what aspects of this success can be applied to other situations and challenges.

- Partner with a colleague to create your own learning-edges maps or diagrams about your teaching. Where is there overlap, and where is there difference? How might you support each other to take incremental steps in challenging areas? If you are inspired, give each other a homework assignment to try a challenging step, and then report back to each other in a week.

Conclusion

In this chapter, we have explored ways we can cultivate our self-observer to learn from our successes and challenges, practice responding rather than reacting, interrupt trigger cycles, and engage with more choice and consciousness with our colleagues and students. We also explored how to develop the self-scientist in our students so that they have the capacity to see and understand more about their own learning process. And finally, we looked at ways to partner with a colleague to deepen our self-reflection. In the next chapter, we will look at the dimension of being present and how we can cultivate our ability to stay alert, flexible, focused, and responsive in the moment.

4 Being Present

If we want children to be less stressed in school, if we want teach-ers to model responsible and caring behavior for our children, we must address and reduce teachers' stress levels. Our thinking and our brains suffer if we are feeling stressed. . . . Reducing stress in the classroom reduces teacher burn-out, improves classroom climate, and leads to better academic outcomes.

—Adele Diamond

Self-Reflection

What typically keeps you from being present in the classroom, in staff meetings, or with your colleagues? What helps you come back to the present moment?

Being present refers to our capacity to be awake, relaxed, and alert in the moment so that we can effectively engage with our students and colleagues. It also relates to our ability to stay flexible and responsive to the needs of the class, while meeting our learning objectives for the day. Finally, being present relates to our capacity to recognize and take advantage of teachable moments, even when they may, at first, seem inconvenient or impractical.

We can cultivate our capacity to be present through specific practices that help us return to the moment, even in times of great distraction or stress. With students, fostering the capacity to be present includes the use of focusing activities and practices that support students to manage distractions, maintain attention and focus, and focus on the day's lesson.

Being Present as a Teacher

When the emphasis in schools is overly focused on bench-marks and standardized tests, we may constantly feel pulled into the future toward our projected learning outcomes. This is natural and understandable in our high-stakes, pressure-filled education system, where we often feel we barely have time to pause. And yet, when we intentionally engage in practices for becoming present and returning to the present moment when we are distracted or triggered, we can enliven

> When teachers use strategies to reduce stress and build a positive emotional environment, students gain emotional resilience and learn more efficiently and at higher levels of cognition. Brain-imaging studies support this relationship.
>
> —Judy Willis

our teaching and engage our students at a whole new level. This allows us to more effectively meet our academic goals and bring more joy, creativity, and vibrancy to the classroom.

Principle: Cultivating Our Presence and Awareness

Many of us have had days when our teaching feels robotic and rote, or when we feel so distracted or emotionally overloaded that we simply do what we can to survive. There are days when the breakneck pace of the schedule simply wears us out—we rush from home to school, class to class, to an after-school activity, and to a staff meeting with barely enough time to go to the bathroom, let alone reflect on our interactions with students and colleagues. In these kinds of situations, how can we possibly enjoy teaching and be fully present with our students?

One of the job requirements of teaching is juggling a variety of priorities. We generally work with twenty to forty students at a time, all with varying learning styles and needs, some of whom are clamoring for our attention while others simply try to melt into the background. If we come to the classroom filled with distractions, it can be nearly impossible to pay attention to what is happening in the moment—we can easily fall into rote ways of delivering content and habitual patterns of reaction to disruptions or challenges. However, there are many practices that can help us come back to the present moment, manage our own stress, and work more effectively with the many needs and priorities present in our classroom.

Practice: Learning to Be Present Through Mindfulness

One way we can manage our distractions is by engaging in regular mindfulness practices, such as the breath awareness practice described in chapter 3. As John Miller (2007) notes, "Mindfulness practice involves learning to be wholly present to what is happening in the moment. Teachers find these practices to be a powerful way to take care of themselves and develop presence, which leads to better student-teacher relationships as students respond to teachers' increased presence and interest" (p. 9).

One teacher speaks of the impact of regular mindfulness practices on her work and personal life in this way:

> I'm much calmer. Even when I'm at home, drinking coffee, my mind's not racing in a thousand different places; I'm just liking my coffee. I've learned how to just take things for what they are and not keep everything on my shoulders all the time. And because I'm not doing that anymore, that allows me to treat my kids better, address their needs better, and try and teach them to be mindful through my example. (Jennings, 2011)

Patricia Jennings (2011), senior fellow at Garrison Institute's Contemplative Teaching and Learning Initiative and a research assistant professor in Human Development and Family Studies and the Prevention Research Center at Penn State University, reports:

Mindfulness may help teachers provide emotional support to students. Mindfulness is associated with perspective taking and empathetic responding, relatedness and interpersonal closeness, emotion communication, and anger management. Therefore, mindfulness may help a teacher be more responsive to individual students and to recognize teachable moments more frequently.

Teaching is an extremely emotionally demanding profession. Fortunately, studies show that mindfulness-based interventions may promote resilience and reduce the emotional exhaustion that precedes burnout. This may promote enjoyment of teaching and help teachers maintain their commitment to the profession and their care and compassion for their students.

The following activities support our capacity to become present through mindfulness.

Activities for Learning to Be Present Through Mindfulness

During nonteaching times throughout the day, instead of checking your phone and email between classes or during lunch or an off period, try taking a mindfulness break using one or more of the following strategies.

- Notice five specific things out your window—clouds, students, a kite, birds, cars—and try to see them with fresh eyes.
- Take three deep, long breaths and release any stress or strain in your body.
- Eat a snack slowly, keeping all your attention on just eating.
- If you have a favorite quote, poem, or piece of writing, take a few moments to read it to refresh your sense of inspiration and connection to what's important now.
- Take a "five-senses walk" across the campus and notice what you see, hear, smell, taste, and feel. This sensory awareness will help you return to the present moment, just as breathing does in breath awareness practice.

Practice: Working With Obstacles to Presence

Working with obstacles to presence involves identifying and addressing the experiences, feelings, events, concerns, and behaviors that distract us from being present in the moment. An obstacle to presence could be a triggering comment that a colleague or student just made that gets our heart pounding. Or perhaps we are worried about an upcoming doctor's appointment or are concerned about a loved one. Maybe we are simply anticipating the weekend or time with friends after work. Simply noticing that we are distracted can help bring us back to the present moment. And, when we observe these patterns of distractions in an ongoing way, we cultivate our capacity to come back into the present. The following activities support us in working with our own obstacles to presence.

> ## *Activities for Working With Obstacles to Presence*
>
> - Make a list of internal and external things that tend to be obstacles to presence. Notice any patterns over time. For example, are you always worrying about a particular student? One of your children? A health issue? Is there a way you can attend to this concern and then let it go for the day?
>
> - Write down three distractions and put them in a bowl or basket at the beginning of the day—consciously giving them up for the time being so you can attend to your class and students. At the end of the day, review the distractions and see if anything has shifted or changed. Ask yourself if there were any downsides to putting aside these distractions.

Principle: Recognizing and Utilizing Teachable Moments

At times we can be so focused on outcomes and lesson-plan goals that we are unable to see the unique and powerful teaching opportunities that arise in our classroom. Sometimes these unplanned opportunities come in the form of a student asking a question that takes the lesson in a new direction. Sometimes the teachable moment comes in the form of meeting a challenge head-on: for example, when we choose to pause in the midst of a lesson to discuss a problematic relationship between two students. It may also mean taking time to respond to a world or school event that is impacting our students' emotions and their capacity to learn. Or it may mean taking time to celebrate or honor a milestone or important moment in a student's life or an exciting event at school. When we are able to embrace these moments, we often find that we can meet our curricular goals in unforeseen ways that engage and motivate students and increase creative and critical thinking.

When we are present to the realities and needs of the moment, we are less likely to miss the proverbial "elephant in the room" that is distracting students from learning. This elephant can be anything from interpersonal conflicts to larger issues in the classroom such as the interplay of race, class, gender, culture, and power dynamics. When we develop an awareness of these dynamics, we can find appropriate ways to address the issues that might be undermining the foundation of trust in our learning community or our students' capacity to pay attention. Our willingness to take advantage of teachable moments also helps students more deeply understand the connection between school and their personal lives. Consider the following example.

In a suburban high school, racial epithets appeared on the walls of the cafeteria, creating a great deal of fear and outrage. As the morning bell rang, a teacher listened to the conversations her students were having as they came into class. Some of the students expressed that they felt the incident was no big deal—just a stupid prank. Other students shared that they were afraid to come to school that day. Others were horrified that this kind of sentiment would be expressed in their school. The teacher began her history lesson but found that her students were distracted and unavailable. She stopped the lesson and then offered them an opportunity to share their feelings and insights about the recent events at their school. In that moment, she was also able to connect this moment in time to historical events in the civil rights movement and offer important information about the impact of racist acts. She then invited her students to take some action in their school. The class then organized a series of unity days to build the trust in the school community.

Principle: Taking Care of Ourselves

When we get on an airplane and prepare for takeoff, the flight attendant reminds us that in case of an emergency, it is essential that we put on our own oxygen mask before helping others. This approach holds true for teaching. If we do not adequately care for ourselves, we will not be able to attend to the needs of our students.

Of course this does not mean we won't have to push ourselves or work long hours at times. But it does mean that it is paramount to create some kind of intentional practice to rejuvenate and renew ourselves throughout the day and year to offset the pace and pressures of the job. Some of these practices may help us discharge built-up emotion—such as physical exercise and the expressive arts. Other self-care practices help us quiet and calm ourselves and become more alert. This may mean closing the door during lunch and taking a break, sitting in silence, or reviewing an inspirational quote, image, or piece of writing.

Throughout the course of the year, it is also important to plan times to take a longer break from our work. Renewal refers to the ways we can "fill our wells" after they have run a bit low. There are many programs such as Courage to Teach (www.couragerenewal .org), Cultivating Awareness and Resilience in Education (CARE for teachers) (www .care4teachers.org), and Stress Management and Relaxation Techniques in Education (SMART in Education) (www.smart-in-education.org) that offer educators a chance to gather with one another to explore their inner lives in the company of other educators. Of course, there are many such ways to renew ourselves. Often, simply heading to a beautiful place in the natural world can help us to clear our minds and feel renewed.

When we are constantly extending ourselves to our students, serving on committees, and juggling our professional and personal lives, we can neglect ourselves and end up in a cycle of exhaustion, frustration, and burnout. When we get caught in this cycle, by the end of the school year we may feel we are simply limping to the finish line. It can take a great deal of discipline and commitment just to get ourselves out of our normal routine. Committing to longer periods of time to renew ourselves at least quarterly can make all the difference in our capacity to be present and to experience satisfaction in our professional lives. The following story, shared by a teacher who attended a retreat for educators, is excerpted from an interview with first-grade teacher Maura McNiff by Lisa Sankowski (n.d.).

My principal told me that after I attended a Courage to Teach retreat, he really saw a change in me as a teacher. I seemed happier to him, and more settled, and he might have even said calmer. This was obvious to me, but it didn't occur to me that it would be something others would recognize. Before the retreat, I was quite judgmental and externalized a lot of the things that I was impatient with. I became more tolerant because I became less focused on looking at the performance of others and more focused on looking at myself. I understood that teaching is about me, and that's where all change and effectiveness emanate from. That was a huge, huge understanding for me. When I first started teaching I saw things very differently. When I saw other teachers who were struggling I would think: "If she'd just put in five more hours a week instead of leaving at 3:00, or if he would just recognize this, or that, or the other thing, we could have a much better meeting, or if she were better organized . . ." —you know, blah, blah, blah. When in fact, that's not how it really works. The reality of a lot of things hasn't changed. What's happened in education in the last few years has been discouraging. But what has changed for the better is my recognition of the sphere of influence I have in my work and of the importance of being present, really present, to the kids.

—Maura McNiff, First-Grade Teacher

Practice: Engaging in Self-Care and Renewal

Our students learn as much, if not more, from what we do and how we act as from what we say. When we are stressed, overworked, or on the verge of burnout, we are less able to support our students' growth and learning. In this way, taking care of ourselves is not selfish. In fact, when we establish healthy habits to take care of our body and mind, we are more available to share our greatest gifts with those who need us most. The following activities support us in caring for and renewing ourselves.

Activities for Engaging in Self-Care and Renewal

- Take time to celebrate successes and major milestones.
- Spend time in nature.
- Take walks and avoid multitasking during this time.
- Run or garden with the intention of relaxing your mind.
- Organize and decorate your physical work environment so that it is uplifting.
- Regularly express gratitude and appreciation to others.
- Do nothing—sit quietly in silence.
- Journal, draw, paint, or create other visual art.
- Make music on your own or with others.
- Engage in a contemplative practice. (See examples at www.contemplativemind.org /practices/tree.)
- Read or study inspirational books.
- Stop work at regular intervals to take even a short break.

- Attend a retreat program alone or with colleagues.
- Reflect on your goals and intentions at the start of the day.
- Take a few minutes at the end of the day to reflect on at least one moment or interaction that went well or that you are grateful for.
- Acknowledge what is going well in your work and life.

Being Present in the Classroom

If students are not motivated, receptive, and ready to learn, all of our best efforts to teach will not create the learning outcomes we hope for. As John Medina (2008) notes, "Does it matter to learning if we pay attention? The short answer is: You bet it does. . . . The more attention the brain pays to a given stimulus, the more elaborately the information will be encoded—and retained. . . . Whether you are an eager preschooler or a bored-out-of-your-mind undergrad, better attention always equals better learning" (p. 82).

Principle: Fostering Learning Readiness and Presence in Students

We often begin class assuming that our students are ready to focus and engage. We may dive into teaching only to discover that our students are distracted and restless or that we, ourselves, are not as present as we would like to be. We may feel frustrated, as if we are losing precious learning time. We may wonder, Why aren't my students paying attention?

Throughout school, students are told to "pay attention," and yet many students simply do not know what this means or how to engage in this way. Because of this it is important to explore what paying attention looks like in our classroom and to give students the opportunities and skills to learn how to focus and attend. This includes sharing our expectations for paying attention. For example, we might share that in this classroom paying attention means not listening to your iPod, or texting, or writing notes to your friends.

The following activities can help students to cultivate their attention and focus.

Activities to Cultivate Attention

First, create some quiet. Then direct students toward an experience using one of their five senses:

- Sound a chime or a note on a musical instrument and ask students to listen closely until the sound fades.
- Ask students to pay attention to the feel of something on their skin: the air, water, the fabric of their clothing.
- Give each student a small piece of something sweet (chocolate, a raisin) and encourage them to let it melt in their mouths all the while paying attention to the changing texture and taste.
- Encourage students to notice smells and to pay attention to them longer than they normally would.

These and similar activities are short, but potent. As you introduce these activities, let students know that these practices can help them learn more about the way their minds work. Reassure students that it is normal to lose focus. Encourage them to notice it is lost and to come back to the object of attention. Let them know that in these moments of noticing they are cultivating their self-scientist.

When we take time to prepare students for learning by waking up their bodies and minds, we are more likely to see surprising connections, creative thinking, and new learning arise. The following story offers an example of how to work with the transition time after recess.

One third-grade teacher uses the time right after recess to have a class meeting as a way to cultivate learning readiness. This is often a time when emotions run high and students can have trouble settling back into learning mode. In class meetings, this teacher asks each student to share one thing that happened at recess. During the circle, there is no cross-talk and students are asked to refrain from directly naming each other in any of the incidents. They are asked simply to share about how they felt about the incident. The teacher finds that by simply giving students a few minutes to share stories from recess, they are less distracted and more able to refocus on the next learning task. This teacher remarks, "I am always struck by the fact that students only need a brief moment to be heard and to express their feelings or issues. Then they feel heard and seen and can be more present and ready for learning."

Practice: Incorporating Focusing Activities

Focusing activities provide support for transitions into and out of class, help students manage distractions, and bring the class to focus so students are ready and able to learn. Focusing activities support students to develop their capacity to be self-scientists by giving students opportunities to reflect on their experiences, feelings, and thoughts. They build community, enhance relationships, and increase time on task by reducing time spent on reactive classroom management and conflict mediation.

Teachers can use focusing activities to support learning readiness at the beginning of class (or in the middle of class if students need it) so that students can become more present, focused, and alert. Starting class with five deep breaths, journaling on a theme, a playful community-building activity, or a deep listening dyad or pair share helps students and the teacher leave distractions behind and tune in to the present moment. (See the appendix, page 159, for full descriptions of focusing activities.)

Focusing activities can be used in any grade level or content area. A high school language arts teacher starts each class with a simple focusing activity. He writes a quote on the board from a novel students are reading for class, and asks them to take a moment of silence to contemplate the quote, and then share their insights with a partner. The students then share one sentence about what surprised them or what they learned. This five- to ten-minute activity often energizes the rest of the discussion that day in class.

The following focusing activity is an example of a playful and active way of bringing a group of students into the present moment.

Ten-Minute Focusing Activity for Grades 3–8

Ask students to arrange themselves in a circle. Explain that you are going to start the day with an activity to support learning and focus:

1. Each student will toss the ball only once and receive the ball only once. A student who receives the ball is invited to share one phrase about how he or she is feeling today (for example, tired from little sleep, worried about a test, excited for a basketball game, and so on) and then gently toss the ball to someone else in the circle who has not yet received it. The group will be creating a pattern with the ball toss, which they will later repeat. Students should remember whom they throw the ball to and receive it from.

2. After everyone has received the ball once, students repeat the same pattern created during the first round, with each person tossing the ball to the same person in the same order. Then the teacher will introduce a second ball into the circle while the first ball is still going around. Then, as the group is ready, the teacher will introduce a third ball, so that soon the group is "juggling" three balls around the circle in a pattern. Occasionally balls will drop and laughter will often follow, as students scramble after the loose balls.

3. After a few minutes, the teacher stops the activity and asks the students some simple questions:

   o How do you feel now? Do you feel more present? Awake? Focused?

   o How might this activity relate to learning? (Students might respond that they have to maintain focus or that when they worked together they could keep several balls going at once.)

   o When did we laugh? (Students might say that they laughed when they dropped the ball—when they made a mistake. As this arises, it is important to take the opportunity to explain that mistakes are part of learning. You can also discuss the challenges of laughter within a group—and how people can be sensitive about being laughed "at" instead of laughed "with.")

4. As you complete the activity, encourage students to take their energy and focus into their next activity and to bring that sense of collaboration and teamwork to all their classrooms and subject areas.

This ten-minute ball toss focusing activity allows students to become more present and ready to engage with content. Students have the opportunity to engage their bodies, awaken their minds, and build community. Including some kind of focusing activity at the beginning of class each day can help students transition into class, clear their minds, and prepare for learning.

Focusing activities can work on both the group and individual levels. At times, we may need to quickly evaluate the needs of the group before deciding which kind of focusing activity is most appropriate. For example, if students are wild and rowdy after recess, using a golden moment of silence or a reflective writing prompt can help them calm their energy. If students are sleepy and disengaged after lunch, beginning class with an activity that gets them up and moving can encourage them to become more alert.

Active focusing activities help students become learning ready by getting students moving and engaging different parts of their brain and body. As Antoinette Yancey notes:

> Kids pay better attention to their subjects when they've been active. Kids are less likely to be disruptive in terms of their classroom behavior when they're active. Kids feel better about themselves, have higher self-esteem, less depression, less anxiety. All of those things can impair academic performance and attentiveness. (as cited in Medina, 2008, p. 18)

Following is another example of an active focusing activity.

The Wild River Runs Focusing Activity

Arrange chairs in a circle, with one fewer chair than there are people in the class. Everyone sits in a chair, except for one person who volunteers to stand in the center of the circle. Demonstrate the activity by standing in the center first. The person in the center chooses a descriptor from the following list or makes up a descriptor, then says, "The wild river runs for everyone who . . .

- Is wearing black shoes."
- Has brown eyes."
- Wears earrings."
- Enjoys playing sports."
- Likes reading novels."
- Likes the summer best of any season."

Everyone who fits in the category mentioned by the person in the middle of the circle must get up and find a new seat. Students cannot take either of the seats immediately to their right or left. The person who does not find a seat (which could be the person already in the middle) will now move into the middle of the circle and call out another descriptive category. Continue this activity for five to ten rounds. After the activity is complete, ask students if they notice anything about their state of alertness.

Reflective focusing activities are intended to quiet the body and mind and draw students' attention inward. This kind of focusing activity may involve writing on a quote or prompt, making art, engaging in stress-management techniques, or taking time in silence. These reflective options help students to settle in and "turn down the volume" of their distractions. As Paula Denton (2008) says, "The skillful use of silence can be just as powerful as the skillful use of words. When teachers use silence, we open a space for students to think, rehearse what to say, and sometimes gather the courage to speak at all" (p. 29). (See the appendix on pages 160–163 for examples of active and reflective focusing activities.) Some teachers choose to start every class with a few moments of silence or reflection time as a way to help students transition from one content area to another. If there is time, pairing an active focusing activity with a reflective focusing activity can support students to connect to themselves and to the community.

One first-grade teacher builds reflective focusing activities daily into her classroom routine. Students come in from recess and immediately get out their journals and find a place in the room where they are not close to any peers. Then they open their journals to a new page and wait for the teacher to distribute several colored pencils to each student. The lights are turned down low, and the room is quiet. Students are given five minutes to write or draw about anything that is on their minds before they gather in the meeting areas to begin their next activity. In these few moments, students are able to quiet their bodies and draw their attention inward, so they can then focus more easily on their next lesson.

Being Present With Colleagues

With the pressure of our workload, we may feel we do not have time for anything beyond our preparation and class time with students. As the cycle of stress and busyness gains momentum, it can be difficult to reach out to others, leaving us feeling ever more isolated and alone in our work. Even if we are actively looking for ways to connect with our colleagues, we may not feel that there are opportunities to do so in authentic ways and productive environments. However, when we have effective practices and meaningful ways of gathering, it can be profoundly nourishing to engage with colleagues to support one another.

Principle: Giving and Receiving Support

Engaging in practices with our colleagues is an essential aspect of sustaining our efforts toward self-care and renewal. When we feel more supported, connected, and less alone, we are naturally able to remain more present in the classroom and in the course of our daily lives. The following activities offer colleagues options to give and receive support in meaningful ways.

Activities for Giving and Receiving Support

- We often rush into faculty or planning meetings without any opportunity to leave behind any stress we have brought with us. In your next faculty meeting, see if your colleagues are willing to begin the meeting with a minute or two of silence or reflection, a reading of an inspirational quote, or with celebrations. Or start team meetings with a simple, ordinary activity such as a brief opportunity for each member to share a positive highlight from their day. This kind of activity is an uplifting way to begin working together.

- Engage a colleague as a "mindfulness partner." In pairs, begin a mindfulness practice and report to each other about your results inside and outside of the classroom. As part of your practice together, share how you are regularly caring for yourself and "filling your wells" so you do not deplete yourself.

- Find one colleague in the building to have a weekly lunch with to check in about how things are going, share challenges and successes, and set goals for the upcoming week. Perhaps engage in a two-way interview to get to know each other's teaching approach and philosophy.
- As part of faculty self-care and renewal, explore opportunities to spend time socially with like-minded colleagues. Consider initiating a monthly gathering of colleagues to engage in an activity that has little to do with school (such as bowling, softball, movie night, and so on).

Conclusion

In this chapter, we have explored ways we can manage our distractions and stress to become more present in the classroom and with our colleagues. We have also shared practices for supporting students to pay attention and become learning ready. In the next chapter, we will delve into the dimension of establishing respectful boundaries, exploring the ways this dimension supports us to take care of ourselves and create safe, inclusive, productive classrooms and schools.

5

Establishing Respectful Boundaries

The love and discipline I bring to my students is based on a belief that there is a core of goodness in each child. I believe there is an innate thrust toward creative growth in each person. If we connect to that core, if we can nourish, affirm and acknowledge it, the seed will grow and flourish into its unique potential.

—Rachael Kessler

Self-Reflection

When you think of the word *boundaries*, what images and ideas come to mind? What stories from your life and your school years contribute to your image of boundaries and boundary setting?

Establishing respectful boundaries is an essential part of our teaching practice, as it calls us to compassionately express our authority, take responsibility for ourselves and our classrooms, and clearly define and communicate our limits. This dimension includes knowing our own internal boundaries or limits; being aware of perspectives and biases that may influence our boundary setting; developing skill and comfort with setting boundaries; being willing to meet resistance, frustration, and pushback about our boundaries; and maintaining caring relationships in the midst of conflict or challenge.

Creating Respectful Boundaries as a Teacher

In helping professions, such as teaching, it can be difficult at times to draw effective boundaries or limits for ourselves. Perhaps we feel we must say yes to the one extra committee that we are being asked to serve on, or we struggle to intervene and set boundaries in tense situations in the classroom. Or perhaps we feel intimidated by colleagues, and so we rarely speak up. Or perhaps our boundaries are so rigid that we tend to close ourselves off or shut down possibilities or experiences that might actually help us grow.

Understanding our own boundaries relates directly to our capacity to know ourselves well, recognize habitual patterns, and see what is sustainable for us. This does not mean that we are inflexible. Knowing our own boundaries allows us to stretch when it is important to take on an extra workload or let go of a point we were making in a meeting. It simply means that we develop awareness of and conscious relationship with our internal boundaries so that we do not burn out, end up resentful, or become less effective in the classroom.

Principle: Understanding Our Own Boundaries

How do we know when a boundary has been crossed? Often, we have a strong physical or emotional reaction—a tightening in our gut, a constriction in our heart, a shortening of our breath, a wave of heat, tears, or anger. Perhaps we feel disrespected, disregarded, unseen, unheard, or even offended. When this occurs, we can take time to ask ourselves about the undercurrents of the situation and make a conscious choice about how to respond. To effectively engage with our own boundaries and respond thoughtfully, we need:

- **Self-discipline**—The capacity to thoughtfully manage our responses and not simply react in habitual ways

- **Discernment**—The capacity to determine whether the reaction has to do with the present or past and whether this issue is one we need to work out with another or just ourselves

- **Skillfulness**—The capacity to skillfully find a way to respond or act when a boundary is crossed

- **Courage**—The strength of heart to enter into situations that make us uncomfortable

As we explore this dimension, it is essential that we also take into account the perspectives and biases that may influence our feeling that a boundary has been crossed. For example, we may make assumptions and create a story about what is behind a student or colleague's action, behavior, or statement based on our worldview or cultural understanding. Perhaps we feel that a student is being disrespectful because he does not make eye contact when he speaks. However, that student may be looking down and away, not out of disrespect, but because respect for elders is shown in a different way in his family or community. Perhaps we feel our personal space is being invaded because a colleague stands very close and talks loudly about a particular issue. This may lead us to avoid or even judge this colleague when this highly expressive style may simply be a natural expression of this colleague's community or family. Or perhaps we assume that a colleague, who is more reserved, does not want to have a relationship with us. Examining our own stories and cultural assumptions can help us to more fully understand our boundaries and to negotiate them effectively with others.

The following activities can help us understand our own boundaries.

Activities for Understanding Our Own Boundaries

- The next time someone asks you to commit to something or take something on, pause and take the time to consider what an answer of yes or no will mean for you and your existing commitments.

- The next time you feel that someone has crossed a boundary that is important to you, use self-inquiry to discover what that boundary is about and how you might respond rather than react. Inquire into your "story" about the situation—do you know that this story is true? Why or why not? How might this influence your response and actions?

- Keep a journal for a month and note each time you feel a boundary of yours has been crossed in your professional setting. Note any patterns that emerge and what information this might offer you about yourself or others.

Principle: Welcoming the Unwelcome

Welcoming the unwelcome refers to the capacity to see challenges and obstacles as opportunities for learning and growth. This principle invites us to lean into (rather than away from) those situations that make us uncomfortable. Often when challenges arise, especially in the form of students acting out, we feel resistant, frustrated, or afraid. Or, when conflict appears in our classrooms or with colleagues, we want to avoid it. If, however, we can reframe the situation and allow ourselves to let go of our ideas about how things should be, new possibilities emerge.

From this perspective of openness, we can then see what lessons or opportunities are being offered to us or our students. The student who is acting out is providing us essential information—either about the way we are teaching or about that student's needs or internal state. The restless student who can't sit still might help us to see that we need to take a five-minute break to stretch and get a breath of fresh air. The "heckling" student in the back of the class may help us consider a new approach to teaching a novel we've taught a dozen times. The student who repeatedly talks back may be asking for attention of any kind—positive or negative. The student who resists any personal sharing may have a painful family situation she is afraid of exposing. The colleague who confronts us about a point we made at a meeting may give us the opportunity to clarify the meaning of our comments or uncover a misunderstanding. When we welcome the unwelcome, we get curious about the jewels that might be present in the muck and mud of an uncomfortable situation.

Welcoming the unwelcome can also remind us to see the opportunities for learning in particularly challenging moments at school. For example, the news of a peer just arrested for drunk driving may have all the students in the classroom distracted—and yet it can open doors to important conversations, if we are willing. On a ninety-degree day when the air conditioner breaks, we may decide to hold class outside under a tree and find that this creates a strengthened sense of community. An administrative change at our school may mean that our job is being redefined in ways that feel stressful to us, and yet we may eventually feel grateful for the new skills and capacities we are pushed to learn.

Welcoming the unwelcome can also help us to find our sense of humor on days when nothing seems to go quite right, and this alone can shift our perspective and engage our capacity to meet challenges.

Practice: Getting Curious About Sabotage

Despite our efforts to create a safe and engaging learning space, inevitably students will behave in ways that undermine our best-laid plans. Students who "sabotage" might test limits, disrespect us or their peers, break rules and agreements, or cause distractions that interfere with teaching time. Encounters with students who sabotage can offer us some of the most powerful opportunities to deepen relationships, invite student voice, and set clear boundaries. This does not in any way mean we allow students to derail the course of the class. But, by getting curious about the sabotage, we are more able to turn directly into the challenge and meet the situation with creativity and openness. On the one hand, the sabotaging behavior might invite us to shift the lesson or approach we are taking or to widen our cultural perspective and consider if we are misreading a behavior. On the other hand, we may be called to provide a strong boundary for a student in a way that opens the relationship, rather than shutting it down. Often, underneath the mask of the saboteur is pain, hurt, insecurity, and cynicism. When we reach out authentically to students who sabotage and recognize their potential as positive leaders and contributors, they often feel seen and known in expanded ways, and this alone can unlock their potential to shift their role.

For example, one tenth-grade teacher was introducing a community-building activity when a student who often resisted these types of activities began to snicker and denigrate the group's work. Instead of asking her to stop or step out of the activity or classroom, the teacher turned to the student and asked her to explain what she was having an issue with. The student was surprised about being asked. Then she got very serious and said that she felt like these types of activities could get sappy or fake. In that moment, the teacher wanted to defend the activities and describe all the ways they related to community building, school, and learning. But instead, he took a deep breath and decided to simply hear her out. He validated her concerns and asked the student if she would assist him by watching out for signs of inauthenticity. She looked at him, surprised, then shrugged her shoulders and said she would. In the following weeks, she became more actively engaged in helping to create an authentic and positive classroom environment and keep the class on track.

In this situation, the teacher took the risk to turn into the challenge and meet it through inquiry and curiosity. He was able to effectively engage the saboteur and invite her to enter the community as a leader and participant, instead of as a heckler on the perimeter.

However, there are situations when our outreach efforts do not shift the behavior of the sabotaging student. And because it is often these students who most need care and compassion, it is important to be aware of our own tendency to "caretake" these students in ways that don't serve the learning community. When we see the pain or hurt behind sabotaging students' behavior, we may develop a tendency to avoid drawing boundaries, hoping that our caring approach will make a difference or that these students will make the necessary changes on their own. However, in order to serve as a guardian for the community as a whole, it is essential that we address students' behaviors directly. We know that if we make continual exceptions for certain students, this will not ultimately serve them. Classmates, in fact, tend to develop resentments toward sabotaging students and begin to distrust our capacity as teachers to create safety and respond fairly.

The following story illustrates one teacher's challenge to balance the needs of the individual with those of the group.

One tenth-grade language arts teacher had a student, Emma, who was clearly troubled. From day one, everything about her attitude and body language said, "Stay away from me!" The teacher soon found out from the school social worker that Emma's brother had been killed over the summer. Knowing what she had been through, the teacher cut her a lot of slack when she misbehaved and offered her extra help when she struggled to maintain passing grades.

Despite these efforts, over time Emma's behavior in class got more extreme and erratic. The teacher told Emma that she knew she was upset and struggling, but that it wasn't okay for her to take this out on other students or treat people with disrespect. Emma agreed to try harder. However, one day she yelled a racist slur at a student in the middle of a class discussion, and the teacher immediately asked Emma to step out into the hall. Emma apologized and began to offer excuses. The teacher told her she had crossed a line and needed to go to the principal's office. Emma pleaded her case and asked for one more chance, saying that if she went to the office, she'd likely get written up or even suspended. She was sincere, and she was struggling with overwhelming emotions and impulses, but her behavior was now negatively impacting the class. The teacher decided to go ahead and send Emma to the principal's office for this offense.

She felt tremendous grief that Emma would likely be suspended and also realized that, because she had made such a personal connection with Emma, she had given her too much leeway for too long. The teacher didn't regret reaching out to Emma, but she decided that in the future, she would draw a line earlier for the safety of the class and for Emma's sake as well.

Getting curious about sabotage reminds us to examine the deeper dynamics in the classroom so we can take the actions we need to take to reach out compassionately, engage sabotage creatively, draw clear boundaries, and serve as the protector and guardian of the class as a whole. The following activities support us in meaningfully engaging students who sabotage.

Activities for Getting Curious About Sabotage

- When there are consistent behavior issues, consider it a request for attention and help, and view the behavior as an indirect form of communication from the student to you.
- Practice seeing the positive leader in the saboteur. Spend time considering his or her positive traits (humor, assertiveness, intelligence) and affirm these as you can. If possible, give a saboteur some kind of genuine role in the classroom that engages him or her in supporting the well-being of the learning community.

- Discover what behaviors of yours tend to trigger students and consider different approaches.
- When possible, meet individually with disruptive students to discuss the nature and impact of their behavior and create a plan for the future.

Creating Respectful Boundaries in the Classroom

Many teachers say that the most frustrating aspect of their job is classroom management. Often, we simply want to teach our content and not have to navigate challenging interpersonal dynamics that arise. However, it is just these dynamics that can interfere with learning. This is why it is so essential to take the time to create a respectful, inclusive learning environment with clear boundaries and expectations. As Carol Ann Tomlinson (Tomlinson & Imbeau, 2010) notes, "Effective teaching and learning are as much social and human endeavors as they are cognitive processes. Investing time in building a growth web of human connections will yield significant dividends in terms of trust, understanding, appreciation, community, and motivation to learn" (pp. 105–106).

Principle: Engaging in Proactive Classroom Management

When we don't develop student-teacher relationships that include clear and consistent boundaries, our discipline can be perceived as haphazard, unfair, or arbitrary. But when we create a proactive approach to classroom management, we can increase the level of trust our students have in our capacity to effectively lead and teach. A proactive approach to classroom management includes creating clear expectations about appropriate behaviors in our particular classrooms, inviting student voice through discussion about boundaries and through a shared agreements process, being direct and clear with our requests, talking about consequences for certain behaviors ahead of time, and developing awareness of how our own actions, beliefs, and assumptions might be contributing to behavior problems.

Practice: Creating a Positive View of Discipline and Boundary Setting

Many people have negative associations with the word *discipline*. The word can conjure up the image of a militaristic drill sergeant or an authoritarian teacher who embarrasses students in front of the class. Many of us have experienced inappropriate uses of power under the guise of discipline. But the spirit of respectful boundaries harkens back to the root of the word *discipline* itself. *Disciplinare* means "to teach or instruct, and it refers to the system of teaching and nurturing that prepares children to achieve competence, self-control, self-direction, and caring for others" (Committee on Psychosocial Aspects of Child and Family Health, 1998, p. 723).

From this perspective, establishing respectful boundaries is essential to creating a caring, safe, and productive community of learners.

For many teachers, it can be difficult to find a positive image or model of discipline. On the one hand, we may have had experiences where discipline was expressed through punishment and humiliation. On the other end of the spectrum, we might have experienced a very loose form of discipline, a kind of "anything goes" approach that leads to constant chaos. Or we might have had experiences of discipline where the teacher (or parent) attempted to be friends with the child—giving up their natural and positive authority.

If we have only had these negative models, how can we develop a positive vision or approach? Simply inquiring about the models of discipline we have experienced in our lives can support us in taking a proactive and intentional approach to discipline. When we are more conscious about what experiences and models inform our style of classroom management, we are less likely to repeat unhelpful models, avoid providing boundaries altogether, or fall into other unconscious patterns. To begin this inquiry process, ask yourself: What kind of discipline was modeled by my teachers and family members? How does this modeling impact my view of discipline today? Where have I seen positive modeling of discipline or clear boundaries in my life—even if it has been in the lives of my friends or colleagues?

One positive image of discipline is that of a guardian or steward. As guardians, we use our positive authority to serve the community. From this view, discipline is not about coercion or obedience. Instead, it is about helping students understand the consequences of their actions, giving them the opportunity to renew their commitment to the community, helping them learn from their mistakes, and offering them the chance to repair any harm. It is also about creating a community in which students learn the skills they need to succeed in school and in life. When we are unwilling or unable to create these boundaries, we often lose our love of the work as we become embroiled in classroom dynamics that sap our energy and sabotage every student's learning.

Researchers who interviewed middle school students from urban schools across the United States summarized their views of what makes a "good teacher." Students consistently noted that good teachers are "strict but nice" and they "don't give up on you" (Wilson & Corbett, 2001, p. 39). When students know that educators will protect the community and hold the line while staying in caring relationships with them, they are more willing to share their authentic selves, open their minds, and take the intellectual risks necessary for true learning. As Rick Smith and Mary Lambert (2008) note, "The bottom line is that when students test us, they want us to pass the test. They are on our side rooting for us to come through with safety and structure" (p. 2).

The following activities support us in creating a positive view of discipline and boundary setting.

Activities for Creating a Positive View of Discipline and Boundary Setting

- Thinking back on your experiences of discipline, identify your positive and negative role models. Take some time to explore what these people taught you about your own approach to discipline.

- Identify what you would still like to learn about child development and how to best establish clear boundaries with students in the classroom. Create a plan for how to get the information and support that you need to implement best practices.
- Read a book about discipline and classroom management, like *Relationship-Driven Classroom Management,* by John Vitto, and discuss the ideas it contains with a colleague.
- Identify a positive image for discipline. Create some kind of visual reminder of this image. Consider using a metaphor, such as mountain climbing or whitewater rafting, to remind you to pause and reflect when resistance, fear, or challenges occur.

Practice: Providing Classroom Leadership

Taking our "seat" as the classroom leader and expressing our positive authority involve both establishing the clear purpose and direction of the class and building positive and trusting relationships. As the classroom leader, we are often challenged to manage myriad priorities, dynamics, and needs. When we develop touchstones for our awareness of the whole classroom, we are better able to work with this complexity, avoid pitfalls, and navigate challenges.

Following are a variety of activities that support us in providing positive classroom leadership.

Activities for Providing Classroom Leadership

- Be alert to teachable moments that lead the class into unscripted but relevant explorations.
- Model for students that difference is an asset rather than a problem to be solved.
- Invite students to help solve classroom problems and participate in decision making.
- Without fanfare, sit or stand next to disruptive students.
- Guide the development of the classroom community and discourage the formation of cliques or subgroups that could undermine cohesion and collaboration. Intentionally shift grouping tendencies by gender, racial or ethnic background, language, and other categories by varying seating arrangements and project groups.
- Establish a trustworthy environment with clear instructions, such as giving students the right to pass or be a witness (engaging as an observer only) during social and emotional learning activities.
- Create a place in your classroom or school where tough conversations can occur and conflicts can be resolved. Model for students how they can use that place, and let them understand your conflict-resolution process before a heated situation arises.
- Create a discipline plan in which you identify the various steps you will use to work with disruptive behaviors, so that you can be both thoughtful and decisive. Create a plan for how you will maintain positive relationships with the students in the midst of setting clear boundaries.

Practice: Developing Shared Agreements

One of the ways we can engage our students in proactive classroom management is through introducing a shared agreements process. Shared agreements are different from adult-mandated, non-negotiable classroom or school rules. They exist alongside established rules and generally overlap with those rules. A shared agreements process involves asking students what they and the group need to create a safe, respectful, productive learning community. When students actively participate in creating a set of agreements and commit to doing their best to follow them, they take more responsibility for the classroom culture. When there is a shared sense of ownership and empowerment, students are often more present and engaged in all aspects of school. A shared agreements process also helps teachers engage students who resist top-down rules. Throughout the school year or semester, and especially when challenges arise, the class can return to their shared agreements as a touchstone to help maintain a productive and respectful community.

Of course, in every class there are times when rules and agreements get broken, and it is the teacher's job to safeguard the physical, emotional, and intellectual safety of the class. However, when we engage in a shared agreements process, we engage all of our students in problem solving and creating a trusting environment. A class might even discuss the challenges and resolve the issue together depending upon the scenario and the group's cohesion. Deciding on a process ahead of time and providing a protocol for class problem solving, including consistent and thoughtful consequences, support students in feeling empowered and included.

It is most effective to begin a shared agreements process after students have had a few weeks of classes, so they understand the format of the class and begin to develop trust and a sense of community.

Activity for Developing Shared Agreements

1. Ask students to brainstorm a list of what they need from each other to learn effectively, speak openly and honestly, and share what is important to them in this class. Write down this list without editing. Engage in discussion about any concepts or words that seem abstract or unclear.

2. Ask students to name themes or categories in which items from the list could fit. For example, no interrupting and no put-downs might fall under a general category of "respecting the speaker." List these three to five major themes or categories.

3. Ask students to commit to the agreements in some way (for example, signing the agreements, giving a thumbs up, and so on).

4. Write up and post agreements where they can be referred to throughout the school year.

Practice: Setting Limits With Care

Setting limits with care involves having the skills to offer clear, fair, and consistent boundaries that protect and sustain the learning environment; the inner discipline and confidence to take positive and intentional action when a student crosses a boundary; the willingness to appropriately use our adult power and authority to convey boundaries; and the humility and courage to admit when we have made a mistake, misunderstood a behavior, or have not skillfully addressed a situation.

Another aspect of setting limits with care is having a clearly thought-out plan for working with disruptions in the classroom, so that we are less likely to become reactive or feel caught off guard. Of course, as with all plans, unexpected situations or reactions can emerge that challenge us to become creative in the moment—to invent a new approach, use our humor, or engage the student in a fresh way.

Consider the following example of one teacher's sequential method for working with challenging behaviors.

1. Name the behavior that isn't working, and ask the student to make another choice.

2. If the student still continues the behavior, let him know that you will next ask him to step out of the activity or step out of class if the behavior continues. Explain that this behavior is getting in the way of other students' learning.

3. If the behavior still continues, ask the student to sit out of the activity, with an invitation to rejoin the community when he is ready to engage respectfully. It is essential to include invitations to rejoin the community, so that the student knows there is a place for him in the learning community and that he can make different choices in the future.

4. Finally, if all else fails, ask the student to go see the principal, counselor, or assistant principal, and tell the student you will talk to him later more directly.

Setting limits with care requires great courage and discernment—as we consider the well-being of our individual students and the classroom as a whole. The following activities support us in setting limits with care.

Activities for Setting Limits With Care

- Create clear expectations about appropriate behaviors at the beginning of the year.
- Be direct and clear with requests.
- Invite student voice through discussion about boundaries and through a shared agreements process (see page 77).
- When possible, create a way for students to re-enter the community after breaking an agreement.
- Talk about consequences for certain behaviors ahead of time.
- Develop awareness about how your own actions, beliefs, and assumptions might be contributing to behavior problems. Consider inviting a colleague to observe your class.
- Continue to revisit the purpose of the lessons and activities that you are introducing and connect that purpose to learning goals.

- Reflect and validate the feelings that are emerging in the classroom, while offering students direction about appropriate ways of expressing those feelings.
- Be compassionately consistent and fair with boundaries.
- Consider the safety and well-being of the whole class as well as the individual.

Practice: Making Direct Requests

Without realizing it, we may adopt an indirect teaching style in which we ask students rhetorical questions instead of making direct requests. This approach can confuse students and lead to unnecessary misunderstandings and conflict. The following story illustrates the importance of making direct requests.

A teacher was talking in the lounge about a particularly energetic first-grade student named James. She couldn't understand why he was so defiant with her. Just that day she had asked him if he was ready to go to the library, and he looked her right in the eye and said, no! She then responded by saying she would need to escort him to the library. The student began crying and protesting, and the situation took twenty minutes to resolve. The teacher later reflected on the situation with a colleague, who pointed out that she had asked James a question, rather than making a request, and that James had answered this question honestly. This colleague then suggested that the teacher try making a direct request instead of asking a question. The teacher had never even thought about this aspect of her communication style before. She was grateful to see that by making direct requests she could avoid misunderstandings and shift the relationship with James and other students.

The following activities support us in adopting a more direct communication style.

> ## *Activities for Making Direct Requests*
>
> - Over the next week, take note of how you make requests and how that impacts your students' behavior and responses.
> - Notice when a student's behavior or response may be directly related to the way you have phrased a request or question.
> - Write down three implicit expectations you have about students' behavior and find a way to explicitly address these expectations (for example, students should pay attention, focus, participate, and so on). You may assume that all students understand what it means to pay attention, but doodling on their papers may actually help some students attend better. For others, interrupting fellow students with their own answers makes them feel as if they are paying attention well. You may wish to open up a discussion about how students best pay attention in class and list these ways on the board.

Practice: Addressing Bullying and Harassment

Most schools have had to develop action plans for managing bullying and harassment among students. These kinds of behaviors are deeply troubling and complex. There are entire books dedicated to the topic, and so a comprehensive exploration of bullying and harassment is beyond the scope of this book. However, our proactive approach to working with this challenging issue is to offer *all* students structured opportunities to:

- Learn more about each other in a variety of ways that break down typical social barriers

- Develop social and emotional learning skills (including stress and anger management skills)

- Collaborate with peers

- Engage in discussion about expectations, boundaries, and consequences for behavior

- Adopt empowering and productive leadership roles with their peers

When we integrate social and emotional learning skills into the classroom, *all* students are supported in moving into more conscientious and compassionate ways of interacting. For many students, this simply is *not* part of the skill set they arrive in the school with, and learning them together with all students prevents the possibility of feeling stigmatized. Once students have learned and practiced these skills, they are less likely to bully each other and more likely to stand up for themselves and others when bullying occurs.

Another essential aspect of addressing bullying and harassment is to work as a school-wide team to develop protocols for responding to incidents and identifying what student behaviors are simply beyond the capacity of the school. For students who have experienced extreme trauma or abuse, aggressive behavior may be an expression of their overwhelming pain and suffering and may require more help than teachers or schools can provide. It is essential in these cases to get help from the school's resource team, as these students simply may not be able to effectively control their impulses or manage their pain without additional support.

Following is an example of an initiative an elementary principal took at his school to address bullying.

Faculty at a rural school in Missouri were seeing signs of bullying among their third graders. Instead of pulling out the identified bullies and placing them into an anger-management group, as had been done before, the principal decided to create a leadership group that had a mix of bullies, victims, and bystanders, though the students were not named as such within the group. The group, along with the principal, met once a week for an hour for the purpose of developing leadership skills at the school. At first, the group did not even talk about conflict or bullying issues. They simply engaged in activities that helped students get to know each other and identify their strengths and challenges. By week five, this group had developed a strong sense of trust and began to discuss issues such as anger, managing emotions, stress, and peer relationships. Both bullies and victims were able to share about their struggles with peers, and this alone led to breakthroughs in understanding and behavior.

At the end of the eight-week session, the students were given the assignment to act as community leaders in the school and to create a plan for how they would step in and advocate in situations where there was conflict, harassment, or bullying. Of course there were still issues and challenges with the third graders, but the principal noted a profound change in this group of students. He noted that they developed a new sense of pride in and responsibility for the community. They felt they had an important role in the school, and that inspired them to be their best selves.

Because each school and community is different, antibullying and harassment plans will necessarily be unique. Integrating an antibullying program in conjunction with teaching social and emotional skills can be a very effective, multipronged approach to working with this complex issue.

In a proactive approach to addressing bullying, we can introduce activities that help all students:

- Get to know each other in new and different ways (beyond cliques and social roles)

- Build social and emotional learning competencies

- Build a "feelings vocabulary" together so students (especially younger children) can identify their feelings (see the appendix, page 168, for more information)

- Learn what anger and other emotions feel like and look like in themselves and others

- Identify anger and stress triggers, and use anger and stress reducers

- Learn to express their anger in healthy, nonviolent ways

- Identify and address things they do that trigger other people's anger (such as teasing or name calling)

- Learn to identify when they have engaged courageously or chosen positive behaviors in difficult situations and build on those experiences

- Learn how to repair harm

Principle: Seeing Behavior as Communication

Students communicate as much through the actions they take as through their words. When we look at the potential messages that exist beneath a particular behavior, we can find ways to address the underlying need and engage the student in problem solving.

Perhaps a student is feeling overwhelmed or doesn't understand what is being asked of her. Perhaps something happened at home and this student's anger has nothing to do with school. Or, maybe something about our class content is a trigger and a student is reacting to the very material we are teaching (for example, a teacher has assigned homework that asks students to write about the Holocaust, and the student's family members are Holocaust survivors).

When we notice when disruptive behavior happens and track what seems to provoke or prevent it, then we can engage students more directly in problem solving. When a student expresses a strong emotion, we can inquire to find out what information is present in that emotion. We can draw a boundary around the expression of that anger ("Sara, I can see that you are upset about this assignment, but please lower your voice and address me in a more respectful way in this classroom"). We can also use inquiry to get to the heart of what is going on for that student ("Now, please tell me what is it about the homework assignment that you are struggling with"). In this way, we begin to stretch ourselves to allow healthy expressions of emotions to come into the classroom, while continuing to offer clear boundaries about appropriate behaviors. When we are able to act from this understanding, we show our students that we are an adult who can be counted on to care, pay attention, set limits, and provide support.

Seeing behavior as communication can also help us avoid taking our students' actions personally. That is, a student may simply be tired or upset that day, and his or her lack of responsiveness in class may have nothing to do with us personally. If a student seems aloof or irritable, he or she may have had a fight with a friend at recess. The student may have missed breakfast that morning or not slept much the night before. Of course we still hold the student accountable or check in with the student individually if needed. But it does mean we can shift our perspective and consider that our students' behavior may have little to do with us and in that way move out of a more defensive posture into inquiry and curiosity.

Practice: Avoiding Pitfalls and Blind Spots

We all have blind spots—where we can't clearly see the situation because we are so close to it. Part of our work as teachers is to engage in practices that help us see what we cannot easily see about ourselves and our classrooms, increase our awareness about our own patterns of reactivity, and inspire us to remain curious about the underlying reasons for students' behaviors. Developing our self-observer and our cultural responsiveness is a critical aspect of this approach—so that we are less likely to misinterpret students' behavior as a challenge to our authority.

The following activities are designed to help us avoid common pitfalls and engage more consciously with student behaviors.

Activities for Avoiding Pitfalls and Blind Spots

- Get curious and inquisitive when students act out.

- Avoid getting defensive about a lesson or activity.

- Don't take student outbursts or cynicism personally. We never know what's behind a student's behavior, and many times, it has nothing to do with us or our lesson.

- Never shame or humiliate a student publicly (using name calling, yelling, put-downs, or ridicule), but do not hesitate to call out a negative behavior that is occurring repeatedly. (For example, "Joseph, when you continue to name call and laugh at other classmates, it is hurtful and disruptive. We have a shared agreement in this class to be respectful, and this is not part of acting respectfully, so you need to change your behavior.")

- Consider sending a student out of class or to the office only after you have tried other interventions.

- Examine your own beliefs, biases, and interpretations of a student's behavior before responding.

Creating Respectful Boundaries With Colleagues

Inevitably in our collegial relationships, boundaries get crossed, conflict arises, buttons get pushed, emotions flare. The current education environment is a veritable pressure cooker, and it is up to all of us to conscientiously attend to our interactions with each other so that these pressures don't tear us apart individually or collectively. Engaging with our colleagues with more intention and compassion also directly impacts our students. Students notice when a school culture is rife with discord, competition, and distrust, and this does not create a productive context for learning and growth. For these reasons, it is essential that we develop skills and capacities to navigate conflict in our adult learning communities.

Principle: Managing Boundaries and Working With Conflict

We often avoid setting boundaries or addressing conflict because these kinds of interactions make us uncomfortable. However, these experiences can be sources of creativity and rich learning if we consider conflict an opportunity for mutual understanding and growth. As Parker Palmer (2009) encourages in *A Hidden Wholeness*, "When the going gets rough, turn to wonder" (p. 218). When we feel a boundary has been crossed or when conflict arises, we can make a choice to approach these situations with curiosity and an openness to learn.

Conflict emerges when one or more people feel that their boundaries have been crossed or disagree about how to move ahead in the school in a way that respects differing perspectives. There are times in meetings and conversations when we may feel we have to choose between saying what we *really* think and risking our working relationships or staying silent about something that is important to us. Is there another option? How might we retain our connection to our values and feelings while maintaining positive and caring relationships? How can we practice creating respectful boundaries with an open heart?

Conflict can alert us to those aspects of our work that are calling out for attention. Perhaps, through navigating this conflict, we become clearer about our personal boundaries or increase our awareness about issues in the school that really matter to us. For some of us, the practice of establishing respectful boundaries with colleagues may involve speaking up with clarity rather than silencing ourselves and stewing in our hurt feelings. For others, it may mean pausing and not firing off an angry email, but rather waiting and responding in a thoughtful way, face to face. For others, it may mean adopting the willingness to truly hear the other person's point of view—even if it is radically different from our own.

When we are able to stay curious and present as we move through challenging times, we may make surprising discoveries. Perhaps our staff realize something important about a habitual way we relate to one another and intentionally commit to changing that pattern. Or perhaps we realize that a conflict is primarily a result of our collective exhaustion and stress and begin to strategize about how we can more directly support each other during intense times. Staying with the discomfort of this process requires a particular kind of courage and strength of heart. But the benefits of engaging conflict together can often deepen the trust within the community and support us in collaborating more effectively and joyfully in the future.

The following activities help us to skillfully navigate conflict.

Activities for Navigating Conflict

- Welcome the unwelcome. When you feel that familiar tightness in your stomach and want to run away from the conflict, take a breath and see the conflict as an opportunity for stretching your capacities. Here is the moment to notice if your heart is opened or closed.

- When you are triggered, sometimes the bravest and wisest action is to call for a break so that you and others involved can come back with an open mind and a fresh perspective. Cultivate your self-observer to note the need for a pause.

- If you are involved in a conflict and are struggling and unable to move it forward, suggest that a neutral colleague sit in to listen and reflect on what he or she hears. This is different than a mediator, which can be a trickier role for a colleague to take on. Sometimes just having a third party deeply listen and reflect back what is said can open up a new point of view and create common ground.

- Introduce specific methods for conflict resolution into your school community. Nonviolent communication, council work, or other practices can support nonreactive speaking and listening.

- Focus on successes as well as problems. Suggest engaging in a success analysis (see the appendix, page 173, for a success analysis protocol) around an issue in the past that you resolved in a satisfactory way. Look at what worked and how you might apply what you learned to the current challenging situation (National School Reform Faculty, n.d.).

- When approaching another colleague about a conflict or misunderstanding, share your perspective and feelings from the "I" perspective, in which you claim your own experience as your own and do not blame the other person. (For example, you may say something like, "When we were in that staff meeting and you made that comment about the math department, I felt disrespected and confused about what I thought you were saying. Can we talk more about this?")

- When in doubt, start with appreciation and gratitude. Many conflicts are based on misunderstandings. Beginning with a generous and genuine gesture with a colleague can create an opening for clarifying some inherent confusion. This may mean that you simply share that you care about your working relationship with this colleague. Naming some of the colleague's strengths can also be very helpful and can shift the dialogue away from defensiveness.

Mark Gerzon, an experienced conflict facilitator and author of *Leading Through Conflict* and *American Citizen, Global Citizen* and other books in the field of global leadership, shares the following insight on dealing with hot and cold conflicts (Mark Gerzon, personal communication, June 10, 2012).

A principal asked me to facilitate an in-service training to help teachers deal with conflict. She told me that the previous year there had been a lot of conflicts, and that if teachers could have handled them better, it might have saved a lot of time and energy. We began at 8:00 a.m. with the entire faculty in the school cafeteria. I asked them to share some of the conflicts from the past year. Nobody raised their hand or spoke up. I realized that the teachers did not want to talk about their conflicts, because naming a conflict that has challenged, upset, or confused us is a vulnerable thing to do. So first I needed to establish some trust. I explained to the teachers that acknowledging a conflict does not mean that you have done something wrong, but rather that you have something to learn. I shared that everyone has trouble dealing with conflicts because we are not taught how to handle them. Then I explained, "There are two kinds of conflicts: 'hot conflicts' where people are overtly expressing anger by shouting, raising their voices, and calling each other names. These conflicts often feel scary. The other kind of conflict is a 'cold conflict,' where nobody shouts at each other or directly confronts each other. Instead, people talk to each other about the issue in the hallways and after school." In organizations like schools— where everyone is supposed to be nice—there are a lot of cold conflicts. At that point, I asked them, "Now that we have redefined conflict and made it clear that it happens to all of us, does anyone have any conflicts they can name?" Suddenly there were a lot of hands in the air, and we began the work of addressing these conflicts. So, I have learned that if conflict is too hot, we need to cool it down. But when conflict is too cold, we may need to heat it up a bit, just to get things moving so the issues can be dealt with openly and honestly.

Conclusion

In chapter 5, we explored how establishing respectful boundaries can support us in honoring our own needs and limits, protecting and guarding the safety of our classroom, and skillfully navigating conflict with our colleagues. In chapter 6, we will discuss how developing our emotional capacity can help us teach with more resourcefulness, effectiveness, and balance and develop an "emotionally intelligent" classroom and adult learning community.

6

Developing Emotional Capacity

We know emotion is very important to the educative process because it drives attention, which drives learning and memory.

—Robert Sylwester

Self-Reflection

Which emotions—in others or yourself—tend to be challenging or uncomfortable for you? Why?

Each day, we and our students and colleagues experience and express a wide range of emotions—joy, anger, sadness, frustration, exuberance, apathy, anxiety. Developing our own emotional capacity gives us the ability to work intentionally and conscientiously with emotions—ours and others'—that inevitably show up and impact the learning environment. Developing emotional capacity includes expanding our emotional range, cultivating our emotional intelligence, developing emotional boundaries, creating emotional safety, and developing positive connections between emotions and learning. When we work with this dimension, we cultivate our resourcefulness, resilience, and effectiveness.

Emotional Capacity as a Teacher

Developing our emotional capacity as teachers means that we understand more about what we feel, develop greater comfort with the full range of our emotions, and learn how to develop healthy emotional boundaries so that we are not constantly overwhelmed or stressed.

Principle: Expanding Emotional Range

Expanding our emotional range means that we intentionally turn our self-observer inward to understand more about our own emotional landscape. It involves identifying which emotions we tend to be comfortable or uncomfortable with in ourselves and others. From this place of understanding, we can work to stretch our capacity to relate to those

"Emotions are the predispositions of actions."

—Julio Olalla

emotions that feel edgy, uncomfortable, or at times unbearable. We can do this by taking daily or weekly inventory of our emotional landscape. In this practice, we can note which emotions tend to arise and which emotions don't. We can also note which emotions we tend to welcome and which ones we tend to suppress or push away, and how this impacts our lives and teaching.

For example, perhaps we are in a particularly challenging time in our personal life and a student's joyful exuberance makes our own struggles more apparent, and so we avoid direct contact with that student. Or perhaps when certain forms of social dialogue happen in our class, we feel afraid that the situation is going to explode, so we shut down what could have been a rich conversation. Or maybe we find that we are so uncomfortable with conflict that we will do anything to keep the peace, including allowing students to violate classroom boundaries. Or perhaps a student's loss of a parent reminds us of a recent loss in our lives, and we avoid reaching out to that student because we don't want to feel our own pain. It is natural for us, as human beings, to have these responses—to want to protect ourselves and avoid discomfort. However, when we open ourselves to the possibility of feeling the whole range of our emotions, we become less reactive and avoidant and have increased access to resilience, joy, and meaning in our lives.

Practice: Working With Uncomfortable Emotions

So how do we develop our comfort with emotions that feel uncomfortable to us? When we don't like what we are feeling, how can we develop our willingness to stay present with those emotions? Let's say we have engaged our self-observer to understand which emotions are challenging for us and discover that we tend to shy away from situations where anger might be expressed. In fact, we see that we tend to suppress signs of intense emotion (in ourselves and others) when they emerge. Perhaps we were raised in a "culture of politeness," where it was taboo to express strong emotions in any context. Or, on the other hand, maybe we were raised in a family where anger was only expressed in dangerous or volatile ways.

Once we become aware of our own tendencies, we have more choices about how to work with anger and intense emotion when they arise in ourselves or in the classroom. Perhaps, rather than shut down the emotions that emerge, we can learn how to express them in a healthy way. For example, we might realize we are feeling grief and sadness about the recent death of a friend and decide to take a weekend off in nature to allow that grief to be fully expressed. Or, during an intense moment in class, we might learn to simply acknowledge a student's emotions and then invite the student to stay after class to share more ("I can see you are really feeling passionate about that issue," or "I can hear that you are angry about what happened on the playground," and so on). When we expand our emotional range, we become less resistant to certain feeling states and more accepting of the various emotional weather patterns that move through us and others.

The following activities help us work with uncomfortable emotions. Seek out support for this work—with friends, colleagues, or therapists—depending on what feels appropriate for you.

Activities for Working With Uncomfortable Emotions

- Notice what feelings you are comfortable and uncomfortable with in yourself and others, and consider *why* certain emotions may be uncomfortable for you.

- Create a list of your emotional triggers and note how you react to these triggers. (For example, "Every time I am interrupted by a student or colleague, I feel disrespected and a surge of anger moves through my chest, and I want to speak out angrily.") See if you can practice the pause when a trigger arises (see chapter 3) and make a new choice.

- Keep an emotional-range journal for a month. In your daily journal entries, note what emotions you tend to experience regularly and what emotions are less present or absent. Note, too, which emotions you tend to shut down or avoid. Take some time to reflect on the ways you manage your emotions. If you are stressed, what do you do to cope? Is this a helpful coping strategy, or would you like to consider other ways for working with stress? Then set some goals for yourself about new strategies you would like to try. Note the effectiveness of these new strategies as you try them.

- When a strong emotion arises, ask yourself: "What is the message of this emotion? What action is being called for?" In challenging moments, try bringing an intentionally positive frame to the situation. Ask yourself, "What is the opportunity here?"

- Read Brené Brown's (2012) *Daring Greatly* or view her videos on vulnerability and uncomfortable emotions, and discuss her work with a colleague or friend.

Principle: Developing Emotional Intelligence

Emotional intelligence (EI), a term and framework first coined by researchers Peter Salovey and John D. Mayer and later developed by author Daniel Goleman, is "the ability to monitor one's own and others' feelings and emotions, to discriminate among them and to use this information to guide one's thinking and actions" (Salovey & Mayer, 1990, p. 189). In this way, emotional intelligence helps us to know what we are feeling, manage those feelings in healthy ways, develop social skills and the capacity to relate to others, cultivate empathy for others, and sustain motivation through times of challenge. Developing our own emotional intelligence directly impacts our students, as we are better able to create and sustain positive relationships, model emotional health, and engage with our class from a place of resource and resilience. In this very direct way, our emotional intelligence supports student learning. As Daniel Goleman (2006) notes:

> The power of an emotionally connected teacher does not end in first grade. Sixth-graders who had such a teacher earned better grades not only that year but the next as well. Good teachers are like good parents. By offering a secure base, a teacher creates an environment that lets students' brains function at their best. That base becomes a safe haven, a zone of strength from which they can venture forth to explore, to master something new, to achieve. That secure base can become internalized when students are taught to better manage their anxiety and so more keenly focus their attention; this enhances their ability to reach that optimal zone for learning. (pp. 283–284)

Practice: Managing Our Emotional States

We can develop our emotional intelligence in an ongoing way by regularly asking ourselves, "What am I feeling now? How is this impacting my teaching? How can I best manage my emotions in this moment?" If we feel anger bubbling up, perhaps we know it would be helpful to spend a few minutes in reflective silence before our class, just so we can cool down and start class with a different perspective. Additionally, when we are experiencing strong and overwhelming negative emotions, it can be helpful to ask ourselves, "In this moment, is there something I am feeling afraid of?" Many times, beneath the layer of our anger, hurt, or anxiety is a fear of losing control, being humiliated, looking bad, or making a mistake. Realizing the different layers of our emotional states can help us take a deep breath and make a more conscious decision about our behavior and approach to a situation.

The following activities help us manage our emotional states.

Activities for Managing Our Emotional States

- When you are unable to identify what you are feeling, take a moment to tune into the "felt sense" or physical sensations in your body. This can assist you in better understanding your emotions. Ask yourself, Is my throat tight, my gut clenched, my face hot? Do I feel choked up? Do I feel like running out of the building? The very act of naming what you are feeling can immediately help you access your own wisdom and practice the pause so you have more choice and awareness.

- Do something physical or creative to express your feeling states. Aerobic activity, time in nature, or time in a creative venture can substantially shift our experience of intense emotion and give us access to the deeper layers of our emotional landscape.

- Identify two or three stress- and anger-management techniques that work for you that you can engage in during hot situations with students or colleagues. For example, you may need to take a two-minute break and then return to the situation. Or you may need to take three deep breaths. Or you may need to take a moment to reaffirm your connection with that person by noticing what you appreciate about him or her.

- Include lessons on stress and anger management in your classroom, and create a common vocabulary that encourages productive communication for all.

- Remember your sense of humor. Humor can be one of the most useful antidotes to stress and intensity.

Principle: Cultivating Emotional Boundaries

When we open our hearts and risk caring deeply for our students, we may also, at times, feel their pain and suffering. It can be difficult to let go of our natural human tendency to want to alleviate another's suffering or resolve their life challenges. In fact, there are times when it is appropriate for us to extend ourselves and support a student to navigate hardship. However, cultivating healthy emotional boundaries helps us to reach out from a place of choice and clarity rather than compulsion or obligation and to empower our students rather than seek to fix them. Additionally, when we have clear emotional boundaries, we are better able to leave our worries about our students behind at the end of the day so we can attend to our own well-being and refresh ourselves. Giving ourselves time and space for renewal then allows us to be more present and available for our students the next day.

Another aspect of cultivating emotional boundaries is understanding what is useful to share with our students and what is not. Although we want to model openness and allow students to know who we are, it is also important to avoid sharing highly personal and intensely emotional aspects of our lives. If we are wondering if we should share a particular story or feeling, we can ask ourselves, "Why am I sharing this story or information—is it going to benefit my students? Is this coming from a balanced place within me? Is what I am about to share personal in a way that will create stress for my students?" Overly emotional or intensely personal disclosures on the part of a teacher can be overwhelming and even damaging for students, as they may feel that they are being asked to take care of us or be the adult in the situation. Developing our emotional boundaries requires us to have enough awareness about ourselves to know when and what to share and when we need to seek out other adults for support and guidance.

Practice: Letting Go of Fixing

Attending to students' emotional safety does not mean we need to fix our students' problems or personal issues. In fact, since this is not the role of educators, treading into the territory of fixer is dangerous both for teachers and for students. We are not therapists. Confusion about our role can lead us into the spiral of being overwhelmed and then burning out, as we feel the heavy weight of our students' personal lives and the inability to alleviate the conditions causing their suffering. However, we can support our students by integrating activities that help them identify and understand emotions and learn how to manage their own feelings, stress, and distractions. We can support our students by providing a steady, caring adult presence in their lives and by being an advocate for their well-being.

The following story illustrates one teacher's journey to let go of his tendency toward fixing.

A fifth-grade teacher shared that he used to be unable to draw clear emotional boundaries with his students. He knew unsettling details about their lives and would often worry about them at night. He spent a great deal of time outside of school trying to figure out how to solve the problems that seemed to interfere with his students' learning.

After months of this, he felt completely overwhelmed and exhausted. He also felt a certain quality of despair and loss of hope and was no longer able to fully express his care for his students. He felt that to function as a teacher, he had to shut down his heart. But after a conversation with a close colleague, he realized it wasn't his job to solve these students' problems. He could be a good listener, offer support, and find students other resources in the school, but he didn't have to feel guilty or hold onto his students' stories after leaving the classroom.

He intentionally practiced leaving his worries and concerns about his students' lives behind him at the end of the day. Over time, he found that he was able to be more present with his students and to feel his deep care for them without getting completely overwhelmed. He discovered that he was actually able to open his heart wider with his students when he had healthy emotional boundaries in place.

The following activities support us in letting go of our tendency to take on too much emotionally or attempting to fix our students' lives.

Activities for Letting Go of Fixing

- Engage in personal practices that help you let go of the school day and release yourself from the need to fix students' lives (for example, finding time for a walk, run, or swim in which you intentionally release the day; taking a few minutes to journal or sit in silence to create a break between work and home; engaging in a debrief with another colleague at the end of the day in which you verbalize your worries and concerns and leave them behind; talking with an interventionist at the school about any serious concerns you have about students so that you know you are taking necessary action).

- Engage in self-observation to become more aware of what emotions are yours and what emotions belong to others (students, parents, and colleagues). If a colleague is frustrated, we might have a tendency to take on that frustration. If a student is sad, we might take on this sadness. Understanding more about our empathetic response can help us recognize when an emotion is not ours.

- Ask for help from colleagues when needed.

- Maintain connection and regular communication with counselors and school interventionists to whom you can refer students. This is especially important if you feel students are experiencing distress beyond what you can address in the classroom.

Emotional Capacity in the Classroom

"Creating a learning space that is not closed down by fearful emotions requires a teacher who is not afraid of feelings. The teacher must make the first move in opening the space for feelings simply because the teacher has the power to do so."

—Parker Palmer

Inevitably, students bring their personal experiences into the classroom. Imagine the student whose parents are getting divorced, who has a new baby sister at home, who just failed a test in another class, or who has a huge track meet after school. Imagine, too, the feelings of the student who is asked to partner on a book report or lab project with another student who regularly bullies him at recess or in the locker room. Consider the experiences of the student who is homeless and sleeps in a car, observes domestic violence regularly, or is the target of racial or homophobic slurs in the halls. These students may try to focus, but if they lack well-developed strategies to identify and manage their emotions, their minds will be elsewhere as we try to engage their attention.

Principle: Fostering Emotional Safety in the Classroom

Every day, we see the ways in which our students' emotional states directly impact their capacity to learn. Distracting emotions can run the gamut from unexpressed grief to fear to exuberance and excitement. Emotional and physical safety are critical to creating the conditions for learning. Without this kind of safety, the brain simply cannot function effectively, and we cannot access our critical and creative thinking.

Learning theorist Renate Caine discusses the way that feeling threatened impacts our learning:

> When we feel threatened . . . we can do some things well, like memorizing, because the brain perseverates under threat and likes to do things over and over again. Repetition provides a sense of safety when you feel helpless. But real thinking, making connections, higher-order thinking and creativity is incompatible with that kind of environment. (Pool, 1997, p. 12)

When we promote a climate of emotional safety, we decrease the negative impacts emotional distress can have on the learning process—such as defeatism, learned helplessness, and confusion. Though we cannot possibly address all the stressors in students' lives, we can create a caring environment where students can share authentically and receive support when overwhelming emotions emerge. When we directly support students to work with emotions that naturally arise in school settings, we empower them to access resources inside and outside of themselves, giving them lifelong tools for resilience.

As we develop more awareness about our students' emotional states, we are also better able to recognize early warning signs in students struggling with unmanageable emotions. When we do see these concerning emotions or behaviors in students (depression, anger, agitation, inconsistent attendance, exhaustion, and so on), we can then help them find other resources within the school. Stepping into this territory with students can, at times, feel overwhelming or risky for us personally, especially if we feel emotionally triggered by a student's problem (such as depression and grief). But, as evidenced by incidents of school violence, dropout, bullying, harassment, and teen suicide over the last decades, the consequences for not paying attention and taking action can be devastating (Aber et al., 2011). Developing proactive measures with a team of colleagues who support our efforts will help us become guardians of school safety and culture and effective advocates for students. It can also be helpful to have an all-staff meeting to discuss these issues, in which counselors and interventionists share the warning signs, and the staff create a plan for working with students in emotional distress.

Practice: Cultivating Students' Emotional Intelligence

Many students enter our classrooms without the basic social and emotional skills to focus and communicate and collaborate effectively. Even if we are not employing a dedicated social and emotional learning program, we can still help students develop basic skills as part of their learning and growth. This may mean that when we talk about the classroom community at the beginning of the school year and develop norms and agreements, we include a few lessons on emotional intelligence and communication. This investment up front normalizes the fact that emotions will show up in the classroom and gives students some sense of how they are expected to manage themselves.

As we explore emotional intelligence with our students, it is important to consider their developmental needs. For younger students, a feelings vocabulary (see the appendix, page 168) can be an important aspect of this process, so students learn a way to notice and name what they are feeling and to identify the body sensations that tend to accompany these feelings. For older students, teaching mindfulness and stress-management techniques (see chapters 3 and 4) can be a doorway into talking about emotions. High school students often respond strongly to a leadership framework in which students are taught how to prepare for life after high school and become strong leaders in their communities. They can explore the role emotional intelligence plays in their capacity to meet their goals and make their dreams reality. The following activities can support students in cultivating their emotional intelligence.

Activities for Cultivating Students' Emotional Intelligence

- With older students, assign class reading on emotional intelligence and leadership. Follow up with a discussion on methods for developing emotional intelligence and leadership and how they relate to success in school and life.

- Create a feelings vocabulary with your students. Use the headings Excited, Sad, Scared, Happy, Angry, and Tender. Then have students brainstorm all the words that are associated with each heading. Ask students to rate on a scale of one to five which feelings they are more and less comfortable with in themselves and in others.

- For younger students, assign a personal feelings wheel. With all ages, you can start the day with a "weather report" as a way to raise awareness of the feeling states in your classroom that day. (See the appendix, page 168, for more details.)

- Ask older students to create a personal map of their own emotional intelligence, including the feelings they are comfortable and uncomfortable with and their current management strategies. Then assist students in identifying management strategies they would like to try in the future.

- With your students, brainstorm ways to manage feelings and impulses during charged interactions or emotionally triggering situations. Introduce practicing the pause or other mindfulness activities (see chapters 3 and 4). Set up a peace corner, encourage journaling, teach focused listening, or bring in a chime or bell that students can ring to indicate a need for a pause.

Practice: Teaching Students About Personal Disclosure

When we invite students' questions, personal sharing, and stories, it is important that we help them understand what is appropriate and safe to share in the classroom. This is not always intuitive for students. In fact, it is a skill we often must teach—particularly for secondary students. Students must learn how to be authentic in a way that is collegial rather than confessional. When we create a trusting learning community, we must realize that some of our students may have had very few authentic, trusting relationships in their lives. As they settle in and learn to trust this particular learning community, they may inadvertently wander into emotional territory that is beyond the bounds of what the classroom can hold. This is natural and not problematic. It simply requires our attention, awareness, and compassionate action.

If a student becomes particularly emotional or begins to disclose information that is highly personal, a teacher may need to interrupt and redirect the student. This is to protect both the student who is sharing and the other students, for whom some information could be overwhelming or disturbing. In such situations, we can respectfully redirect the student by saying, "Thank you so much for speaking up so honestly. What I hear you saying is so important and personal that it requires more time than we have here, so let's take some time after class to discuss this." It is essential to clearly intervene in this situation without shaming the student in any way. Although it may feel counterintuitive to stop a student in the midst of an overly personal sharing, it actually fosters greater safety and trust in the class when students see us assuming our natural role as protector of the learning community. This will allow deeper and more authentic connections to emerge.

The following story illustrates how one teacher worked with a student who began to share highly personal experiences.

An eighth-grade teacher shared that, midway through the year, a student named Miranda, who hadn't spoken much throughout the year, decided to share during community circle time. The day's topic was "pearls of wisdom," and students were sharing stories about life lessons that significant people in their lives had taught them. The teacher was thrilled that Miranda finally felt safe to speak and inspired to share a personal story.

Miranda began to share, "One of the most important people in my life is my older brother, who's in college now. He has taught me so much about determination and perseverance because he has bipolar disorder." Miranda went on. "He told me that life really isn't about being good at everything—it's about still trying even when you feel like everything is stacked against you." At that point, Miranda started to get emotional, and the teacher instinctively began worrying about where the story was going. Miranda continued with a shaky voice, "That meant so much when he said this. We were all so worried because he had just tried to kill himself by taking . . ."

At this point, with the intense emotions rising in Miranda and the introduction of the theme of suicide, the teacher knew he had to intervene. "Let me stop you there, Miranda," he said, "because you made a beautiful point, and I really want to take more time to discuss this issue with you more in person after class. The issues you raise are so important, and I am grateful for your willingness to share this with us. And we don't have the time in this class period to really give these issues the time they need. Let's plan to talk more after class."

Miranda nodded, took a deep breath, and gathered her emotions. Before the next student spoke, the teacher affirmed Miranda and reminded the class of the prompt: "That was a powerful story Miranda just shared. Let's take just a moment to honor her story and then move on to the next person. I want to remind you that our topic is 'pearls of wisdom,' and we are sharing stories about the teachings we have received from people in our life. All kinds of stories are welcome, because, of course, pearls of wisdom can be very funny too."

The student who spoke next did tell a funny story, and by the end of the circle time, all kinds of stories had been shared—sad, funny, poignant. After class, the teacher spoke with Miranda, who agreed to see the school counselor to talk about the impact her brother's challenges was having on her life.

The possibility of encountering tricky emotional terrain with our students may concern us deeply. We may fear that by creating a community of trust we will open a veritable Pandora's box of emotions. But this is hardly ever the case. Most often, students share meaningful stories that are appropriate for the classroom. But when students do spill a highly emotional story, it generally points to an issue that needs attention. In these situations, we need to have the supports in place to help students access resources beyond the classroom. It is important to note that with the influence of highly confessional media forms, such as reality television, Facebook, and so on, students often need even more support to understand what is appropriate to share in classrooms. You may wish to engage a specialist or counselor to discuss this with your students. The following activities will help you teach your students about personal disclosure.

> ## Activities for Teaching Students About Personal Disclosure
>
> - Create a compassionate and nonshaming way to intervene with a student who is revealing more than is appropriate for the classroom.
> - With older students, clearly define the purpose of personal sharing in the class—it is in the service of learning and building relationships. With older students, at times it is important to stress that the purpose of personal sharing is not for dramatic impact or to impress or shock others. You can then discuss the consequences of this kind of sharing for that person and the people around him or her.
> - Discuss the limits of confidentiality and your legal obligation to report (see chapter 7).
> - Engage in a discussion about the impact of media on our sense of what to share and what not to share about ourselves.

Practice: Addressing Global Issues and Fear of the Future

With the number of local and global crises students hear about and experience—war, poverty, school and gang violence, climate change—it's no wonder they often feel overwhelmed and disempowered. And with the ongoing bombardment of media and increased access to technology, it is all too common for students to become numb, desensitized, or "checked out." Our youth regularly experience "too much, too fast, too soon" (Melissa Michaels, personal communication, 2001), and these feelings and conditions inevitably impact students' desire and capacity to engage in school. Sensory overload can compromise students' capacity to learn and contribute to a sense of alienation. Feelings of hopelessness and helplessness lead to disengagement in school and in life.

When students are continually operating on sensory overload, they tend to cope in a few ways:

- They shut down and numb their system because they cannot process or integrate any more information. This often leads to depression, apathy, or the inability to feel.

- They seek ways to discharge the agitation, anxiety, and fear through hyperactivity, aggression, or risk taking.

- They engage in thrill-seeking in an attempt to feel something authentic or "real," which can lead to self-destructive behaviors and unhealthy risk taking. In its most extreme form, this can lead very desperate students to commit violent acts—toward others or themselves.

From a young age, many students see and experience intense levels of pain and suffering in their own communities and in the world around them. As adults, in our efforts to keep our students informed, we may, at times, give students information about events and conditions in our world without also helping them to integrate this knowledge into their lives. When this kind of information is given without the space and time to process it, it can strike fear in students and leave them with a sense of hopelessness. In these situations, students may think, "There's nothing I can do, so why try?" When students become numb or shut down in this way, they are much less available for real learning.

The following story illustrates the impact of world events on students.

One high school student watched a devastating film on climate change as part of a geography class. Afterward, she felt a great deal of confusion and fear. The teacher did not offer students a chance to discuss the film or to talk about actions they could take to mediate global climate change. The students left the class feeling that they were helpless in the face of grave circumstances. While the student was given important information about the state of the world, she was not given guidance or direction about what to do with this information or how to apply it or integrate it into her life. In this situation, the teacher could have helped students to process this information by giving them opportunities to critically engage with the issue, ask good questions, develop creative solutions, and understand why they are learning the information. By including some time for this kind of conversation, we empower our students rather than discourage them.

Another high school science teacher took a different track to exploring climate change. Over the course of a week, she showed a series of twenty-minute sections of a documentary film to her students. After each section, she stopped the film and asked students to engage in reflective writing and pair-shares on questions the film raised. At the end of the week, students were asked to define one action or a set of actions they would commit to in the next month that related to climate change and to explain how their choices linked to the science of climate change. Students then wrote reflective papers on the month-long experiment they were engaged in. They shared their reflections with each other. As a class, they decided what the most effective strategies had been, and they shared that learning with the rest of the school in a series of posters titled "What You Can Do." Students were actively engaged in thinking, learning, and problem solving.

The following activities will help you address global issues and fear of the future in your classroom.

> ## Activities for Addressing Global Issues and Fear of the Future
>
> - When including challenging topics in your lesson (such as climate change or war), give students an opportunity to share personal reactions and responses to the material.
> - Create ways for students to creatively express what they are seeing, feeling, and noticing in the world. One eighth-grade language arts teacher gives students an opportunity to create notebooks with visuals and words that represent events and movements in the world that feel positive and hopeful and those that feel challenging or painful.
> - If you notice that students are particularly subdued or down after a lesson's content, make sure to follow up with the class, have a short conversation, address their feelings, and offer action steps that they can take. You might conclude class with a lighthearted active focusing activity. (See the appendix, page 160, for sample classroom activities.)
> - When possible, invite students to share about issues in the world about which they feel strongly. Ask students to speak about how they would like to be change agents. This conversation can be connected to a variety of content areas, from social studies to language arts to science.

Practice: Working With Agitation, Numbing, and Grief

Agitation, grief, and loss inevitably show up in our schools, whether a student is experiencing a move, the loss of a parent or teacher, a divorce, or a shift in identity. Grief can also emerge from losses associated with developmental or school-initiated transitions—such as the shift from elementary school to middle school. Grief may also be triggered when students experience school or world events that are traumatic or troubling.

Students often come to school with reservoirs of unexpressed fear and grief that directly interfere with their learning. When students are not given healthy ways to express grief and fear, they tend to numb these emotions. This process of numbing is prevalent throughout much of our culture—as the adult community often lacks the skills, time, and resources to manage our own and each other's grief in healthy ways. However, the costs of this cycle of numbing are great, as both individuals and the community suffer. When we numb our feelings, we diminish our ability to be present with ourselves and each other and lose access to our passion for life and learning.

Student numbing directly impacts our school communities. When students numb, they can begin to lose their capacity to feel compassion or empathy for others or to find meaning in school or life. This desensitization can then contribute to an inability to engage in school, causing students to check out of life, bully others, and at times feel such desperation that they commit destructive, hurtful, or even deadly acts. Sometimes, in an effort to simply feel *something* again, students enter into extreme behaviors in which they hurt themselves or others (for example, cutting or bullying) or take huge risks to break the feeling of numbness (for example, binge drinking, reckless driving, or casual sex).

Because of widespread cultural discomfort with grief and loss, young people are often expected to navigate this terrain without sufficient adult support. One teacher shared that when his mother died when he was sixteen, he went through the entire school year without a single adult acknowledging this loss or offering him resources or support. He shares, "This was devastating to me. I felt alone and isolated in the experience. Looking back I know that these teachers simply didn't know what to do or how to reach out to me. But even one caring adult reaching out would have meant a lot to me." Many students have had this experience of utter isolation in the face of loss or change. Imagine the difference it could make, in this situation and others, if a student had a caring adult in school to turn to at times of grief, loss, vulnerability, or fear.

One middle school student's story illustrates the power of a caring adult.

When Mr. Carroll, the school counselor, first called me down to his office, I thought I was in trouble. But then he said that my mom had contacted him to let him know that my mom and dad were going through a divorce. He said he was very sorry to hear that and that he wanted me to know I could come talk with him whenever I needed to. At first, I felt a little embarrassed. I wasn't sure what to say. But he didn't ask me to explain anything about my family. He just asked me if I wanted to talk and said I could stop by his office any time. And I did. Over that year, I stopped by a number of times just to say hello.

Consider another example of the impact of a caring adult.

A bus carrying thirty members of the high school band crashed on an icy highway in the middle of winter, and a number of students were injured. The next day, a language arts teacher noticed many of his students were having a difficult time focusing on their course work. After recognizing the elephant in the room, this teacher gave his students the opportunity to talk openly about the situation. After fifteen minutes of conversation, the students decided they wanted to do something to help the families impacted by the crash. They used the rest of the class period to design letters, cards, and an action plan to offer meals to the families.

Later that year, when the language arts teacher was discussing the literary theme of ethics and service in community, he was able to refer to this moment in their year when the students took this powerful initiative. They then reflected on what their actions showed about human nature in times of crisis and connected this theme to novels they had read that year. At the end of the semester, students commented that the experience was one of the most memorable aspects of their year.

We are teachers, not therapists or counselors, and yet we can learn to tune in to the emotional landscape of our students to facilitate their learning and foster school safety. When we acknowledge students' grief and loss, they are more likely to feel supported, cared for, and able to access the internal and external resources they need to move through their grieving process in a healthy way. When we develop our understanding of the signs of agitation and sensory overload, we can more readily see when a student is struggling and needs more help than we can offer. When we make emotional well-being a priority and provide specialized resources as needed, we can create a safer and more effective learning environment for all.

The following activities can support us in working with students' agitation, numbing, and grief.

> ### *Activities for Working With Agitation, Numbing, and Grief*
>
> - Have a counselor come to your class in the first part of the year to discuss resources in the school and common challenges for students (including stress, feeling overwhelmed, depression, and so on) and some coping strategies.
> - Engage in your own research and reading about grief and numbing. You may want to read Rachael Kessler's chapter "Grief as a Gateway to Love in Teaching" (Kessler, 2004) about working with grief in schools. If possible, read and discuss this article in pairs or in a group.
> - When you know a student has gone through a major loss or life transition, take a few moments at the beginning or end of class to check in privately, see how he or she is doing, express your care, and help the student find resources.
> - If a major event has occurred in the school or in the world, create a forum for students to express their thoughts and feelings about this event through talking or writing. Students may or may not want to express their feelings about the event, but creating an opportunity for discussion is important. If you notice a student is struggling excessively emotionally, offer to take the student to a counselor.
> - Acknowledge that grief, fear, and sadness come up in our lives and in school. Include content that provides a forum to discuss grief and sadness—whether a book or a discussion of a global topic.

Principle: Developing Emotionally Rich Curricula

For a moment, think about a book, movie, or song that impacted you in a significant way. See what kind of details you can remember. Chances are, you can still remember the story, melody, or characters clearly today because of the emotions connected with the storyline and images. When we are emotionally engaged, our brains retain information more effectively. When we design and utilize an emotionally rich curriculum, we can more easily ignite students' passion for the subject matter—students naturally become riveted and alert, remember details and nuances they might otherwise forget, and are more open to learning new material. As John Medina (2008) notes in his book *Brain Rules*, "Emotionally arousing events tend to be better remembered than neutral events" (p. 79). Maurice Elias, Harriett Arnold, and Cynthia Steiger Hussey (2003) note, "We pay immediate attention to, and we recall more readily, experiences that have strong emotional overtones" (p. 61). And finally, as Nancy Frey, Douglas Fisher, and Sandi Everlove (2009) note, "Students experiencing positive emotions have an improved flow of academic information and a heightened state of learning" (p. 25). Engaging students' emotions positively can be a powerful catalyst for learning.

In the following sections we will focus on how to create emotionally rich curricula that foster a sense of personal relevance and engage students' creativity and imagination.

Practice: Fostering Personal Relevance

Often, students look at an assignment and ask, "How is this ever going to help me in real life?" Even students too young to articulate this question display varying levels of engagement depending on their personal connections to subject areas, activities, skills, or content. However, we can encourage students to make personal connections to any subject area by using innovative teaching methodologies that foster a sense of relevance. In language arts and literature or social studies and history classes, we can pick up on important themes in a text or moments in history and design activities that link our students' lives to that theme or event. For instance, we can design a project, writing assignment, or discussion that explicitly asks students to make a connection between their own personal experiences and those of fictional or historical figures.

For example, when reading Kate Chopin's classic novel *The Awakening* (a story about a woman who feels trapped by social standards and expectations in the late 1800s), one teacher had her high school students bring in images representing ways in which women feel socially or culturally "trapped" today. Each student shared an image, and then the class taped their images onto a drawing of a giant birdcage (an image that is symbolic in the text). Not only did this assignment make the protagonist's struggles more personally relevant to each student, but it also engaged multiple intelligences and helped students remember key motifs (the birdcage) and themes (the search for personal freedom) in the story.

We can also create ways for students to engage personally with the major themes of our core content. Consider the following examples. In one middle school earth science class, students were studying the impact of trash on the environment. To encourage students to understand more about the "disposable lifestyle" most Americans lead, the teacher asked students to carry their trash around with them for the week and to then weigh the trash bag and relate their personal habits to current statistics about waste. The students then wrote a reflection on the experience and shared these with each other.

In a first-grade class, students were troubled to learn that their milk cartons were not recyclable and thus were going into the trash and harming the earth. Their teacher decided to give students a persuasive writing assignment on the topic. Each student wrote a letter to the milk company asking them to change its policy. Then the teacher mailed all the letters to the company in hopes of creating positive change. Some of the most reluctant writers were excited by the purpose of the task and happily participated by doing their best writing. The students were thrilled when they got a personal response to their letters, letting them know that the company would seriously consider their concerns in their policies going forward.

The following activities are also helpful in fostering personal relevance in the classroom.

Activities for Fostering Personal Relevance

- At the end of class, ask students to jot down one phrase about how that day's lesson relates to their life or what the implications are of the lesson for their life, their community, or the world.
- Regularly help students draw personal connections to the content area. For example, you could take five minutes of open-forum comments in which students make a connection to the content or lesson.
- Include project-based learning that allows students to connect their work in school to the community—letter writing, an environmental project, community interviews, a study of students' own town or neighborhood, and so on.
- Consider inviting students to create modern-day adaptations of literary themes, historical events, or social movements from other time periods. Invite them to think about what these themes, events, or movements would look like now, in their world, in their lives, and in their communities.

Practice: Inviting Creativity and Imagination

Creativity is "the ability to transcend traditional ideas, rules, patterns, relationships, and to create meaningful new ideas, forms, methods, interpretations" (Dictionary.com, 2013). Engaging students' creativity and imagination is a critical aspect of developing an emotionally rich curriculum. Though we know that creative thinking is a critical part of learning, schools rarely focus on giving students regular opportunities to foster and practice creativity itself, with the exception of the fine and performing arts. Creativity then tends to be associated solely with the arts or with a specialized group of students who are designated "creative." However, creativity is an inherent capacity in all human beings that requires encouragement, and teachers can assist students in bringing creativity to all that they do in school.

Logical, rational, linear thinking has an important place in our lives and in the classroom. However, even when students can master test taking and memorize important facts, if they don't have the skills to apply this information, take intellectual leaps, and explore new ways of perceiving and expressing, their learning will be limited. Explicitly developing creativity and giving students the tools, time, and space to express their creativity bring learning to life and connect students' passions with the content. Consider the following examples.

A middle school teacher kicked off a unit on the Norse epic poem *Beowulf* by having students discuss common traits of monsters in literature. She then asked students to consider the ways society creates concepts of the monstrous other and how this shapes actions, behaviors, and policies. Students explored examples in racist policies, violence, and genocide. Students were then asked to create an original story based on the Beowulf myth that engaged these themes.

An elementary school teacher had students create inside-out masks of their own faces as part of a unit on identity and culture. She tied this art project to students' book groups in which they were all reading literature that explored social identity. Students were asked to decorate the outside of their masks in a symbolic way to illustrate what they tend to show to the world. The inside of the mask was to symbolize aspects of themselves that were more hidden or invisible. Students wrote a poem for each side of the mask and then shared their masks and poetry with their peers.

The following activities are other examples of how teachers have used creativity as a teaching methodology.

Activities for Using Creativity as a Teaching Methodology

- A middle school teacher divided his students into two groups and created a mock trial for *Brown v. Board of Education*. Students had to use their creative and critical-thinking skills to develop arguments from the historical perspectives they were representing.
- A fourth-grade teacher studying the Renaissance had her students create a Renaissance fair. Each student came costumed as a historical figure from the Renaissance and was asked to interact with family members, peers, and teachers from the perspective of this historical person.
- A ninth-grade language arts teacher had his students write their own versions of *Romeo and Juliet* with modern-day storylines and versions of the characters.
- A seventh-grade language arts teacher assigned the Sandra Cisneros book *The House on Mango Street* and asked students to write their own vignettes about their lives.
- A high school science teacher asked her students to memorize the periodic table by creating their own rap or rhyme.
- An American government teacher asked students to create an annotated and illustrated timeline of the civil rights movement with small, significant symbols drawn next to key dates and events and to write their own civil rights speech related to one of the dates on the timeline.

Each of these teachers met core content standards and goals and inspired creative thinking in students. Developing creativity helps students break out of habitual ways of thinking, process information in multiple ways, and apply their learning. The following activities help foster creativity and imagination in students.

> ### *Activities for Inviting Creativity and Imagination*
>
> - Ask students to role-play or enact mock situations in which they have to creatively share about content and solve problems (such as for a famous historical event or meeting).
> - Invite students to develop metaphors or symbols that relate to their personal lives or academic content.
> - Engage students in personal or mythological storytelling during which they are asked to bring a scene or situation to life in vivid, innovative ways.
> - Ask students to write their own myth based on an ancient myth that represents the journey of their lives. This personal myth could also include other literary devices.
> - Have students create their own speeches based on famous speeches of times past.
> - When learning about poetry or different aspects of literature, have students write their own versions of a published work that mirror a particular style or form.
> - Include other expressive art forms when learning facts in math and science (bring in music, visual arts, and symbols). For example, ask students to create a song or rap that helps them memorize multiplication tables or the water cycle. Have them create a short story or symbolic representation of cell division.
> - In any subject area or for a major project, include at least one expressive art form; for example, give students the option of writing a poem or song, drawing a picture, making a collage, creating a mask, or building a diorama to represent or express a major concept or theme. It is essential to make materials available to students so there is not an issue of resource inequity.

Emotional Capacity With Colleagues

We often feel we have to manage our emotions and difficulties alone and that there is no place to express our feelings in a school setting. Reaching out to colleagues can go a long way toward creating a more caring and supportive adult learning community. This does not mean that our faculty or team becomes a therapeutic support group, but rather that we take the time to know each other as human beings and share our humanness.

Principle: Reaching Out to Colleagues

As in our classrooms, a whole range of emotions can emerge in the faculty community—despair, exhaustion, outrage, elation, joy. When we intentionally make space for this in the school community and take the personal initiative to reach out to others, we may find that not only do we feel less alone, but that the business matters of the school run more smoothly. Impasses and factions within schools often emerge from core misunderstandings and hurt feelings. Taking time in faculty meetings, staff lunches, and department meetings to check in briefly and learn how each person is doing can assist us in working better as a team and in being aware when someone is feeling particularly challenged, exhausted, or burdened by a personal issue.

One teacher shares the following story about the power of reaching out.

When my father died suddenly, I was in the middle of preparing students for state tests. I buried myself in my work and closed my heart to the comfort offered by friends, family, and colleagues. My unresolved pain grew and grew. One day a trusted colleague invited me out to dinner and conversation. That was a turning point for me. The opportunity to be heard reminded me of how important it was for me to slow down and take care of myself in this very challenging time of my life.

Finally, taking time to share both our celebrations and challenges can help us manage our emotions more effectively so we are better able to do our jobs. Often schools can inadvertently foster a culture of complaint—where it is more comfortable and acceptable to share what is wrong rather than what is right. By intentionally including time to celebrate successes and accomplishments as well as challenges and struggles, we can keep a more balanced perspective. In this way, gratitude and celebration help us to build our resilience, while sharing our challenges helps us find resources inside and outside of ourselves.

The following activities will help us to foster emotional intelligence with our colleagues.

Activities for Fostering Emotional Intelligence With Colleagues

- The next time you find yourself feeling overwhelmed by strong emotions at school, ask a trusted colleague to support you by simply listening without feeling any need to fix you or your issues. Conversely, if you see someone who seems to be struggling, reach out and offer them your support—coffee, a walk, or time to listen during lunch or planning period. You may wish to use a deep listening practice to support this process. See the focused listening practices (in the appendix, page 164) for examples.

- Find a colleague you can check in with regularly so that you have at least one person in the building who is keeping track of you in this way.

- Start meetings with a faculty weather report, in which each person shares his or her own personal weather. If you don't wish to use weather as a metaphor, each person can simply share one word about how he or she is feeling or what issues he or she arrived with that day.

- Start meetings with an opportunity for each staff member to partner with another colleague to share one celebration and one challenge from the day or week.

- Engage your faculty in a discussion about emotions, risky behaviors, and possible interventions. Confronting the emotions of your students in school is less overwhelming when you have a team approach.

Conclusion

In this chapter, we looked at the many ways developing our emotional capacity directly impacts growth and learning. Now that we have explored each of the five dimensions individually, in chapter 7, we will look at how we can integrate these dimensions into the classroom throughout the arc of the school year. Chapter 7 will offer a developmental approach we call the Learning Journey to describe this process.

7

The Learning Journey: Putting It All Together in the Classroom

The function of education is to teach one to think intensively and to think critically. Intelligence plus character—that is the goal of true education.

—Martin Luther King Jr.

Self-Reflection

When you think of your teaching experiences thus far, what metaphors come to mind?

In chapters 2 through 6, we explored each of the Five Dimensions of Engaged Teaching in depth. In this chapter, we discuss how to integrate the five dimensions over the arc of a term or school year as a way to improve social, emotional, and academic learning outcomes. We will introduce a framework of group development called the Learning Journey that includes three stages, each with its own characteristics, challenges, opportunities, and goals. This developmental approach applies to any classroom and content area as well as to classes explicitly dedicated to social and emotional learning (such as an advisory, morning meeting, SEL, or transitions program). Whether we are teaching kindergarten or fourth grade, a high school math class, or a middle school advisory, integrating and applying the five dimensions through various stages of development helps us as we create and sustain thriving learning communities. Additionally, as our classroom communities develop over time, so do our capacities as an engaged teacher. In doing so, we also model and encourage these capacities in our students and in one another.

The Learning Journey includes the following stages:

- Stage one—Cultivating a caring community

- Stage two—Strengthening community and connection

- Stage three—Creating positive closure and anchoring the learning

Understanding these stages of the Learning Journey can help teachers:

- Design and sequence lessons in a way that appropriately and effectively fosters relational trust and builds a sense of community

- Attend to the needs of each individual and the group

- Anticipate challenges and plan accordingly

- Maximize academic learning opportunities

- Appreciate and acknowledge both individual and group progress

- Support students during transition times

Throughout this chapter, you will see icons that represent each of the five dimensions. They indicate which dimension a particular principle or practice supports, as shown in table 7.1.

Table 7.1: The Five Dimensions of Engaged Teaching

	Dimension 1: Cultivating an Open Heart
	Dimension 2: Engaging the Self-Observer
	Dimension 3: Being Present
	Dimension 4: Establishing Respectful Boundaries
	Dimension 5: Developing Emotional Capacity

Stage One: Cultivating a Caring Community

Each student arrives in the classroom with a different personality, background, learning style, and skill level. When we take steps at the beginning of the term to intentionally gather students into a cohesive whole and give them a clear sense of purpose and direction, we are investing in the foundations of our learning community. This initial investment then supports students in effectively communicating and collaborating with each other, participating in their own learning, and feeling as if they belong to a community they are also responsible for. As Stephen Covey (2009) notes, "Helping students to feel connected is what prevents and removes many of the discipline issues before the year is scarcely underway" (p. 93).

In stage one of the learning journey, we focus on developing trust, promoting a caring community that respects differences, fostering cooperation and companionship, and creating a climate of focus and academic rigor. Students will:

- Get to know and trust each other

- Begin to explore their own identities, interests, and personal goals

- Explore their learning goals for the school year

- Develop a sense of cohesive community

- Learn skills to focus and apply themselves to schoolwork

Creating a caring community requires that we are aware of and attentive to the full range of diversity that any given group might contain. This means creating a norm of respect for both more-apparent differences, such as gender and native language, as well as less-visible differences, such as socioeconomic status and religion. (See Developing Cultural Responsiveness in chapter 2 for some specific strategies). Throughout the stages of the Learning Journey, it is important to use language that is inclusive of all students in the classroom (for example, using gender-neutral language and not assuming students are from two-parent households), to protect all students from hurtful language and behaviors (for example, racist slurs, insults), and to avoid assumptions about what students have in common (for example, that they are all heterosexual or share the same cultural context).

Sue Keister, president of Integral Vision Consulting, shares the following story about building trust and a sense of belonging (S. Keister, personal communication, April 10, 2011). Sue provides consulting and professional development services for the Collaborative for Academic, Social, and Emotional Learning (CASEL); Lions Clubs International Foundation; and the PassageWorks Institute.

I was teaching a class in which we were exploring the impact of our words and actions on others. I opened the lesson by explaining how genuinely affirming words and actions tend to strengthen us, and negative ones tend to weaken our confidence. I held up a sheet of paper and asked the students to contribute words and actions that they might hear in the course of the day. I then tore a piece of paper from the sheet when the words and actions were negative, and I added pieces back on when the words were supportive. Soon I was down to one little piece of paper.

One student said, "What happens when you get down to your last piece?" The class became silent, and I knew that it was a critical moment for learning.

Staying with this inquiry, I asked, "Have you ever felt like you were down to your last piece? What did you do?"

Another student remarked, "You would hold on for dear life because you disappear if you lose your last piece." So I closed my fist around the piece of paper.

Another student said, "Look at your hand. It's a fist. When you get down to your last piece, you present a fist to the world. You have nothing to give. You have to fight and keep people away, because you're not going to let anyone take your last piece."

Continuing with the metaphor, I asked, "What do people need who are down to their last piece?"

Another student responded, "We have to add to that person's last piece so that they have enough to give away again. Then they can open up."

Another said, "So, when someone approaches us with anger or hate or sadness, they may be on their last piece. It may have nothing to do with us. Our responsibility is to add something positive to their lives. Next time, we could be on our last piece, and it will be good if people understand that and help us instead of returning fists with fists."

From that point forward, the metaphor of the "last piece" became our touchstone for the power we have to support each other and help open the "fists" of the world with kindness and support rather than negativity and reactivity.

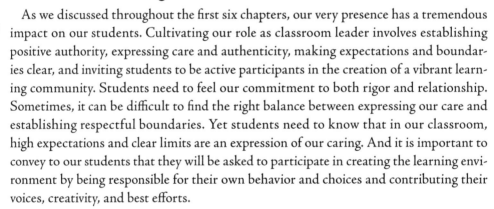

Practice: Establishing Our Role as Classroom Leader

As we discussed throughout the first six chapters, our very presence has a tremendous impact on our students. Cultivating our role as classroom leader involves establishing positive authority, expressing care and authenticity, making expectations and boundaries clear, and inviting students to be active participants in the creation of a vibrant learning community. Students need to feel our commitment to both rigor and relationship. Sometimes, it can be difficult to find the right balance between expressing our care and establishing respectful boundaries. Yet students need to know that in our classroom, high expectations and clear limits are an expression of our caring. And it is important to convey to our students that they will be asked to participate in creating the learning environment by being responsible for their own behavior and choices and contributing their voices, creativity, and best efforts.

As students are first getting to know their teachers and peers, they will often test limits as a way of understanding the boundaries of the particular classroom. When we engage our students with a balance of caring, high expectations, and fair and consistent boundaries from day one, students can more easily relax and settle into the term or year. As Rudy Crew (2007) notes, "Setting clear expectations in the classroom frees both students and their teachers from having to guess what their goals are and lets them get down to the hard work of reaching them" (p. 70).

The following activities help us establish our role as classroom leader.

Activities to Support Classroom Leadership

- Each day, greet students at the door or from your desk or make eye contact with them when calling roll. In some way, make a brief personal connection with each student.

- At the beginning of the year, share several personal stories that help connect students to you as a teacher. Appropriate stories about your experience as a student around their age can be very effective.

- Provide a context and purpose for the class and revisit this purpose occasionally throughout the year.

- Invite student voices, passions, and interests. Take time to get to know your students.

- Be clear about your expectations for the classroom environment (for example, in regards to cell phones, texting, email, doing homework in class, food and drink in class, and so on). Invite students to participate in creating these expectations.

- State clearly that in this class, we will respect differences, and hurtful language will not be tolerated. Collectively explore all the kinds of differences that will be respected in the group.

- Encourage divergent thinking by gathering a variety of viewpoints and asking open-ended questions.

- Do not let behavioral issues go unaddressed. Set a tone of firmness and care early on.

- Establish wait time: give students three to five seconds of thinking time before asking them to respond to a question you have posed.

- Notice if you are providing equal opportunities to all of your students. Notice if you find yourself falling into a pattern of calling on certain students and not others, and make a conscious effort to remedy this.

- When appropriate, move chairs and groupings of students so different students sit in the front and back of the class.

- Make one-on-one personal connections with students: set up office hours, encourage your students to come see you in the first few weeks, and consider making home visits to students before school begins. For elementary students, consider a preschool family picnic or gathering of some kind.

Practice: Providing a Context for Social, Emotional, and Academic Learning

The principles and practices embedded in the Five Dimensions of Engaged Teaching can be applied to a variety of different classroom and youth development contexts. Some teachers might have the opportunity to implement a social and emotional learning curriculum or a once-a-week advisory program, health class, transitions program, or leadership class. Other teachers may choose to integrate these principles and practices by weaving them into their regular classes throughout the term or year. Others may integrate social and emotional learning standards with academic standards and teach the skills and dispositions as part of their core curriculum. Whatever the context, it is essential that students understand how these principles and practices relate to their social, emotional, and academic success. When students understand the reason for including a focusing activity or a community circle or a discussion on transitions, they are more open to these experiences and less likely to resist or undermine them.

Figure 7.1 shows a sample of a chart used in a classroom to clarify the purpose of a ninth-grade leadership class that was implementing a social and emotional learning curriculum.

What This Class Is	What This Class Is Not
A place for engaged learning	A friendship group
A place to improve our communication skills	Therapy or counseling
An environment of shared responsibility	A place for secrets
An opportunity to develop our social, emotional, and academic intelligences	A place to exclude, bully, or create cliques
A place for collaboration and cooperation	A place without rules or guidelines
An opportunity to know ourselves and one another better	A place to check out and disengage

Figure 7.1: Sample chart for clarifying the purpose of a ninth-grade leadership class.

Practice: Developing Shared Agreements

Developing shared agreements is an essential part of stage one (see chapter 5, page 69, for a full description of this practice). In this section, we provide a story to illustrate what the process of developing shared agreements might look like in a classroom. This activity can be adapted for any age group, and though the language and tone may shift, the themes of the agreements are often the same. It is most effective to introduce the shared agreements process after students have had a few weeks of classes so they understand the format and some of the content of the class and have had a chance to begin to develop trust and a sense of community. It is important for students to understand that shared agreements coexist alongside school rules—they do not replace school rules.

A teacher explains to his students, "Today we are going to talk about the kind of classroom community we all want to create together. As we discussed earlier, there are some non-negotiable rules for this classroom and for our school, but now I would like us to develop our own set of agreements for this class. This is a chance for each of you to speak about what matters to you. To start, let's each brainstorm a list of ideas. I want you to write down three to five things you need to be able to trust each other, speak honestly and openly, and take risks to learn."

He then asks his students to write for five minutes before reconvening them to discuss their responses. One student, Jerome, speaks up: "Respect. Without respect, nobody's going to talk."

"Thanks, Jerome. That is so important," the teacher responds. "But what exactly does respect look like? How do we show respect?" He listens and writes down students' ideas on the board, adding his own ideas as well. "For me," he says, "respect means listening to each other. And I know you are listening to me when you aren't talking to each other when I'm talking and when you're not writing notes or poking each other with pencils. To me, listening means we give each other our full attention."

Joshua raises his hand. "I hate it when kids laugh at each other and put each other down," he says. Then, Elena, a shy girl who often sits in the back of class, raises her hand. "Sometimes it seems like only some people speak in this class. Or kids get interrupted and can't finish what they're saying."

While continuing to gather ideas and allow for conversation, the teacher is conscious of inviting comments from all the students, not just the ones who most often speak.

After five minutes, Felicia, a boisterous girl who often challenges her teacher, raises her hand. "So how are we supposed to have any fun with all these rules?"

The teacher smiles. "Of course we will have fun. In fact, I think having agreements about how we treat each other will help us have more fun."

"But Joshua said he doesn't like when people laugh, and I like when we laugh," Felicia continues. The teacher then leads his students in a discussion about the difference between laughing at and laughing with someone. He discusses how creating and honoring shared agreements will be an ongoing process of listening and learning from each other.

Ten minutes later, the group has a list of twenty ideas. The teacher says, "Now let's see if we can create a short list of agreements from all these ideas. What themes do you see in this list of ideas on the board?"

"Well, a lot of them have to do with respecting each other," one student comments.

"Yes, I see that too. And we talked about all the different ways we show respect. Okay, we'll make respect one of our categories." They create a list of five shared agreements: respecting, listening, taking responsibility, having fun, and including others. The teacher then asks students to give a thumbs up or thumbs down for each of the agreements to indicate if every student is willing to abide by and stand behind the agreements. All of the students give a thumbs up, except for Henry, who sits back in his chair with his arms folded across his chest. The teacher asks Henry to speak about his objections.

"Well, what if we mess up? I mean, what if we get mad or say something stupid?" says Henry.

The teacher responds, "I'm glad you brought that up. Of course we will make mistakes. That is part of learning. These agreements are a way of reminding us to bring our best selves to this class, but we all have tough moments and tough days. So perhaps we should add something like 'the willingness to learn from our mistakes.' How does that sound?" Now, the class gives a unanimous thumbs up. He then asks for two student volunteers to create a colorful poster for their agreements that will then be hung on their classroom wall.

Classroom Agreements

Listen to one another.

Include one another.

Do not put others down.

Be engaged.

Respect yourself and respect others.

Learn from your mistakes.

A note about confidentiality: During a shared agreements process, older elementary, middle, and high school students will sometimes request a confidentiality agreement. While it is natural for students to want confidentiality, it is important to share (in age-appropriate ways) that there are limits to confidentiality for these reasons:

- As educators, we have a legal obligation to report any comments or behaviors that suggest students may do harm to themselves or to others, or that they are being abused or physically threatened in some way.

- Parents, colleagues, and administrators may feel that a confidentiality agreement in a classroom creates an unsafe environment for students because it then resembles therapeutic environments where students are more likely to share information that is not appropriate for school.

Instead of mandating confidentiality, ask students to agree to *respect each other's privacy* and discuss exactly what this means. Respecting each other's privacy includes not sharing stories or information that are not ours to share, not gossiping or using information about others in hurtful ways, and not probing or pushing others to share personal details. We also encourage students to speak from the "I perspective," to not attribute any names to stories that are shared, and to not use, adapt, or interpret someone else's stories for their own purposes. If students are not respecting each other's privacy, address this in the classroom immediately through community dialogue or community circle.

Practice: Scaffolding Activities to Build Trust

Cultivating a caring community—the overarching goal of stage one of the Learning Journey—requires building trust. We are best able to build this trust when we invite students to take small steps toward a larger goal. We can sequence activities and themes in a way that helps students get to know one another over time and to gradually develop deeper connections within and across peer groups. As students begin to trust each other and their teachers, they naturally begin to take more risks—to try new things, face challenges, recover from failures, and explore or share new aspects of themselves.

At the beginning of the year, we introduce community-building activities and focusing activities (see chapter 4, page 57) that allow for quick success and low emotional or intellectual risk. We offer developmentally appropriate "getting to know you" activities that allow students to learn about each other gently and by invitation. It is important to choose developmentally appropriate themes or questions that support students to build trust with their peers. This is not always as simple as it may seem. A dyad question such as "What is your neighborhood like?" may seem straightforward, but students from different socioeconomic backgrounds who have not yet built trusting relationships with their peers may feel self-conscious about the differences between their neighborhoods. Questions such as "What's a book or movie you have recently enjoyed?" or "What's one of your favorite foods, animals, songs, or kinds of music?" or a request to "Talk about a place you love" or "Talk about a season or time of the year (besides summer) that you like and why" provide a more level playing field. Later, in stage two, we might introduce deeper themes, but when a group is first coming together as a community, it is important to give students low-risk ways to learn a bit about themselves and each other.

As we learn to scaffold and sequence activities to build trust, it is helpful to be aware of a behavioral pattern called "skirt and scout" that often occurs in early stages of group development. This behavior involves the tendency in newly forming groups for individuals to skirt away from revealing too much about themselves while simultaneously scouting for more information about others. If, through this process, students feel that the group situation is safe, they are often willing to share more about themselves and to take intellectual risks. Ice-breakers and activities like "trust falls" (when one person falls back into the arms of another) or "hot seat" (when one person is put on the spot and asked to respond to questions in front of the group) that push students to trust each other beyond what is appropriate for a particular stage in the term or year can backfire. In the heat of the moment, students may reveal more than they intend or try something they later regret. In reaction, they may subsequently shut down or become even more distrustful in order to protect themselves from future risk or overexposure. When we allow students to build trust slowly, meaningful compassion and connection occur and the learning community naturally evolves and deepens.

As the classroom leader, it is important to continually assess where students are in their process of developing trust and to choose activities and prompts that are appropriate for the group's stage of development. The same activity that can catalyze the deepening of the community when introduced halfway through the term or year may create a backlash of caution and suspicion in the first few weeks of class. For example, in a unit on coming of age, we may ask students to write and speak about a childhood belief they had but no longer hold as true. Sometimes these kinds of themes elicit stories that bring up deeper emotions such as loss, rejection, or embarrassment. Early on in a group's development (stage one), there is often not enough safety and trust in the group for certain activities or themes to be meaningful or safe. However, once we have developed a foundation of trust, themes such as the two just mentioned can take students to profound places of connection to themselves, to others, and to academic content.

Stage one of the Learning Journey gives us the opportunity to build a strong foundation for the school year and prepare our community of learners for the more complex territory of stage two. During stage one, students often experience a range of emotions from eagerness and excitement to impatience, fear, and anxiety. As we create a culture of safety and engagement in our classrooms, our students' intellectual curiosity, compassion, and authentic self-expression will naturally emerge. As we devote time to the goals and practices of stage one, we simultaneously support students' social, emotional, and academic learning. And, more specifically, as we model the Five Dimensions of Engaged Teaching in our own practice, we encourage students to develop these capacities within themselves so they become more reflective and present with each other, focused on academic learning, responsible for their behaviors and for the classroom climate, able to identify and express emotions appropriately, and compassionate to themselves, others, and the world around them.

Summary of Stage One

To support students during stage one of group development, we can:
- Establish our role as classroom leader
- Provide a context for social-emotional and academic learning
- Build in a shared-agreements process
- Sequence activities to build trust

Stage Two: Strengthening Community and Connection

In stage one, we created a caring and inclusive classroom community as a foundation for the rest of the learning journey together. In stage two, groups generally experience a strengthening of relationships, a deepening sense of community, and a willingness to take more creative and intellectual risks. As students develop a sense of trust in themselves and one another, they express themselves with increasing authenticity and can manage more complex emotional and academic territory. Although all communities will enter this more complex territory of stage two at some point, it is important to gauge the level of trust and safety in the classroom so we don't expect or push a level of depth or risk that students are not ready for. This period of time can look very different depending on the size, chemistry, and context of each group as well as the duration of time the group is together.

Along with the greater depth and connection typical of stage two, we may also see students becoming restless with topics that felt timely and appropriate in early weeks and months but now feel overly simplistic or superficial. In addition, because depth and connection often invite greater openness and vulnerability, it is not uncommon for students to again begin to act out and test limits. During stage two, it is paramount to continue to hold clear boundaries and respond with consistent, appropriate consequences.

At this stage, sometimes unconscious stereotypes, which unintentionally violate the agreement to respect all differences, surface among peers. These classroom experiences are indicative of the larger contexts in which we live, as stereotypes are pervasive throughout our society, media, communities, and work life. Such moments are powerful opportunities to explore where and how students learn and internalize stereotypes and to offer alternative perspectives. With older students, these teachable moments can lead to a rigorous exploration of the gap between commonly held beliefs, the statistical reality, and the real experience of people who are the targets of prejudice. See chapter 2 on page 21 and the references and resources section of this book for resources for working on cultural responsiveness.

Typically, students become more empowered during stage two as the level of their participation, connection, and authenticity increases. The learning community now has potentially created enough trust and safety to explore themes and topics such as stress and anger management, peer relationships, communication and problem solving, larger societal issues, and world events. This might be a time when we engage in a regular practice of community circles or council in which students have a chance to speak, one at a time, on a theme that connects to content and their personal lives. Stage two is also often a time when students are able to take more initiative and work together on collaborative projects.

The following practices help us apply the Five Dimensions of Engaged Teaching to meet the goals of stage two. These practices are not exclusive to stage two, but they are described here because their depth and importance increase significantly during this phase.

Practice: Engaging Student Voices

Effectively engaging student voices requires time and thoughtfulness, as well as openness on the part of the teacher to appropriately share ownership of the class. There are many opportunities to invite student voices into the room, such as dialogue and discussion, inquiry, collaboration, personal storytelling, sharing and reflection, and personal response to content. As students learn more about each other and reflect on deeper themes and subjects, community connections emerge and appreciation for each other's differences often increases too. Also, when students feel seen and heard, they are less likely to act out to get our attention or the attention of their peers. When we engage student voices in multiple ways, motivation increases as students want to participate, share, think, and stretch their own capacities.

Sometimes teachers feel wary of soliciting too much student participation or feedback because they are concerned about losing control of the class or opening the floodgates to negative feedback. However, when we skillfully ask for feedback, our students feel empowered and most often respond in a positive and helpful manner. We can also orient student feedback toward a strengths model, in which we ask students to identify what is working and how we can build on those strengths. And we can include a weekly, monthly, or quarterly check-in when we ask students to write down on a note card plusses and minuses of the class for them. These methods can help us gauge how our students are doing and how we might need to adjust our teaching methods and content.

The following instructional practices give students opportunities to be seen, heard, and known by explicitly inviting their perspectives and unique voices into the classroom.

Activities for Inviting Student Voice

- **Know, wonder, learn (KWL):** Invite students to ask questions pertaining to a subject of study. For example, at the beginning of a weather unit, ask elementary students to write down what they know about weather and what they wonder about weather. At the end of the unit, ask students to record what they have learned about weather. The beginning questions help guide your lessons according to students' background knowledge and curiosity. The follow-up questions help to anchor the learning for longer-term memory and future application.

- **Class debrief:** Provide debriefing sessions at the end of an activity in which you ask for students' feedback and reflection about how the activity went for them—what they liked, did not like, learned, or remembered; what they felt challenged by; what learning edges they experienced; and so on. For example, a debrief may follow a challenging math homework assignment, a community circle on childhood memories, a focusing activity involving teamwork, or a required social studies text. In all cases, student learning is often anchored or expanded as students share and listen to others. At the same time, your future teaching plans are informed by the students' responses.

- **Dyads, wheel within a wheel, and community circles or councils:** Ask students to share on a chosen theme (either a social-emotional theme or a subject-specific content theme) in pairs or with the whole group. Each person is invited to share without being interrupted for a certain amount of time. (See the Summary of Instructional Practices on page 134 for more ideas.)

- **Oral presentations:** Ask groups or individuals to share in front of the class on a certain theme or subject. For example, in younger grades, offer sharing time so that students can bring in special objects from home and talk about them.

- **World cafés:** In these activities, students respond to three open-ended questions related to social and emotional themes or academic content, answering one at each four-person café (table). As students rotate among the tables, they record notes from their dialogues and then report out at the end of the session (Brown & Isaacs, 2005).

- **Check-in note card:** On a weekly, monthly, or quarterly basis, ask students to write down one to three aspects of your class that are working for them and one to three challenges (plusses and minuses).

- **Strengths and opportunities map:** Invite students to create a strengths and opportunities map for the class in which they identify strengths and opportunities for growth in terms of classroom community, peer dynamics, academic learning, and any other factors you want to add. Ask students to identify favorite and least-favorite lessons, projects, and topics and share why they feel this way. Then share the results.

- **Brainstorming:** Opportunities to brainstorm can be individual or group in nature. Topics can be social-emotional or academic. For example, brainstorm solutions to a current classroom community issue such as exclusion or name-calling, ideas for a class play or field trip, or possible science quiz questions on rocks and minerals. In some cases, teachers make a decision based on the class's ideas, or the class may vote. Brainstorming gets students' thinking going and helps solidify learning.

- **Asking for feedback:** Elicit feedback in debriefing sessions, during one-on-one conferences, or through online or paper surveys (with the option of responding anonymously); depending on the context, you may use the feedback to select your next steps, refine lessons, guide class meetings, or meet with individual students to problem solve.

Remember that students may express their voice through speaking, writing, art, or other means. These expressions may remain private (as a personal reflection), or they may be displayed or shared with the teacher, a peer, or a small group.

Practice: Fostering Deeper Connection With Self, Others, and the World

Another essential aspect of stage two of the Learning Journey is supporting students to foster deeper connections with themselves, peers, teachers, and the world around them. We define *connection* as a web of caring, authentic, and meaningful relationships. Connection includes the experience of belonging to a larger community and of being truly seen and known as a whole person. When students feel connected, they are often better able to access their skills, gifts, passions, wisdom, curiosity, and capacities to learn.

Many students regularly feel a sense of separation, isolation, and lack of belonging. This experience of alienation is often at the heart of risky behaviors, violence to self or others, school dropout, and academic failure. There are many contributing factors to this—the overuse of technology, shifts in family structures, pressures of a consumer culture, and an overall lack of a sense of true meaning, purpose, and relevance.

The experience of authentic connection is a powerful antidote to the experience of alienation. This kind of connection is fundamentally different from the superficial contact and relationships offered by and through media, technology, and consumer culture. As Kessler (2000b) discusses in *The Soul of Education*, when true opportunities for connection are not offered, young people tend to seek a sense of meaning and purpose through what can be bought and sold; joy and transcendence through drugs, sex, and other risk-taking behaviors; and initiation through destructive rituals of self-mutilation and hazing. When we create communities of authentic connection, students are more likely to see that they are not alone in their questions, challenges, and search for purpose. When they are given opportunities for self-expression, they are more likely to appreciate and express their own unique gifts and discover how they can contribute to their community and world in meaningful ways. When students feel connected, they naturally access their own resilience and capacity to skillfully navigate change.

One high school senior shared the following story from her advisory class.

During my freshman and sophomore years, my father was in Iraq. It was a really hard time for me in my life, because it was just me and my mom and my three younger siblings at home. It was hard because I had to take on more of a leadership role within my family. Our advisory class definitely changed the way I thought about that role and my own life, because it made me realize that the same kinds of hardships that were happening in my life were happening for other students in other ways. And I understood that, maybe it stinks that you have something hard that you need to overcome, but there are so many other people in school that can relate to you and can relate to the problems that you have, so you should never feel alone. You should always know that you can overcome the hardships in your life—you can overcome adversity. And, you can be who you want to be, and you can be a happy person.

The following elements and practices help create a sense of connection in students.

What Creates a Sense of Connection to Self, Others, World?

- An awareness and appreciation of our profound uniqueness, exquisite differences, and surprising commonalities
- Dialogue and exploration about what is unique about our particular learning community and configuration of students: our skills, capacities, personalities, viewpoints, perspectives, dreams, and visions
- Opportunities to explore our passions, dreams, visions, and big questions
- Opportunities to be seen and known beyond our typical roles
- Experiences of reciprocity and interconnectedness: giving and receiving appreciation and support within a community, sharing reciprocal responsibility within a community, and developing an understanding of our inter-relatedness
- Exploration of where we come from: our lineage, roots, heritage, and people
- Personal links and emotional connections to curriculum and content
- Encouragement to bring our unique views and voice to the classroom
- Integration of student interests and passions into curriculum themes and content
- Opportunities for students to understand themselves as part of the communities they live in (from family to neighborhood to region)
- Opportunities for students to contribute to something bigger than their own personal lives (such as community projects, service learning, and so on)

If we wish to effectively improve the health, well-being, and growth of our students, it is essential that schools become places where authentic connection is *central* to the mission of the institution of learning itself. When students feel connected, their ethical impulses naturally emerge—students want to contribute and engage. And although we are not our students' family members or counselors, we can form significant, caring relationships with them and create learning opportunities in which meaningful connection is more likely to occur. Following are some practices that can support students in deepening their sense of connection to self, others, and world.

Explore Interconnections

Helping students continually make connections between their own individual lives and the concentric circles of community they live within—from family structures, to school community, to neighborhoods, to the state, national, and global community—cultivates a deeper sense of connection and belonging. Just introducing the idea of interconnection can be a catalyst for greater awareness, empathy, and engagement. For example, exploring with students our relationship to the environment can be a rich science unit as well as an exploration of interconnection.

Include Deeper Themes and More Complex Content

In our discussion of stage one, we noted the importance of sequencing activities to gradually and steadily build trust. In stage two, we have the opportunity to incorporate deeper themes and more complex content. This deepening applies to both social-emotional and academic situations. For example, during morning meeting in third grade, we may introduce focusing activities that require more trust and collaboration. In a transitions program for fifth graders, we may introduce a theme about the challenges and opportunities of making the shift to middle school. In a high school language arts class, we may introduce community circle themes that relate to overcoming challenges, sharing memories from childhood, world events, peer relationships, or gender issues.

Give Students Opportunities to Collaborate

Although there may be plenty of opportunities for students to work collaboratively during stage one of the Learning Journey, in stage two, as connections and trust build, students often have a greater capacity and desire to work together. When students know themselves and one another better, they can work together more effectively and for longer periods of time on more complex projects. It is essential to provide support and structures for collaborative learning that help students include all voices and distribute the work among the team in an equitable way. It is also important not to assume that all students have equal access to resources, so providing materials for projects is important.

Give Students Opportunities to Explore Meaning and Purpose

Another way to support students in stage two is to give them opportunities to explore their own sense of meaning and purpose. When students connect what they are doing in school to their own identities, lives, and internal sense of meaning, they engage more deeply and care more about their learning. It is helpful to give students opportunities to explore their own sense of purpose in school and in their lives and to explore such questions as:

- What do I want for myself in school and life?

- What are my gifts, and how can I express them and share them with my community?

- What gives me a sense of purpose in school and in my life?

- How does this particular content area support my greater goals or visions for myself?

- Where in my life do I experience meaning and purpose?

We can ask students to explore these questions through writing, art, collage, music, public speaking, dance, and the spoken word. We can also incorporate this kind of exploration into a theme or topic relating to class content (for example, identity, gender, coming of age, or culture)—especially in language arts and social studies or history.

Give Opportunities to Explore Passions, Hopes, and Dreams

We can also deepen a sense of connection in students by giving them the opportunity to explore and share their passions, hopes, and dreams through verbal, visual, and symbolic expression or through dyads, circles, or councils. For example, we can invite students to bring in a symbolic object representing what they are currently passionate about in their lives. Students might bring a stone from a favorite river, a necklace from a family member, a photo of a friend, a piece of sheet music, or a baseball representing a sports team. Alternatively, as part of a language arts class, students might create vision boards for their future on which they collage images to represent where they see themselves as older students or adults. This collage can then be paired with a writing activity in which students explore their hopes, dreams, and visions for the future.

Honor and Include Student Questions

Wondering about our own selves, our existence, our peers, our culture, and the nature of life is a natural and universal part of being human. This innate curiosity is at the root of authentic education, for it links learning to the deepest of questions within us. Developmentally, of course this inquiry about ourselves and our lives shifts over time. The wonder of elementary students curious about a caterpillar climbing a tree shifts to middle school curiosity about who we are and how we belong or do not belong to our peer group. High school students often begin to wonder about the purpose of their lives and their place in the world.

The capacity to ask questions, to inquire, and to wonder keeps us from falling into old, habitual patterns that close down possibilities and new insights. Encouraging students to ask all kinds of questions helps them develop both their critical thinking skills and their capacity to make connections between academic content and their lives. We can encourage students to ask questions about our subject matter, and we can also invite them to ask questions that are more philosophical in nature. These philosophical questions, or questions of wonder, may not have concrete answers. As we teach students to welcome their own questions, we increase their capacity to tolerate ambiguity, paradox, and the realm of the unknown.

This process of sharing our questions and wonderings also helps us understand our connections and our common humanity, as people often share the same fundamental questions about themselves and about life. This can profoundly impact students (teens in particular) as they realize they are not alone in their questions and that other students are exploring the depths of life in a way that might not always be visible on the surface.

We can help students value questions, as much as the answers, in all aspects of school and life. For example, as students begin the school year, we can pass out note cards and ask them to anonymously write down what questions they have about the upcoming school term and to identify what challenges and opportunities they anticipate. Students may share questions like, Will I make new friends this year? Will I fail math? With older students, when reading literature and exploring themes such as gender, we can invite students to anonymously write down what they wonder about the other gender. Questions that often arise are: Why do guys find it harder to share their feelings? and Why do girls tend to talk behind each other's backs so much? In elementary school, we can begin a unit on physical science by gathering the questions students have about the earth (What do you wonder about the earth?). Some of these questions may have answers (Where does lightning come from?), while others may remain the source of ongoing inquiry (How can we live sustainably on our planet?). The following examples of questions of wonder come from fifth- through twelfth-grade students.

Sample Questions of Wonder

- How do I discover who I am? And when I do, will I know it? Will anyone else notice the change?
- Why does beauty affect me so much?
- Am I weird or is everyone else?
- Do teachers really care about us, or do they pretend? Do they really believe what they teach us?
- Why is it so hard to get along with others at this age?
- What in life makes certain people so much more giving and loving than others?
- Why do people go against what they believe to fit in?
- What is it like to be old?
- I wonder if the universe ever stops.

Practice: Skillfully Navigating Challenges

In stage two, new challenges may surface. When students start to express themselves more fully, share more deeply, and open up to others, they may also feel an increased sense of vulnerability and may pull away from the community or push back with behaviors so as to avoid that feeling of being vulnerable. Additionally, by the time we enter stage two, the "honeymoon period" of stage one may have passed. The class may then be challenged to work with the rich and complex dynamics that can occur when students more fully share their authentic selves. Because of the trust we have built, students may now feel safe to share more personally. If a student veers into territory that is too emotionally intense or personal for the classroom setting, it is important for us to remain clear about our limits as a classroom teacher and to redirect students in compassionate ways. (See chapter 6 for more on specific practices connected to emotional boundaries.)

Additionally, academic pressures and stress may be catching up with students at this stage, and we may need to introduce more stress-relieving activities—a focusing activity, a mindfulness activity, or a community circle on stress and stress reduction. If we feel stretched or tested by students' exuberance as they feel more empowered and engaged, we can help students find positive outlets for this exuberance and continue to bring them back to the tasks at hand (see chapter 4 on being present). Finally, challenges may simply arise from unique and unpredictable events and experiences in our lives and the lives of our students. These unexpected situations are often an opportunity to "welcome the unwelcomed."

If classroom management becomes an issue during stage two, this is a good time to revisit the goals and purpose of the class or activity and the group's shared agreements and non-negotiable rules. Depending on the intensity of the challenges, it may be useful to hold a class meeting or discussion about the issue at hand, addressing potential causes and strategies for getting back on course. This is also a good time to reflect on respectful boundaries and model for students that we, as classroom leaders, are ultimately responsible for holding firm boundaries and being explicit with expectations and follow-through. See chapter 5 for more specific practices.

Summary of Stage Two

To support students during stage two of group development, we can:

- Engage student voices—
  - Invite students to develop their own prompts or themes to explore.
  - Encourage students to engage in problem-solving discussions when issues arise among peers.
  - Ask students to revisit their learning goals and to stretch their learning edges.
- Foster deeper connections with self, others, and world—
  - Give prompts and themes that help students connect to themselves, each other, and the content on a deeper level.

Summary of Stage Two

- ○ Allow more opportunities for students' passions, visions, and interests to be a part of learning.
- ○ Invite students to share their questions and wonderings.
- • Skillfully navigate challenges—
  - ○ Revisit the purpose of class.
  - ○ Welcome the unwelcome.
  - ○ Re-establish boundaries and revisit shared agreements.
  - ○ Use inquiry.
  - ○ Get support.

Stage Three: Creating Positive Closure and Anchoring the Learning

At the end of a year or term, creating an intentional closure process for students can support them in anchoring their learning, experiencing a sense of completion, and smoothly transitioning to summertime, winter break, or the next term. When we do not create opportunities for positive closure, students can sometimes feel a lack of completion or experience confusing endings. Without some way to synthesize their learning and review the arc of their academic journey, students may simply feel overwhelmed by the academic projects and events that subsume the last days or weeks of class. Positive and intentional closure can have a significant impact on students' learning and experience of the class and community.

Practice: Creating an Intentional Closure Process

As we assess what kind of closure process to introduce, we can consider the trust level of the group, the amount of time this class has spent together, and what social, emotional, and academic themes we have explored. In a standard content class, such as social studies or science, the most appropriate approach for stage three may be to offer students the opportunity to review what they have studied and learned and to engage in some self-assessment. In other situations, such as an advisory, seminar, or class dedicated to supporting transitions, leadership, or social and emotional learning, it is important to offer more extended time for closure. (See www.passageworks.org for references to transition curricula.)

Whatever our particular situation, we can dramatically impact our students' experience of endings by giving them opportunities to review what they have experienced, reflect on what they learned, express their emotions associated with this particular ending, and give each other meaningful feedback and appreciation. In some cases, we may simply reflect upon our time together and share important memories or key learning experiences. In other classes, we may spend several weeks talking about the impending change and transition. See the following sample classroom activities for ideas for intentional closure.

Sample Classroom Activities for Intentional Closure

- Give students the opportunity to review their work, projects, and assignments and assess their progress. Provide a checklist or questionnaire for students to fill out that is appropriate for their age. Ask them to summarize what they learned and share these learnings with their peers. These assessments could relate to social, emotional, or academic learning, depending on your class.

- As a group, review the arc of your content learning—where did you begin and end, and what was learned throughout the process? Then relate this learning to social and emotional learning. This group assessment of the term can be helpful in a different way from the individual assessments.

- With an advisory, seminar, transitions, or SEL class—consider the activity "I Remember . . ." in which the group sits in a circle and one by one shares a story or memory from their time together. These memories can be short. If there is time, multiple rounds of this story sharing can occur—as one memory often spurs another. This sharing of memories can also be done through a group mural or collage or any other expressive format.

- As a class (grades K–5), create a memory book in which each student writes and draws about a special memory of the year. Make a copy for each student and keep the original in the classroom for classroom history and to share with future classes.

- Ask each student to pull three names out of a hat and write (or draw, depending on the age) notes of appreciation for those people. Or, as a class, spend time appreciating each person. For younger students, you may wish to record sentiments on large chart paper for each student to take home.

- Ask students to write a class letter to the incoming students telling them about the opportunities, joys, and challenges of being in that grade (What do they like about being a first grader? What's challenging about being a first grader?). Older students can write letters with the same purpose. For older students, consider using a prompt such as, "What I wish I knew about being a first-year high school student when I began the year."

- In small groups, prepare how-to booklets about being in the class or grade that is about to end (for example, "How to Be in Second Grade at Commons Elementary"). Highlight the joys and challenges found along the way.

Practice: Anchoring Learning—Making Time for Review and Reflection

When we offer opportunities to anchor learning, we help students retain and apply key experiences and concepts from the year. The anchoring process may involve reflection, review, self-assessment, and sharing and celebration of what has been learned. Supporting students in anchoring their learning helps them carry this learning into the next phase of their schooling. Students may review and reflect individually or collectively. They can share their reflections with the larger group, and that reflecting can involve expressing verbally, in writing, or with symbols (artwork, music, and so on).

Some review and reflection questions to use with students of any age include:

- What do you remember most about our time together?

- What did you most enjoy?

- What aspects of this term or class were challenging?

- What did you learn?

- How will you use or apply what you have learned? (This is less appropriate for younger elementary students.)

- What were your goals, and how did you meet or not meet them? How would you like to continue your learning in the future?

- What is different now than at the beginning of our time together—personally and for the group?

- What have you learned about yourself personally and as a member of a learning community?

Practice: Normalizing the Full Range of Emotions

If there has been a deep sense of connection and trust within the learning community, a whole range of emotions can arise during endings—for both teachers and students. Transition years between elementary, middle, and high school can be particularly intense times. As we near the end of a semester, a year, or a more extended period of time together, students may feel excitement and anticipation, as well as sadness around the loss of this particular community or this time in life or school. We can support students by identifying and normalizing the full range of emotions that might show up at this time. In a conversation about the upcoming ending, we might say something like, "This last term, we've shared important things about ourselves and learned a lot from each other. As we come to the end of our time together, some of you might be feeling ready and excited and some of you might be feeling a bit sad about the change. I want you to know that all of that is welcome here." We can continue this dialogue by giving students the chance to articulate what they are feeling and thinking. We can also ask them to name what they will gain in this transition and what they are carrying forward with them from this time together.

With more pronounced "endings," like the end of elementary or high school, students may not know *how* to manage the emotions they are feeling. As a way to avoid these feelings, they may inadvertently participate in a pattern of "negative goodbyes." We live in a culture that tends to avoid meaningful goodbyes. Small losses can remind us of big losses. And because most adults have had little support or education in dealing with the grieving associated with endings, they often feel awkward or ambivalent about goodbyes in general. Consequently, students have few models for constructive closure. When we give students the opportunity to create healthy closure, we not only give them tools for this particular transition, but we also support them to make transitions in a healthy way in the future.

The following are common ways that students create negative goodbyes. By simply discussing these tendencies to avoid or spoil goodbyes, we can invite a more intentional closure process and bring awareness to unconscious behaviors during these times. We can also offset the tendency toward negative goodbyes with the practices named in the box "Sample Classroom Activities for Intentional Closure."

Common Negative Goodbyes

- **Denial and trivializing:** In an effort to avoid their own feelings, some students might deny or trivialize the "ending" we're in the midst of. "We're not really saying goodbye. Just because this group is ending, we'll all see each other in classes next year (or in high school, or at Christmastime). What's the big deal?" If this occurs, we can acknowledge the feeling and also make space for other feelings and experiences of this particular ending.

- **Withdrawal:** Some students pull back from the group as the ending is in sight. Consciously or unconsciously, they believe it will be easier to part if they have already shut down emotionally. "Gee, I'm sorry I forgot to come to our last class or meeting. I had this project I had to get done for another class." Or, "I don't really have anything to say about all of this. I don't want to really talk about the end of the school year." If this kind of behavior occurs, we can reach out to the student individually and also name the importance of showing up for the last class sessions—for each other as well as for ourselves.

- **Spoiling:** Teachers and students often unconsciously say or do something in the last few weeks or hours that sours the closeness and good feeling in the group, often because of the feelings associated with loss. There can be the unconscious sense that it will be easier to part ways if we are angry at each other or if we deny the closeness or learning that's happened. If a student says or acts in a way that "spoils" the closeness, other students may feel strangely relieved. "Thank God we have only one more class. I can't wait to get out of here." Because spoilers often only act out in the final days or meetings of a class, they can easily distort a class evaluation if it's done on the last day of class. The spoiler then rewrites the history of the class or his or her experience in the class, emphasizing the negative aspects of the time together, which makes it easier (less sad or difficult) to part ways. If "spoiling" happens, we as the teacher can name the tendency toward this in the moment, and invite students into a discussion or activity around closure that surfaces the range of emotions and experiences within the class as a whole.

Practice: Taking Time for Appreciation and Gratitude

As part of a positive closure process, we can ask students to take time to acknowledge and honor their own learning and contributions to the learning community, appreciate one another, and appreciate the group as a whole. This kind of appreciation and gratitude can be offered through reflection and writing or through a group-focused listening practice involving dyads, a community circle, or a council. For example, we can ask students to identify three things they have learned about themselves that year and one thing they appreciate about the group or their peers and to share this in a closing council. Before beginning such an activity, it is helpful to spend some time talking about how to give and receive appreciation, as this experience can be quite unusual in many school and peer cultures.

The following sample closure activity can take an entire class period. This activity requires that students know each other fairly well and that class members have developed trust in one another. As always, it is important to adapt this activity for our particular age group and community. Additionally, if we do not trust that students' appreciations of each other will be positive, we can also ask students to write appreciations ahead of time, even anonymously, and then share them with the group later after we have screened them.

Closure Activity: Appreciations Council or Circle

1. Ask each student to write his or her name on three different pieces of paper and then place them into a basket.

2. Each student draws the names of three people to whom he or she will give appreciations.

3. Ask students to put back any doubles or slips with their own name and redraw.

4. Let the students know that their appreciation may come from knowing this person only in this class or from other times and places they have seen or known the person. It is helpful to give examples of appreciations before you begin: "Julie, I really appreciate how you reach out to everyone and help them feel included. Robert, I appreciate your courage and how you always say what's true, even if it's hard."

5. Give students three to five minutes to write down an appreciation for the people whose names they have drawn.

6. Convene a council (see the Classroom Council Practice that follows). If you have a council object that you pass to designate who is speaking (like a ball or talking stick), that object can be passed to indicate who is to be appreciated. Then, one by one, each person is appreciated by the three students who drew this student's name. It is also powerful if the teacher or teachers offer an appreciation of each student.

Classroom Council Practice

Council is a practice that encourages deep and honest communication. It is integrated into classrooms; counseling offices; and faculty, parent, and community meetings. Based on indigenous, worldwide "cultural dialogic" practices (including Native American traditions), council is a formal, structured, circle-based process that includes sitting in a circle and passing a talking piece in response to a prompt. In a broader sense, council is also about a heightened awareness of self, other, and the natural world. Classroom council practice can include play, movement, rhythm, mindfulness, visual arts, technology, and spontaneous improvisation, as well as fundamental listening and speaking skills. Council is practiced to convey content, to develop social-emotional competencies, and to elicit what students themselves want to understand. Teachers and students may decide to determine their own guidelines for the circles or use the four intentions of council, as developed through the Ojai Foundation and *The Way of Council* by Jack Zimmerman and Virginia Coyle:

1. Listen from the heart—Practice the "art of receptivity" by suspending judgment, reaction, and opinion.

2. Speak from the heart and with heart—Learn to "speak into the listening."

3. Speak spontaneously—Speak without planning and only when holding a talking piece.

4. Keep it lean—Learn to speak to the heart of the matter so everyone has time to participate.

Adapted from Joe Provisor (personal communication, February 7, 2012), MFT Advisor, Los Angeles Unified School District Council in Schools Office Director, Ojai Foundation's Council in Schools Initiative.

Practice: Addressing Developmental Transitions

Students' lives are filled with transitions—transitions into and out of the school year, into and out of development phases, and into and out of each class or day. The transition years into and out of elementary, middle, and high school are particularly vulnerable times for students (Weaver & Kessler, 2011). When educators have an increased awareness of both the challenge and the opportunity of these times, we can more effectively and compassionately help students discover new capacities within themselves to deal with transitions.

In Western culture, youth are rarely intentionally or consciously initiated into the next milestone developmental stage of life (such as puberty and adulthood). When young people are not supported by adults during their transitions or initiated in intentional and constructive ways, they often invent their own initiations. Gang violence, teen pregnancy, binge drinking, reckless driving, cutting, and hazing are all examples of attempts at self-initiation. These attempts are risky at best and deadly at worst. You can read more about this in "Six Passages of Childhood," in *Educating From the Heart* (Weaver & Kessler, 2011) for more on this topic. So, how can we support our young people during these vulnerable transition times?

As educators, we can take many approaches to working with transitions. By simply acknowledging transitions and building in curricular themes that connect to students' transitions, we can normalize the process and give students tools to navigate these times. We can also include content-related themes that address transitions and cycles of change. We can include a community circle or council activity in which we ask students to share about the challenges of the main characters in a book who are "coming of age." Or we may wish to address the ways a study of life cycles can be used as metaphor for how students change, grow, and evolve over time.

Ideally, we also take the time to address developmental transitions more directly—especially in the transition years between elementary, middle, and high school. If we are able to do so, we can then create activities or opportunities for students to explore the impact of transitions in their lives—both past and present. We can help them to remember how they have "stretched" themselves in the past to meet challenges or make changes or go beyond what they thought was possible. We can help them recognize the stress, anxiety, and excitement that often accompany transitions. We can teach social and emotional skills that help them reflect on their own journey, develop their emotional capacity, and utilize self-discipline to make good choices. We can offer community circles, councils, writing and art activities, and projects that give students a chance to share how they are feeling about this particular transition, to speak about what memories and qualities of themselves they wish to leave behind, and to claim the qualities of themselves they wish to carry with them or even reclaim as they transition to a new phase.

The following questions or prompts can support students to more directly explore the transition they are in the midst of—through reflection, writing, and art. Students can explore these questions on their own, in pairs, or in a group. As always, select questions that work for your age group and adapt the questions to meet your own particular learning community and context.

Questions to Support Students as They Explore Transitions

- What are you leaving behind? What aspects of yourself as a student and person do you no longer want to carry with you?
- What aspects of yourself do you want to bring with you, or grow, or expand, or reclaim as you move into this next phase of your life?
- What do you want to honor or acknowledge about the importance of the period of time you are leaving behind? In what ways have you grown, and what have you learned?
- What opportunities for growth are there for you in this next phase?
- What concerns do you have about this next phase? How might you be stretched and tested?
- What qualities do you want to cultivate in yourself in this next phase? In other words, what kind of person do you want to be in this next phase of your life?
- What obstacles might get in the way of that?
- What resources do you have or need to have (inside yourself and in your family or community) that can help you overcome these obstacles?
- What is your vision for yourself in this next phase?
- What commitments do you need to make to yourself and others to support this vision?

The following story, in which one parent shares the experience of her son's transition from elementary to middle school, illustrates the power of involving the parent community in the process of acknowledging and honoring students' transitions.

Landon, along with the rest of his class, was nervous, excited, and ready for a change, but also terrified of the older kids and bigger middle school environment he was just about to enter. His fifth-grade teacher brought in a transitions curriculum to support the class during this time. They dedicated one hour a week to building their community, talking about transitions, and exploring what they were ready to leave behind and what they wanted for themselves in middle school. The semester culminated in a parent-child witness circle. The students, witnessed by their parents, shared what they were thinking and feeling about the transition to middle school.

Then it was the parents' turn to share. Parents were asked to verbally acknowledge the growth and change they had seen in their child over the last year. It was very moving. Everyone could see how much it meant for each student to have this kind of reflection—especially in front of their peers. There was laughter and tears and, most of all, a warm-hearted feeling of community support. Wherever these students were going from that point, they knew their authentic selves had been seen and understood. This alone gave them a foundation for making conscious choices for themselves in the years ahead.

Whatever our situation, committing to engaging in some kind of intentional closure process can greatly support our students to understand and anchor their learning, honor the community as a whole, and transition in a healthy way.

Summary of Stage Three

To support students during stage three of group development, we can:

- Create an intentional closure process
- Normalize the whole range of emotions
- Take time for appreciation and gratitude
- Anchor the learning
- Address developmental transitions

Conclusion

In this chapter, we have explored the importance of taking a developmental approach to our teaching, in which we address the three stages of the Learning Journey: (1) cultivating a caring community, (2) strengthening community and connection, and (3) creating positive closure and anchoring the learning. The reproducible chart The Stages of the Learning Journey Overview can serve as a navigational tool for our teaching path, as we integrate the Five Dimensions of Engaged Teaching across the arc of the school term. In chapter 8, we will explore how to create an action plan for implementing the Engaged Teaching Approach.

The Stages of the Learning Journey Overview

Stage	Goals	Tasks	Things to Try
Stage one	Cultivating a caring community	• Establish your role as classroom leader. • Provide a context for social, emotional, and academic learning. • Develop shared agreements. • Scaffold activities to build trust.	• Simple focusing activities • Shared agreements • Focused listening and pair-shares • Wheel within a wheel activities • Activities that help students get to know themselves, their peers, and the community • Simple community circles • Privacy agreement (rather than a confidentiality agreement)
Stage two	Strengthening community and connection	• Engage student voices. • Foster deeper connection with self, others, and the world. • Skillfully navigate challenges.	• Focusing activities • Community circle or council • Exploration of meaning, purpose, hopes, dreams, visions, and big questions • Inclusion of more complex developmentally relevant themes (if appropriate) • Collaborative and interactive student activities, such as World Café, Socratic dialogues, and projects revisiting purpose, context, and shared agreements, if needed
Stage three	Creating positive closure and anchoring the learning	• Create an intentional closure process. • Anchor learning—make time for review and reflection. • Normalize the full range of emotions. • Take time for appreciation and gratitude. • Address developmental transitions.	• Favorite focusing activities • Appreciation circles • Portfolio reviews • Teaching about negative goodbyes (if appropriate) • Student assessments of progress • Memory books • Student letters to self or to the upcoming class • Family-child witness council • Rites of passage ceremonies appropriate to your community context

The 5 Dimensions of Engaged Teaching © 2013 Solution Tree Press • solution-tree.com

Visit **go.solution-tree.com/instruction** to download this page.

Summary of Instructional Practices

1. Focusing Activities

Active and reflective focusing activities awaken the mind, revitalize and settle the body, increase our capacity to pay attention, and build community.

Examples

- Active: Playful, engaging team-building activities that wake us up and give the community a common goal to work towards (such as Wild River Runs, Ball Toss, and How Many of You. . .)

- Reflective: Writing, drawing, a few moments of silence, relaxation and breath work, creative expression, and mindfulness practices (such as journaling on a prompt or quote, progressive relaxation, and feelings wheel)

2. Symbolic and Creative Expression Activities

Symbolic and creative expression activities give students opportunities to know themselves and each other through a "third thing"—a symbol, metaphor, or image that expresses something they are feeling, thinking, or experiencing in their lives or in relation to content. Symbolic and creative expression develop critical and abstract thinking skills and allow students to indirectly (and sometimes nonverbally) share feelings, thoughts, and perceptions that might be difficult to speak about in a more direct way.

Examples

- Symbolic objects: Students bring or choose a symbolic object that represents something they are feeling, thinking, or value in their life. This activity can also be used to make content-area connections. For example, ask students to bring or choose an object that best represents a character in a book or a concept in math.

- Creative expression through the arts: Invite students to draw, paint, sculpt, or collage an image that represents aspects of themselves, their goals or hopes for themselves, or a connection they have to the content.

- Focusing activities, such as improv or drama exercises: These activities often involve symbolic and creative thinking.

3. Focused Listening Practices

These practices provide students with opportunities to speak and listen to each other in new ways. In focused listening, the speaker shares on a theme while the listener listens without offering questions, prompts, or feedback to the speaker. For a prescribed period of time (usually thirty seconds to three minutes, depending on age and context), the speaker is invited to share his or her own thoughts, feelings, stories, or wisdom on a particular theme. Then the role of the speaker and listener shifts, so that each person has an opportunity

The 5 Dimensions of Engaged Teaching © 2013 Solution Tree Press • solution-tree.com
Visit **go.solution-tree.com/instruction** to download this page.

to speak and listen. These practices also foster critical thinking, as students often make new discoveries when they speak to another person without interruption or feedback. Focused listening practices also augment and support other communication practices, such as active listening, nonviolent communication, constructivist listening, and Socratic dialogues.

Examples

- Dyads and triads: Focused listening on a prompt in pairs, trios, or small groups

- Wheel within a wheel: Focused listening in a series of dyads

4. Community Circles and Councils

Community circles and councils offer students a simple and structured format to engage in respectful communication, storytelling, and personal sharing around relevant themes. Students and teachers sit in a circle of chairs and are invited to speak one at a time on a theme, without interruption. All participants are given the option of "passing" or adding their silence if they do not choose to speak out loud. Depending on the community and context, an object or "talking piece" may be used to designate who the speaker is. Additionally, participants are encouraged to listen and speak openly, honestly, and without judgment and to speak from the "I" perspective.

5. Silence, Solitude, and Reflection

The integration of periods of silence, solitude, and reflection in the classroom cultivates awareness, concentration, intellectual integration, and personal resiliency, giving students a much-needed pause in their day.

Examples

- Golden Moments: One to two moments of silence used throughout the day or to begin and end an activity or lesson or to provide a break when students are unfocused or rowdy

- Solo time: Opportunities for longer periods of silence and solitude in the classroom or in nature

- Reflection: Quiet moments of reflection that can involve stillness, observation, journaling, or drawing

6. Incorporation of Relevant, Developmental Themes

Integrating themes that relate to the developmental stages of young people supports them to feel the relevance of their school experience. Such themes address the transitions students are going through and offer them the opportunity to reflect on their own values, identity, visions, and goals. Additionally, students are invited to make connections between academic work and their personal lives and to engage in multiple-perspective taking—a key critical- and creative-thinking skill.

The 5 Dimensions of Engaged Teaching © 2013 Solution Tree Press • solution-tree.com
Visit **go.solution-tree.com/instruction** to download this page.

8

The Journey Is the Destination

Education is not filling a bucket, but the lighting of a fire.

—William Butler Yeats

Self-Reflection

For a moment, picture yourself in the future on the final day of your teaching career. As you walk out of the building for the last time, reflecting on all you have experienced and accomplished, what is it that you are most proud of?

Imagine a rich and rewarding educational system in which teachers are supported in cultivating an open heart—where they can naturally express their care, compassion, and high expectations for their students and effectively connect with the diverse cultures of the students they teach. Imagine classrooms where both teachers and students have the skills to observe themselves, manage distractions, return to the present moment, and attend to the tasks at hand. Imagine classrooms where respectful boundaries are established and honored to protect the safety and well-being of every student—where students and teachers alike understand that these boundaries are an essential part of maintaining caring relationships and a productive learning environment. Imagine classrooms where students' passion for learning and growth are naturally ignited because content and practices are emotionally engaging and relevant. Imagine schools where students excel academically, feel seen and known, and experience deep connection within themselves, with their peers and teachers, and in their school community. The Engaged Teaching Approach is designed to support just such a vision.

In chapter 1, we explored the roots of the Five Dimensions of Engaged Teaching and made the case for the Engaged Teaching Approach. In chapters 2 through 6, we explored each of the dimensions in depth and discussed the associated principles and practices. Chapter 7 focused on putting the principles and practices together in the classroom to form the Learning Journey. In this final chapter, we will explore how we can create a vision for ourselves and our schools, measure our progress, and achieve both intermediate and long-term outcomes.

Beginning With the End in Mind

So what *are* we educating our young people for? When creating a vision-to-action plan for our ourselves and our schools, it can be helpful to think about the core purposes of education, so we can create a vision that builds on this purpose and reflects these goals.

Our world has changed dramatically since the early 1900s, when modern public education first emerged. And yet much of our educational paradigm still reflects an industrial revolution model—when students were being educated for a very different kind of life. So, how can we create an education system that *supports* teachers and serves *all* children in the 21st century? How can we create a system that educates and prepares our young people for the global, interconnected world we all live in—a world of rapid change and resource challenges, increasing inequities and ever-evolving technologies, global economies, and political turmoil? Technical skills alone will not suffice. Knowledge and information need to be integrated with social and emotional skills so that students can meet the pressing issues of our times and live and work in the world in productive and ethical ways. As we offer students a more holistic paradigm of education, we support them to develop just the skills and capacities needed to envision and enact ways of living on this planet that are meaningful, just, and sustainable.

Leading From the Inside Out

As teachers, we may wonder: given our sphere of influence, given all the challenges in our profession and our students' lives—what can *we* do in the current educational environment to impact students' experience of school? The underlying premise of this book is that when we shift our own practice and presence, we profoundly and positively impact our students, schools, and communities. Of course we may or may not be able to change policy, address resource inequities, or shift entrenched societal patterns. But, we can change our own practice and approach, collaborate with colleagues and students' families, and impact our communities. We can develop and sustain our own social and emotional capacities and model and teach these capacities to students. With this kind of ripple effect, we can shift our educational system from the inside out.

To support you in developing your own vision and action plan, we offer the following profiles of schools that have developed their own unique ways of implementing an Engaged Teaching Approach. Hopefully, these profiles will inspire you to see the variety of ways schools have addressed their challenges and built on their strengths so that you can discover your own authentic way to bring these principles and practices into your classroom or school.

Each of the stories focuses on schoolwide actions that had the support of school leaders. Though you may be working only on a classroom level, these profiles illustrate what schoolwide approaches can look like and achieve.

Walton High School, Rural Iowa

Walton High School is located in a rural Iowa town with an economy centered on agriculture. The school's population consists of students whose families are third- and fourth-generation Midwestern farmers and students who have recently immigrated from Mexico, Central America, Sudan, and Somalia. In the summer of 2008, a few weeks before school began, the leadership team gathered to discuss the challenges and strengths of their school. Through these conversations, they realized that many of their students struggled with the transition into high school. They decided they wanted to address this issue more directly by offering a leadership course for all incoming students. This course, offered every day throughout freshman year, integrated a social and emotional learning curriculum for the transition years with study and literacy skills. Activities included storytelling, group discussion, the development of self-awareness, self-reflection, artistic expression, and cooperative and small-group learning. Faculty teaching this course were offered an introductory training in social and emotional learning and reflective teacher practice, as well as ongoing follow-up professional development and coaching. Additionally, the school offered a day-long all-faculty retreat to create a schoolwide vision and to develop a common language and set of goals for their school. After implementing the leadership class for a year, the school saw greater student engagement, stronger teacher-to-student and peer relationships, increased understanding of the gifts of cultural diversity, and a healthier transition for students moving into and out of high school.

> "After one year in the program, virtually every staff member was strongly supportive of the program; after two years, it is considered an invaluable, necessary part of our culture."
>
> —Walton Leadership Team

Some key goals and objectives of the class included:

- Improving social and emotional skills for ninth-grade students

- Developing a forum for students of different cultures and backgrounds to get to know each other in new ways

- Supporting students during the transition into and out of high school

- Supporting student resilience and fostering learning readiness

- Providing adult mentorship and advocacy

- Providing a safe, supportive, and culturally respectful environment for all students and staff to speak and learn about social, emotional, and cultural diversity

- Introducing a curriculum that encourages the building and reinforcement of life skills and social competencies, including effective communication skills, goal articulation, critical thinking, collaborative problem solving and decision making, organizational skills, stress management, intrapersonal and interpersonal skills, appreciating cultural diversity and cultural contributions, and community service

Components of their approach included:

- A ninth-grade transition and leadership class that combined social and emotional learning with literacy and study skills

- An introductory program with the whole-school faculty

- An in-depth training for the leadership class faculty cohort including SEL skills and capacities, reflective practices, and specific content on working with transitions

- A twelfth-grade Senior Passages transitions course as an elective

- Dedicated professional-development time for faculty

- Regular and ongoing collaborative planning time for faculty

They achieved the following outcomes (based on student surveys and faculty reports):

- A greater sense among students of connection to self, others, and the community

- Increased student engagement

- Student development of social and emotional learning and leadership skills

- A dramatic decrease in the dropout rate for ninth-graders

- Among faculty, an increased capacity to effectively collaborate and sustain a supportive collegial community

- After a three-year period, a leadership course for incoming students is considered among teachers to be an essential part of Walton High School

Their challenges included:

- Finding time for necessary leadership course staff meetings, planning, professional development, and ongoing support to teachers

- Developing initial buy-in from all staff members

- Working with students who regularly sabotaged the purpose and vision of the class

- Finding the right balance of SEL activities and academic content

- Meeting the differing needs of all students

- Developing meaningful, constructive common assessments

Ponderosa Elementary, K–5 Public Focus School, Suburban Wyoming

This arts-integrated public school of choice in a suburban town in Wyoming has been committed to integrating social, emotional, and academic learning from its inception. Based on a philosophy of "head, heart, and hands," this school offers a whole-child approach and integrated arts lessons in every content area.

After Ponderosa first opened its doors, the school flourished and waiting lists grew. As successful as the school was, the staff continued to notice that students and families were often challenged by the transition into and out of elementary school. So, they decided to implement a one-semester transitions program for fifth-graders and a kindergarten transitions program to support incoming kindergarteners. Along with these specific transitions programs, the school also offered all of their teachers training in social and emotional learning and engaged teaching to develop a common language and set of goals throughout the school. Classroom teachers coordinated with each other to decide which social and emotional learning activities were most appropriate for each age group and to provide a clear sequence for their students. They also incorporated project-based learning, outdoor education, seasonal celebrations, lessons that specifically addressed multiple intelligences, and a looping system that kept students with the same teacher for grades 1 through 3 and a different teacher for grades 4 through 5. Additionally, the school emphasized the importance of community building and family involvement through a variety of events and projects—from school vegetable gardens, to all-school fundraising dinners, to regular student presentations of their work, to a graduation day that involved a parent-child circle. As a result of all of these efforts, the school found that school climate improved and that students transitioned between grades more easily, achieved better test scores, and felt safer and more included at school (as indicated through district-sponsored school-climate surveys).

> "At first kids can be a little resistant to community building. But what I really appreciate is that by about midway through the year, the kids who had resisted it before have begun to crave it. They now sink in—and just love it."
>
> —Ponderosa Elementary Teacher

Some key goals and objectives included:

- Creating a healthy transition for incoming kindergarten students, including their families

- Creating a healthy transition for outgoing fifth-grade students, including their families

- Fostering a positive school climate

- Supporting the social, emotional, and academic development of all students

Components of this school's approach included:

- Professional development for all teachers that included social and emotional learning and many of the practices of the Engaged Teaching Approach

- A once-a-week, one-hour transitions program for incoming kindergarten students and outgoing fifth-grade students

- Educational evenings for kindergarten and fifth-grade parents helping them develop their own social and emotional skills and an understanding of their children's transition

- Open enrollment lottery preference for students who qualified for free and reduced lunch

- An English as a Second Language program

- Regular teacher planning and collaboration time

- A looping system in which a teacher stays with the same cohort of students in grades 1–3, and then a new teacher teaches the grades 4–5 loop

- Investment in community with regular community events involving families, including parent nights and community dinners

- Outdoor education

- Project-based learning

Outcomes (based on faculty reports and a district school-climate survey) included:

- Increasingly positive school culture and climate survey results (in 2009, 98% of students indicated "I feel safe on the playground")

- A high degree of collaboration between faculty and families

- A high degree of collaboration among faculty

- Increased percentages of students scoring in the proficient or advanced proficient categories on standardized state tests

- Being named as a School of Excellence for academic achievement

Challenges included:

- Working to scope and sequence the SEL activities across the different grade levels so they did not feel repetitive to students

- Making time for the additional work involved in designing evenings for families

- Finding resources and time to invest in training for faculty

Parkside High School, Urban Illinois

Parkside is an urban high school with a high percentage of students receiving free and reduced lunch. Under the leadership of a new principal, Parkside faculty looked at the challenges in their school community and saw that they were struggling to keep students on schedule for promotion from ninth to tenth grade. They saw that if students remained on track in ninth grade, they had a far greater chance of graduating within four years. To address this challenge, they decided to implement a ninth-grade academy program to create more support and connection for students and teachers. This academy approach paired cohorts of students with teams of teachers so that there would be smaller learning communities and more opportunities for teachers to build community and relationships with and among freshmen. This academy also included a once-a-week advisory program for all ninth-graders. As part of this initiative, ninth-grade academy teachers participated in professional development that offered skills for developing a reflective practice and teaching social and emotional learning. They also engaged in shorter quarterly professional development days and consulting to support their teaching and advisory work. The ninth-grade academy teachers met weekly for lesson planning and coordinated with each other to track the progress of students. The school also invested a great deal of time and energy in engaging in community outreach, building faculty relationships, and developing a respectful, positive school community.

One of the challenges the academy teachers faced was that the fall advisory was implemented as part of teachers' content classes, so every week content teachers had one hour less of content teaching time to make time for advisory. This created a great deal of stress for these teachers, even though they saw the benefits of the advisory class. The schedule was changed

> "What I appreciated most about the advisory class was that I got to meet new people and that I really got to know my friends."
>
> —Ninth-Grade Parkside Student

for the spring semester, and it was decided that, in the future, the school would find a different way to schedule an advisory class so it did not take any time from content teaching.

Despite the challenges, after one year of implementing the academy program and the associated initiatives, the school saw the percentage of students who remained on track for promotion from ninth to tenth grade rise by 16 percent—from 64 percent to 80 percent. Teachers also noted that students were more engaged in school, benefitted from the focus on leadership, and appreciated the opportunity to get to know their peers and teachers in new ways.

Some key goals and objectives included:

- Increasing the ninth-grade to tenth-grade promotion rate to ultimately improve graduation rates

- Creating a school climate of respect among students, teachers, and staff

- Providing leadership training and transition support for incoming ninth-grade students

- Providing mentoring for each student

Components of this school's approach included:

- An academy approach in which teams of teachers taught the same cohort of students throughout the school year in all subjects

- An advisory program held once a week for an hour, taught by one of the students' core content teachers

- A family outreach program

- A schoolwide respect program

- Ongoing collaboration between teachers and administration

- Regular team planning time for teachers, including a once-a-week late start for students (when teachers met for planning)

- An outside evaluator from a university who reviewed and analyzed student and teacher pre- and post-survey data

Outcomes included:

- An improvement in promotion from ninth grade to tenth grade from 64 percent to 80 percent from the prior year

- Students and teachers who self-reported significant improvements in teacher-student relationships

- An increase in the number of teacher-to-family contacts

- Teachers who self-reported significant improvements in relationships with their colleagues

Challenges included:

- Integrating advisory into already existing content areas was not sustainable and added too much stress and pressure for teachers.

- Under the stress of possible school closure, this school had seen many leadership turnovers. At the end of this one-year program, the principal moved on to another position and the formal academy program ended. However, a teacher at the school later reported that many teachers continued the principles and practices introduced in the advisory program after the official program ended.

From Big Picture to First Steps

In each of these situations, educators collaborated to create visions, build capacities, produce outcomes, and select measures that tracked and evaluated their progress. As we know, every classroom and school situation is unique. And though we can learn from other schools and examples, finding our own authentic approach that is responsive to the needs and culture of our students and community is critical to faculty commitment and successful systemic change.

To help facilitate this process, this section offers ideas to support you as you:

- Articulate your own vision for the future of your classroom and school

- Commit to the long-term outcomes that connect to that vision

- Conduct an inventory of current strengths and needs in order to identify intermediate outcomes that reflect the skills and capacities necessary to achieve your long-term outcomes

- Identify the principles and practices from this book that can support this capacity and skill building in you, your students, and your school

You may be engaged in these processes on your own, with a colleague, or as a whole school, so you will need to adapt the practices to support your circumstances.

Practice: Developing a Vision

Consider your own unique situation. What aspirations do you have for yourself, your students, and your school? How do these connect to your school's improvement plan, mission, and vision? Reflect on these questions on your own or in collaboration with others—either way, visioning opens up our thinking, allowing us to see the big picture and develop an integrated and holistic approach to our practice.

It can be powerful to engage in visioning work as a whole faculty. In some situations, we may feel inspired to also include students in this process—to hear what kinds of classrooms feel most supportive and relevant to them. When educators have the opportunity to create a shared vision, there is increased buy-in and responsibility for the vision and the projected outcomes.

One of the schools highlighted in the previous section took a half-day of professional development time to engage their faculty in a visioning process using the following scenario and questions:

> A newspaper article is written about your school three to five years from now. What do you hope the headline says? What are the key points of the article? What will you have accomplished by then?

What questions feel relevant for your classroom or school? Following is an activity you might adapt to explore your vision.

Visioning Activity

1. Imagine that you have continued to develop your own social and emotional capacities and that you are actively modeling and supporting these same capacities in your students. Imagine that you are observing yourself and your students a few years from now. What do you notice? What has changed? What differences do you see in yourself and your students? Consider these questions:

   - What are your students engaged in? How do they work alone and together?
   - How are they relating to one another?
   - How do they relate to you, and how do you relate to them?
   - What are they learning? How are they learning? How can you tell they are learning?

Now imagine you are observing these future students as they leave your classroom and head into the hallways or onto the playground:

- What do you see happening in the hallways or on the playground?
- What are the interpersonal dynamics of the students?
- What is hanging on the walls, and how does this impact the students?
- What is the atmosphere in the school?

2. Considering your answers, write down a vision statement that includes what you would like to see in the next three to five years for yourself, your students, and your colleagues.

3. Review your school's or team's annual plan and look for places of alignment and difference. Note these.

4. Consider sharing your vision with others, or if appropriate and possible, work with other teacher leaders or school leadership on an all-staff visioning process.

5. Identify how you might get support for your vision from your principal, assistant principals, other faculty, and students' families.

Practice: Committing to Long-Term Outcomes

Developing a clear vision can support you to articulate and commit to the long-term outcomes you want to achieve. Perhaps you already have a personal improvement plan that can be adapted to include ideas from this book that resonate with you. Perhaps you can integrate the long-term outcomes in your school's annual improvement plan with some of these ideas.

Some examples of possible long-term outcomes include improved staff culture and collaboration, increased teacher satisfaction and retention, improved school climate and safety, improved academic achievement, and improved student resilience. You can adapt or add to this list for your school. What matters most is to develop outcomes specific to your context and community so you feel personally committed and motivated to seeing these outcomes realized. The long-term outcomes activity that follows is one way to approach this process.

Long-Term Outcomes Activity

1. How would you describe the long-term outcomes that connect to your vision?

2. Adapting these examples and considering the already existing goals for your school, list your own personal or schoolwide long-term outcomes.

3. Meet with individuals (or your team) to share your visions and long-term outcomes.

4. Make a list of the long-term outcomes you (or you and your colleagues) identify as most important for your classrooms and school.

5. If you are working on this process with colleagues, consider setting a regular time (monthly or quarterly) to check in on your progress toward these long-term outcomes.

Practice: Identifying Intermediate Outcomes—Capacities and Skills

Intermediate outcomes include the skills and capacities needed to successfully meet long-term projected outcomes. Some intermediate outcomes that emerge from implementing the Engaged Teaching Approach include increased teacher self-efficacy, enthusiasm, and motivation; increased self-management and stress-management skills in students; and improved teamwork, cooperation, and relationship skills within the school. You may wish to explore what intermediate outcomes/capacities apply to your situation. Where are you and your school currently in relation to these outcomes? What are the capacity-building steps you and your colleagues might begin to take? See the capacities and skills inventory that follows to support this process.

Activity for Developing a Capacities and Skills Inventory

1. Make a list of the specific skills and capacities that you, your students, and your colleagues will likely need to achieve your long-term results.

2. Which of these skills and capacities are currently strengths for you, your students, and your faculty? Which of these could use further development? (The section on assessment on page 150 addresses ways to think about tracking your progress in these areas.)

3. Using the tools in this book or other tools you have discovered, create a rubric that illustrates where you are now with these skills and capacities and where you aim to be in the future. Create a one-year, three-year, and five-year future timeline. Repeat this process for three categories: yourself, your students, and your faculty community. Place your intermediary outcomes and long-term outcomes along this timeline.

Practice: Building Capacity and Skills—Principles, Practices, and Next Steps

Having walked through a visioning and planning process, we will now explore how to connect the principles and practices of this book with intermediate and long-term outcomes and vision. This will help identify what next steps are needed to move into action. For example, if you know you need to develop cultural responsiveness or build your capacity to develop positive relationships with students, you may choose to focus more intensively on the principles and practices in chapter 2. If, in the inventory and needs assessment in the previous section, you identified developing emotional capacity as important, you may wish to focus on the principles and practices of chapter 6. If your school has high rates of student referrals and suspensions, you may wish to focus on chapter 2 and chapter 5, since they directly address classroom management and the building of community to support the establishment of respectful boundaries. See the following process for developing an action plan.

Activity for Developing an Action Plan

1. What principles and practices in this book will directly support your intermediary outcomes and feel relevant to your particular situation?

2. What programs, professional development, mentoring, coaching, implementation steps, and processes might support the development of the intermediate outcomes and capacity building that will lead you toward the projected long-term outcomes you are aiming for?

3. What principles and practices might immediately help you build capacity and shift your teaching practice?

4. What practice will you implement this week? What other steps could you take this week to move toward your intermediate outcomes?

A Map of the Engaged Teaching Approach

Throughout this book, we have explored the underlying premise of the Engaged Teaching Approach: when we actively and intentionally cultivate our own social, emotional, and inner life skills and capacities (through the five dimensions) and integrate specific practices to cultivate these capacities in students, this transforms our teaching and directly impacts our students' learning experience and outcomes. This is not a formulaic approach, and it will look different for every educator and in every setting.

This approach to teaching and learning helps us make the connection between our daily work in the classroom and our long-term vision and outcomes. As shown in the tree diagram in the introduction (page 6), the roots of this approach consist of (1) integrating social, emotional, and academic learning, (2) investing in relationships and community, (3) responding to cultural contexts, (4) fostering connection, meaning, and purpose, and (5) addressing developmental stages.

The Five Dimensions of Engaged Teaching and the associated principles and practices serve as the practical action path that connects the foundational roots with the desired outcomes. The Map of the Engaged Teaching Approach (figure 8.1) illustrates how an implementation path proceeds from vision to action. (You can visit **go.solution -tree/instruction** to download a copy of the map.)

The following activity offers one way to begin synthesizing and summarizing your responses to the reflective questions throughout the previous sections and to create your own personal map.

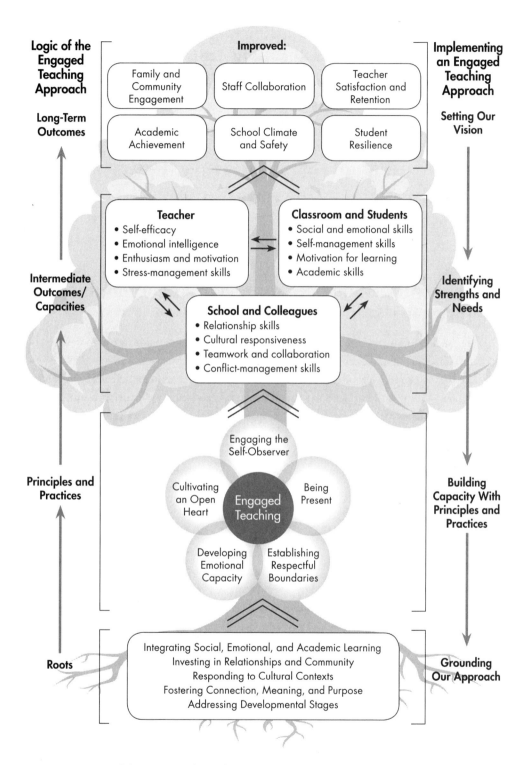

Figure 8.1: Map of the Engaged Teaching Approach.

Visit **go.solution-tree.com/instruction** *to download and print this page.*

Activity for Creating a Map of Your
Engaged Teaching Approach

1. Using the Map Worksheet for the Engaged Teaching Approach (see the reproducible, figure 8.2), write down at the top of the map a brief statement of the vision you have articulated.

2. Below your statement, list and describe the projected long-term outcomes that are critical for you, your students, and your school.

3. List the intermediate outcomes and capacities that you have decided are important to reach your long-term outcomes.

4. List the key principles and practices that you are going to focus on in your practice, in your classroom, and with your team (for example, student-teacher relationships, emotional capacity, or cultural responsiveness).

Assessment: Gathering Information to Inform and Guide Your Journey

After creating your own personal map, you may want to consider how to gather the necessary feedback and information about your particular approach. How will you know if you are on track to develop the skills and capacities you have identified as important to your journey? How will you know if this approach is working for your students? What evaluation methods and tools might help you reflect, learn, and make adjustments along the way? With the emphasis on standardized testing, data and assessment have become a ubiquitous presence in our schools. In many districts, these summative assessments drive policy, curriculum, hiring and firing, and a multitude of other decisions. Because of this, as educators we are expected to prepare students to take state tests and to respond to the results of these tests. However, there are many additional ways to engage in meaningful assessment.

Many teachers find the continual-improvement model of assessment particularly helpful. In this approach (which is aligned with the double-loop learning discussed in chapter 3), we (1) reflect upon and assess where we are (through formative and summative assessments) and identify goals for the future (we need to improve math scores, we need to help our students resolve conflicts, we need to address dropout or attrition, and so on); (2) use a variety of methodologies to get a 360-degree view of our instructional programs and our teaching; (3) ask for feedback and learn collaboratively; (4) note our challenges and successes and identify areas where we need to shift our practice and where we need additional resources; (5) make shifts to our approach and note these results; and (6) then revise our teaching practice to include this new learning. This kind of ongoing assessment creates a process in which we are continually reflecting on and learning from our own practice and the practice of our colleagues.

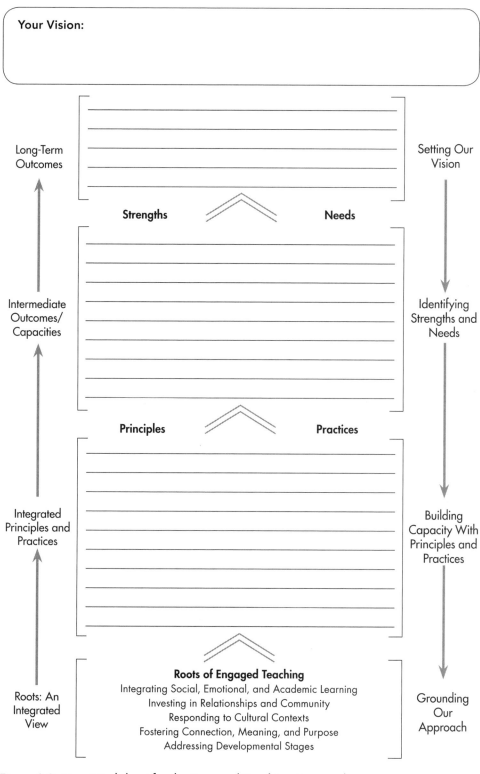

Your Vision:

Long-Term Outcomes

Setting Our Vision

Strengths   **Needs**

Intermediate Outcomes/ Capacities

Identifying Strengths and Needs

Principles   **Practices**

Integrated Principles and Practices

Building Capacity With Principles and Practices

Roots of Engaged Teaching
Integrating Social, Emotional, and Academic Learning
Investing in Relationships and Community
Responding to Cultural Contexts
Fostering Connection, Meaning, and Purpose
Addressing Developmental Stages

Roots: An Integrated View

Grounding Our Approach

Figure 8.2: Map Worksheet for the Engaged Teaching Approach.

Visit **go.solution-tree.com/instruction** *to download and print this page.*

In the following sections, we will offer some examples of other ways to assess the learning and growth in ourselves and our students. In particular, we will focus on methods to help us identify progress in different areas of the Engaged Teaching Approach.

The Process of Assessment

In the beginning of a school year or program, we can gather baseline data so that we have a basis for comparison down the road. After we begin a class, we can use formative assessment methods to begin gathering information to help us make adjustments and course corrections throughout the term. Finally, at the end of a semester or school year, we can reflect on the formal summative data as a basis for making changes in subsequent years.

There are many ways to collect and understand data to improve practice and impact student learning outcomes—self-reflection forms, student surveys, parent/guardian feedback, standardized tests, performance assessments, scoop notebooks, tours through buildings—all these provide us with important information about our vision and outcomes. Of course, every method of assessment has its own blind spots (see McMillan, 2000). If we rely only on self-reflection, we do not have the benefit of feedback or peer observation or student learning data. If we look only at standardized tests, we do not necessarily accurately measure students' learning—especially those who are poor test takers or who might simply misunderstand the question. Additionally, standardized tests can include cultural bias that impacts test results. And, when we rely solely on standardized tests, we are not evaluating other kinds of learning and expressions of knowledge. In his 1989 article, "A True Test," Grant Wiggins uses a medical metaphor: "Our confusion over the uses of standardized tests is akin to mistaking pulse rate for the total effect of a healthful regimen."

It is important to consider different kinds of tools so that we can see beyond these blind spots. There are a growing number of valid and reliable assessment methods and tools that measure school climate and the social and emotional learning of students. By using a variety of assessment methods, rather than a single metric, we are more likely to effectively measure our progress and our students' learning, and thus develop a more accurate whole picture of progress that includes cultural influences and indicators of social, emotional, *and* academic development.

Assessment Methods

Following are three examples of formative assessment tools that could be used to track progress with the engaged teaching skills and capacities you have identified as important. These three examples represent a range of ways to gather information about your teaching and your students. Each of the methods could be used to provide you with ongoing feedback on a wide range of outcomes.

Tools for Reflective Teachers

In *Becoming a Reflective Teacher*, Robert Marzano and his coauthors (2012) offer tools to design and assess forty-one elements in their effective teaching framework. As you think about gathering information on your progress, remember the importance of collecting evidence related to both the teacher and the students. Marzano and his colleagues' framework provides specifics for gathering teacher and student evidence and includes a teacher self-rating scale. This assessment tool, portions of which are shown in figure 8.3 on page 154, is an example of a tool for obtaining feedback about progress in developing a specific aspect of relationship building (in this case, affection for students). *Becoming a Reflective Teacher* offers similar scales and survey questions that relate to setting learning goals, establishing respectful boundaries, teacher awareness, student motivation and progress, and many other elements of effective and engaged teaching.

The Scoop Notebook

To collect evidence regarding how emotionally rich or culturally responsive our curriculum is, we need to gather data from many different sources and get feedback from other teachers and staff. One powerful tool is a classroom artifact method called the "scoop notebook." Professor Hilda Borko and her colleagues (Borko, Stecher, & Kuffner, 2007) describe the scoop notebook as "a procedure for gathering a collection of instructional artifacts and teacher reflections" (p. 10) that would enable someone to review the materials as if they were an observer in the classroom.

The artifacts for a scoop notebook are typically collected during one week and include lesson planning and other materials created before class, student work produced during class, and homework and project work that students generate outside of class. The notebook also includes formal classroom assessments such as tests, quizzes, papers, and reports, and the associated grading rubrics. Teachers take photos of the class and any noncollectable work, such as constructed projects and artwork.

The teacher includes three representative examples of student work for each assignment from class and from homework. Teachers rate the work examples as high, medium, or low quality using a sticky note and include their reasons for the rating and what they learned about the student's understanding from that assignment.

The scoop notebook also contains daily calendar notes and the teacher's answers to daily reflective questions, such as:

- What were your objectives and expectations for student learning during this lesson?

- How well were your objectives and expectations for student learning met in today's lesson? How do you know?

You may also want to include the kinds of self-observer reflections in chapter 3: What assumptions were you making about teaching, learning, and your students during these lessons? What were you feeling before, during, and after the lesson?

Design Question: What will I do to establish and maintain effective relationships with students?

37. What do I typically do to use verbal and nonverbal behaviors that indicate affection for students?

When appropriate, the teacher uses verbal and nonverbal behaviors that indicate affection for students.

Teacher Evidence	Student Evidence
❑ Teacher compliments students regarding academic and personal accomplishments. ❑ Teacher engages in informal conversations with students that are not related to academics. ❑ Teacher uses humor with students when appropriate. ❑ Teacher smiles or nods at students when appropriate. ❑ Teacher puts a hand on students' shoulders when appropriate.	❑ When asked, students describe the teacher as someone who cares for them. ❑ Students respond to the teacher's verbal interactions. ❑ Students respond to the teacher's nonverbal interactions.

© 2012 Robert J. Marzano

How Am I Doing?

	4 Innovating	3 Applying	2 Developing	1 Beginning	0 Not Using
Using verbal and nonverbal behaviors that indicate affection for students	I adapt and create new strategies for unique student needs and situations.	I use verbal and nonverbal behaviors that indicate affection for students, and I monitor the quality of relationships in the classroom.	I use verbal and nonverbal behaviors that indicate affection for students, but I do so in a somewhat mechanistic way.	I use the strategy incorrectly or with parts missing.	I should use the strategy, but I don't.

© 2012 Robert J. Marzano

Teacher Self-Evaluation:					
Element	4 Innovating	3 Applying	2 Developing	1 Beginning	0 Not Using
37. What do I typically do to use verbal and nonverbal behaviors that indicate affection for students?					

Student Survey: Middle School (Grades 6–8)

Directions: For each question, circle "I disagree," "I agree," or "I strongly agree."

37. My teacher likes me.

  I disagree.   I agree.   I strongly agree.

Becoming a Reflective Teacher © 2012 Marzano Research Laboratory • marzanoresearch.com

Figure 8.3: Sample assessment tool.

Source: Reprinted from Becoming a Reflective Teacher *(Marzano, 2012, pp. 222, 45, and 65) with permission from Marzano Research Laboratory and Robert J. Marzano.*

Teachers are also asked to describe the lesson in enough detail so evaluators can understand how the scoop materials were used or generated. At the end of the week-long scoop notebook process, teachers respond to questions that ask how the class lessons relate to their long-term goals for their students and if the scoop notebook accurately represented their instruction. Teachers conclude by offering suggestions about what artifacts might be included in a future scoop to create a more accurate portrayal.

The notebooks are then reviewed and assessed according to rating scales. The authors of the scoop notebook method developed rating scales for middle-school mathematics and science, which are available at the National Center for Research on Evaluation, Standards, and Student Testing (CRESST) website (www.cse.ucla.edu). These existing scales provide examples of how to connect the scoop to identified outcomes.

Using Video in Classroom Assessment

It is not an easy task to observe and assess teacher-student dynamics in a live classroom setting. It can be difficult to find effective and productive ways of evaluating complex outcomes, such as improved classroom culture and climate. Video observation of classrooms can be an effective way to recognize and learn about complicated teacher-student interactions. And though the prospect of being observed on video can initially feel intimidating and make us feel vulnerable, when we use clear design principles and caring practices, we can create professional and positive learning processes.

One example of using video is Daniel Willingham's method for giving and receiving feedback (Willingham, 2009). Willingham outlines a simple video observation method that two teachers can organize themselves. Teachers begin by finding a colleague whom they trust and respect and then follow a series of carefully sequenced steps. They begin by watching videos of other teachers in their classrooms and share observations about what they are seeing. Once they develop familiarity and skill with this process, they then record themselves in the classroom and review each other's taped sessions. Finally, the teachers discuss how to integrate their learning into future lessons and classes.

A second example of using video recordings of classrooms was developed by Robert Pianta, Bridget Hamre, and colleagues at the University of Virginia (Curry School of Education, CASTL, 2013). The Classroom Assessment Scoring System (CLASS) is an observation instrument to organize, describe, and demonstrate effective teacher-child interactions. Hamre and Pianta recognized the challenges inherent in using video as an assessment tool, and so they have carefully designed the process of video observation used in their research and their work with teachers (Hamre et al., 2012). In *A Practitioner's Guide to Conducting Classroom Observations* (Stuhlman, Hamre, Downer, & Pianta, 2010), they comment:

> Teachers may be initially apprehensive about the practice of videotaping, but with sensitive support, they often come to see this as a tool that is extremely empowering. They are able to see, first hand, exactly what happened, rather than relying on someone else's retelling of the event. (p. 34)

These types of tools can support us to effectively employ video observation, learn from one another, and develop our teaching practice.

Learning Communities and Assessment

As with video observation, getting feedback about our teaching can feel vulnerable and risky, and yet working with fellow educators is essential for meaningful ongoing formative assessment. Willingham (2009) notes that we "need to work with at least one other person. Someone else will see things in your class that you cannot, simply because she is not you" (p. 259). So what can we do to set up an assessment process that is both trustworthy and effective?

Investing time and energy in building trust and respect in adult learning communities is critical to creating environments where assessment feels supportive and productive. When we establish this foundation of relational trust, and we practice clear and consistent protocols for giving and receiving feedback, we also create opportunities for honest and skillful assessment. The principles and practices of engaged teaching can support us to build trusting adult learning communities and engage in mutual feedback in compassionate and effective ways. Cultivating an open heart, engaging the self-observer, being present, establishing respectful boundaries, and developing emotional capacity all directly support us to build our core competencies to listen and speak with an open mind and heart. (See chapters 2 through 6 for specific principles and practices for working with colleagues.)

Each of the assessment methods discussed in this section offer different ways of collecting information that will help us develop our capacities for engaged teaching. We hope that these examples of formative assessment tools inspire you to take a fresh look at how feedback methods, when engaged in with precision, care, and compassion, can actually build trust among colleagues and support us to effectively collaborate and learn from each other.

Laying Down a Path

This book offers a practical approach to enlivening our own teaching, engaging students in meaningful and effective ways, and creating rewarding and productive adult learning communities. It includes the wisdom and experience of a great many educators and contains research on best practices and emerging scientific insights that illuminate the connection between emotions, attention, memory, and learning. We hope that you found this approach useful to your own situation and setting and that you see your own wisdom and experience reflected in these pages.

At a time when pressures in the teaching profession could drive educators further into isolation or despair, we also hope that this book supports you in reaching out to fellow educators, implementing important practices, having conversations about what is working and what is not, and building meaningful collegial relationships that facilitate growth and learning for all.

When we approach our professional lives as lifelong learners, we inspire this same love of learning in our students. When we bring our authenticity and brilliance into the classroom, we evoke these qualities in our students. When we commit to the practices that sustain us, we are better able to engage, meet, and empower our students. It is our hope that the Engaged Teaching Approach can serve as a guide to support you in walking your own particular teaching path, day by day, with greater intention, efficacy, and joy.

"Caminante, son tus huellas el camino, y nada más . . .
Al andar se hace camino.

Wanderer, the road is your footsteps, nothing else. . . .
In walking you lay down a path."
—Antonio Machado (Translation by Francisco Varela)

Appendix

Active Focusing Activities

Group Juggling

10–15 minutes, grades 4–12

Gather together five pairs of balled-up socks or five soft balls; it is very important that the balls are soft and cannot hurt anyone and that they are not too light to be effectively tossed. Tell the students this activity is about being fully present and ready to learn.

If you have not already done so, discuss "presence." Ask students what it means to be present and what keeps people from being present (worry, preoccupation, fatigue, indifference, chemicals, and mental habits like daydreaming or always focusing on the past or future). Explain that one of the goals of this class is to understand more about how to manage our distractions and be present for our learning.

Hide all but one sock or ball near you (in a bag on your chair, for example). Form a standing circle with enough room so that students can swing their arms easily. Tell them you are going to toss the ball and make a pattern that the group can remember. Each person gets the ball once and only once. As the teacher, you will go first, saying the name of the person you are going to toss the ball to. If you do not know his or her name, make eye contact and ask the student to share his or her name. That person will again make eye contact and call out the name of another person he or she is going to toss the ball to, and so on. Remind students to remember who they are throwing to and who is throwing to him or her. Ask students to put their hands behind their backs after they have received the ball. (Watch carefully as the group creates a pattern—if someone gets the ball a second time before you have completed the pattern, you must stop and correct or the game will not work.) When everyone has had the ball, the last person tosses the ball back to you, the facilitator.

After you create the pattern, ask the group to toss the ball again, creating the same pattern they just made. Emphasize that it is important to toss the ball so that the others can catch it (no fast pitches) and to help each other out if someone forgets who he or she threw the ball to originally. The goal is to work together to have success and fun as a group. After the group has completed the pattern a second time, ask them to repeat the pattern quickly, this time without names. Give lots of positive feedback.

At this point, ask students, "Do you think you could handle two balls?" Remember: the pattern stays exactly the same. You always throw to the same person and receive from the same person. Start the first ball and wait a few seconds. Then start a second ball. After an experience of success with two balls, introduce the third ball. Keep adding balls if the group is succeeding, until you are tossing all five at the same time. The activity ends when you have received all five balls back again. Then congratulate the group.

You can expect a lot of laughter and zaniness and, if students hold their focus through the laughter, lots of success. If students get critical when someone drops a ball, encourage them

page 1 of 3

The 5 Dimensions of Engaged Teaching © 2013 Solution Tree Press • solution-tree.com
Visit go.solution-tree.com/instruction to download this page.

to stay positive and help each other out. Remind them that it's okay to make mistakes and that they can just pick up the ball and go on.

Take just a few minutes to debrief when the game is over. Ask students what they think this game has to do with being present. With creating community? With learning? This is a good time to make a statement about welcoming mistakes: "Perfection is about no mistakes, but this class is about excellence, and excellence welcomes mistakes, because they can bring laughter and learning." Students will often talk about the importance of learning to focus with lots of distraction. Have a conversation about how the principles of group juggling apply to learning (cooperation, focus, being present, learning from our mistakes, and so on).

20 Things on a Tray

15 minutes, grades 5–12

This exercise demonstrates different styles of learning. Before coming to class, gather twenty objects from around your house. Pick objects that are different but similar in some ways. For example, some objects could be the same color, others could begin with the same letter of the alphabet, and some could have the same function or usage (such as scissors, needle, thread, and material). Display the objects on a tray so they are all visible, and cover the tray with a cloth.

When students enter, ask them to sit in the circle. Have the tray of objects completely covered. Pass out a pencil and paper to each student. Tell the students that in a moment you are going to uncover the tray for 2 minutes. During those 2 minutes, students must try and remember as many objects as they can. Then you will cover the tray of objects again and students will have a few minutes to write down everything they remembered. They will keep their lists to themselves. After 2 minutes, go around the circle and ask students to share one thing on their list and how they remembered it. The one rule is that students are not to shout out, "I remember seventeen objects," or "I remember nine." What is important in this activity is not how many objects we remember, but *how* we think and remember.

After everyone has had a chance to share the objects he or she remembered and how he or she remembered, uncover the tray of objects and ask students to notice which objects they remembered and which they overlooked. Remind them that this is not a competition. You can also have the students collaborate to create as long a list as they can together, and then move to the discussion on ways of remembering.

Ask different students to raise their hand and explain how they remembered what was on the tray. After three or four different memory styles are described, ask, "What did you notice about the methods people used to remember?" Some may say they counted the different colors (for example, they saw four blue, three red, a green, two blacks, and many multicolored). Someone else might say he or she took a picture of the whole tray and recreated it when recalling the objects. Someone else might have looked for the connections between objects, or alphabetized them, or created a story connecting the objects. If you have time, you can invite a person who created a story to tell the story. Talk about the different ways

The 5 Dimensions of Engaged Teaching © 2013 Solution Tree Press • solution-tree.com
Visit **go.solution-tree.com/instruction** to download this page.

we learn and how this activity relates to the classroom. Explain that this is a class that honors our differences and encourages us to look at our individual approaches to life and learning.

Pop Up
5 minutes

In this simple focusing activity, students "pop up" or stand up if a particular statement applies to them. For example, say, "Pop up if you play a sport" or "Pop up if you enjoy reading science fiction." Identify a series of questions that is relevant for your group. This exercise will help you get to know everyone in the room.

Variation: "How Many of You . . . ?"

In this variation, bring your group into a standing circle. Ask the students to take a step into the circle if the question or statement applies to them. For example: *How many of you play sports? How many of you play an instrument? How many of you were born here in this state?*

Gotcha
5 minutes

Gather your group into a standing circle. Let students know we are going to engage in an activity that will build our reflexes. Ask everyone to extend his or her left arm with the left palm opened. Then ask participants to take the index finger of their right hand and place it into the left palm of the person next to them. Say that on the count of three you are going to ask everyone to try to catch the person's finger that is in his or her palm and not be caught by the other person. Count 1, 2, 3, and see what happens. Generally this leads to a great deal of laughter. Then reverse hands and do the activity again. This is a great way to gather a group at the beginning of class or after a break.

The 5 Dimensions of Engaged Teaching © 2013 Solution Tree Press • solution-tree.com
Visit **go.solution-tree.com/instruction** to download this page.

Reflective Focusing Activities

Hot Pencil
Grades 3–12

Hot Pencil gives students a chance to write about a theme or question in an unedited way. In Hot Pencil, students write without stopping for 1 to 3 minutes on a particular question or theme. They are not to worry about what they write, as this writing is only for themselves. The point is to see what emerges when we write about a theme in an unedited way, letting go of our inner judge and editor.

Quote and Reflection
Grades 2–12

Write a quote on the board, and ask students to write about the quote for 3 to 5 minutes at the beginning of class. Then ask a few people to share a short excerpt from their writing or something they realized in the process of writing about the quote. This quote could relate to the content you are teaching.

Silence or Mindful Breathing
Grades K–12

Begin class with a "golden moment" or a few moments of silence in which students simply sit in silence together. Students can open or close their eyes. You may also ring a chime or bell and ask students to put their attention on the bell and notice when they can no longer hear it. Additionally, ask students to take five full-body breaths—breaths that expand their belly and ribcage.

Focused Listening Practices

Listening Dyads and Triads

Grades K–12

Deep listening activities can be done in groups of two or three. Count off so that everyone is included in a dyad or triad. It is best not to ask students to find partners on their own, but rather to let them partner randomly. Let students know that the group is going to engage in a different kind of listening and speaking; it is not better or worse than any other kind of communication, but it offers another communication tool.

Students will take turns listening and speaking on a particular theme for a prescribed period of time (usually between 30 seconds and 2 minutes, depending on the age group and subject matter). Partner A will speak first on the theme for a prescribed period of time. During this time, partner B will simply listen without interruption or questions. Then the facilitator will give a signal that time is up, and partner A and B will switch so that partner B is speaking, while partner A simply listens without interruption or questions. The dyad/triad can experiment with eye contact. (This can be an opportunity to share that different cultures feel differently about eye contact.)

After partner A and B have each had a chance to speak and listen, take a few minutes to debrief the experience, asking students to share how it was for them to listen and speak during the exercise. You can then ask students to partner with another student and try this practice again a second time. If you do so, have students note how they feel the second time around.

This activity can also open up a rich discussion on communication and the benefits and challenges of engaging in focused listening and authentic speaking.

Wheel Within a Wheel

15–30 minutes, grades 3–12

Tell students that they will now explore the practice of focused listening with a variety of different people. Let them know that you are asking them to be self-scientists—to notice how they feel when asked to communicate in a new way with each other. Remind them that this is not a better way of communicating, just a different way. It is a skill they will build on throughout the year.

Ask students to count off by ones and twos. Ask the ones to form a circle of chairs in the middle of the room facing out and the twos to form an outer circle facing the inner circle. Keep the pairs of chairs close, but allow for as much space between the pairs of chairs as possible. Let students know that they will be partnered in a series of paired dyads with different people. Introduce the first theme, and let the inner circle know that in this round students will speak first and their partners second. Instruct students to speak quietly throughout this exercise.

page 1 of 4

As timekeeper, you will ring a bell or raise a hand to indicate that time is up (a timer with a beeper or buzzer is helpful). Explain to the listeners that they are to listen without giving a verbal response. After the time is up, ring the chime or give a hand signal to indicate that the first speaker's speaking time is up. Then ask the second person in the dyad to begin speaking on the same theme (say the theme again, so everyone is clear about the prompt). After both members of the dyad have had a turn to speak and listen, ask the students sitting in the outside circle to stand and move one chair to the left. For the next dyad round, the outer circle begins as speakers.

Decide ahead of time how many dyads will be part of your wheel within a wheel. We generally recommend four to seven rounds—each with a different question. At the end of the wheel activity, take some time to debrief. It is important to remind students that they can share about what they said, but not what their partner said, unless they have explicit permission.

After students have completed the wheel questions, ask them to bring their chairs back into a circle. Facilitate a dialogue with questions like:

- What was it like to listen without interrupting? To speak without interruption?

- What were the hardest and best parts about this activity?

- What did you learn about yourself? About your dyad partners? (This is a chance to share process, not content.)

- What other questions would you have liked to talk about?

This activity can be used for personal sharing and storytelling, to prepare for a quiz or test, to make connections to a novel or text, or to invite students to share their thoughts about the content area. For example, if you are teaching the book *Seedfolks* by Paul Fleischman, you might ask students to share which character they most appreciate and why, or what the underlying lessons of the book are. If you are studying a period of history, you might construct a series of questions related to the time period.

Before you begin the activity, spend some time going over what it looks like to be a respectful listener (not interrupting, not making faces, not making fun of the speaker in any way, and so on). Taking the time to do this before you begin will help you in future activities, when students are in other sharing situations. Talk about body language and facial expressions—students are free to nod or smile, as long as they don't talk. They may experiment with making and not making eye contact.

It is important that both the speaker and the listener are on the same level physically (both sitting in the same kinds of chairs or both sitting on the floor). Never allow members of groups to have higher or lower physical positions from one another. This can imply power status, and is inappropriate for peers sharing from the heart. Share this reasoning with students.

The 5 Dimensions of Engaged Teaching © 2013 Solution Tree Press • solution-tree.com

Visit **go.solution-tree.com/instruction** to download this page.

It is important that the teacher witness and facilitate the activity and not participate in it (unless you have two facilitators, in which case one person could participate). From the position of facilitator, you can watch and ensure that students are respectfully listening and speaking and not interrupting each other. If you see any disrespectful behaviors occurring, it is essential to step in and investigate what is occurring, reminding students of the guidelines of the activity.

Use a timer to keep time. In general, give students 30 seconds each to respond to each prompt. If you have a particularly mature or trusting group, you may be able to extend this time to a minute or 90 seconds.

Choose four to seven questions and adapt them for your age group. Some examples are as follows:

- What kind of music, movies, or books do you like?

- What is your favorite game? What do you like about it?

- What is a favorite place of yours? What does it look like? Feel like? What do you appreciate about it?

- What was something memorable that happened during the summer or your last school year?

- What are some of your interests inside and outside of school?

- What classes do you like and dislike so far?

- Who is one person in your life or in the world that you admire and why?

- What holidays do you enjoy? What do you like to do during those holidays?

- If you could travel anywhere in the world, where would you go and why?

- What is something you really enjoyed in elementary school—a teacher, a friend, or an experience?

- If you could have any superpower, what would it be and why?

- What is a story you can tell about a life lesson you learned in the last year?

- If money was no issue, what would you do with your life?

- What is one issue in the world that is important to you? Why?

Sharing Circles or Community Circles

Grades K–12

Sharing circles or community circles bring focused listening and authentic speaking into a circle format so that the whole community is engaged. In this practice, the teacher or facilitator introduces a theme, and each student and teacher is then invited to share about this theme. It is essential that adults are not simply creating the space for this circle, but fully

The 5 Dimensions of Engaged Teaching © 2013 Solution Tree Press • solution-tree.com
Visit **go.solution-tree.com/instruction** to download this page.

participating. (It can be helpful for a teacher to speak first to set the tone.) As soon as the theme is set, each person in the circle speaks, one at a time, without interruption. If a student is not ready to speak or does not wish to speak, he or she can pass to the next person.

After the whole circle has had a first opportunity to speak, students who have not spoken can be given a second chance to speak, but this is always invitational. Generally, because of time constraints in the classroom, keeping time is essential. One to 2 minutes per student is often sufficient. If you have 45 minutes and twenty students, each student will have no more than 2 minutes, though he or she need not take the full time. You can use a timepiece and a chime or hand signal to note when a student has 15 seconds remaining, so he or she can wrap up the sharing. Some communities opt to use a talking piece of some kind to indicate who is speaking. This talking piece can be a stone, shell, stick, or stuffed animal—whatever is meaningful to the community.

Council

Adapted from Joe Provisor (personal communication, February 7, 2012), MFT Advisor, Los Angeles Unified School District Council in Schools Office Director, Ojai Foundation's Council in Schools Initiative.

Council is a practice that encourages deep and honest communication. In schools in the United States and around the world, it is integrated into classrooms, counseling offices, and faculty, parent, and community meetings. Based on indigenous, worldwide "cultural dialogic" practices, including Native American traditions, council is a formal, structured, circle-based process that includes "sitting" in a circle and passing a "talking piece" in response to a prompt. In a broader sense, council is also about a heightened awareness of self, other, and the natural world. Classroom council practice can include play, movement, rhythm, mindfulness, visual arts, technology, and spontaneous improvisation, as well as fundamental listening and speaking skills. Council is practiced to convey content, to develop social-emotional competencies, and to elicit what students *themselves* want to understand. Teachers and students may decide to determine their own guidelines for the circles or use the "four intentions" of council, as developed through the Ojai Foundation and *The Way of Council* by Jack Zimmerman and Virginia Coyle:

1. To listen from the heart—practicing the "art of receptivity": suspending judgment, reaction, and opinion

2. To speak from the heart and with heart—learning to "speak into the listening"

3. To speak spontaneously without planning and only when holding a "talking piece"

4. To "keep it lean," to the "heart of the matter," so everyone has time to participate

The 5 Dimensions of Engaged Teaching © 2013 Solution Tree Press • solution-tree.com
Visit **go.solution-tree.com/instruction** to download this page.

Working With Emotions

Feelings Vocabulary

Grades 1–8

Divide the class into six groups. Each group will get one feeling category and then brainstorm as many words as students can think of that fall into the same category. The categories are Excited, Sad, Scared, Happy, Angry, and Tender. Our feelings can be quite complex. So some of the words under one emotion will also have flavors of another. Some words, like *frustrated*, could show up under more than one category—like *sad* and *angry*.

Option One

After groups have had time to come up with their list, write each category on the board or a large piece of paper and call on each group to give its list of words while you write them down for everyone to see. After you finish writing, ask the rest of the group members if they have any words they would like to add to that feeling.

Option Two

Give each group a large sheet of newsprint (easel size sticky notes are ideal). Using one color marker, students write all of the words they can think of for their feeling word—with that word at the top. After about 10 minutes, ask them to post their sheets on the wall, or lay them on the floor. The whole group does a "gallery walk" in silence in which students look at each list and can add, in another color marker, words they feel are missing from the list.

After about 5 minutes, ask someone from each group to read the whole list and notice what each feeling category evokes.

Feelings Wheel

Grades K–5

Pass out blank paper and pencils. Ask students to fold the paper in half the wide way— folding the top of the sheet down to the bottom. Participants will draw a circle on the top half of the paper and divide the circle into four quadrants. Participants then write one feeling word in each quadrant. Each word will express something that they are feeling right now. Then, on the bottom part of the page, they will choose two of the words to develop more fully, writing: "I feel . . . because . . ." for each of those two feelings. Let students know this is just for them—they will not be asked to share it unless they wish.

The other ways the feelings can be shared include:

- A quick circle activity in which each student may choose to share one of the words from his or her feelings wheel

The 5 Dimensions of Engaged Teaching © 2013 Solution Tree Press • solution-tree.com
Visit **go.solution-tree.com/instruction** to download this page.

- A deep listening dyad in which students have 1 to 2 minutes each to talk about anything they want to related to what they wrote or how they felt about doing the activity

- A drawing, sculpture, or other symbolic form of expressing the feelings students just identified

Weather Report

This activity is another tool for helping students become present. It introduces the concepts of symbol and metaphor, and is a tool for getting a quick read of the group at the beginning of the day.

Ask students to sit or stand in a circle. Let them know the group is going to be giving a "weather report": each student will have the chance to speak about how he or she is feeling or doing today using weather images. Weather is used as a metaphor for students' state of being at the moment. Give participants examples of some weather report options, like "sunny now, with a storm approaching" or "heavy cloud cover," or "raining, but clearing later today," or "blue skies." Then ask students to close their eyes, if they are comfortable doing so, and quietly reflect on how they are feeling today. (If you just did the feelings wheel activity, you can refer back to it by saying, "You might reflect on the feelings you just identified during the feelings wheel activity or notice if you're feeling something new now.")

Give participants 15–30 seconds, and then ask them to open their eyes. As the facilitator, you should go first in this exercise, modeling your weather report for students. Then proceed around the circle until all students have completed their weather report. Let participants know that the purpose of this activity is to allow them to have more awareness of their internal state and to give them a different kind of language to discuss emotions.

Note: As the facilitator, you may want to comment: "As you may have noticed, I am introducing you to a variety of tools for helping you become present. We started with an active stream with the feelings vocabulary exercise, but today we're primarily working with the reflective, expressive stream of focusing activities."

Pairing Strategies

Later in the semester, you may want to invite students to choose their own partners for dyads. But in the early weeks, students are likely to either choose familiar friends or to feel a lot of anxiety about revealing themselves through their choices or feeling rejected, not chosen, or left out. It can be a relief for them to not have to make these choices.

You may want to choose the dyads, keeping a record of who pairs with whom each week so that over the semester you give them the opportunity to make personal contact with as many different students as possible. Or you may want to use a variety of methods that rely on chance. The simplest of these involves determining the total number of the group; for example, if there are twenty students and adults total, each member of the group counts off—from one to ten and then from one to ten again. Each person then seeks the person with the same number to form his or her dyad.

There are more elaborate ways of creating pairs. You can bring in two decks of playing cards so you have doubles of each number and suit. Students pick a card and find the person with the matching card. You can also use any other paired images or categories.

Using a pairing activity early in the period has many advantages. It allows students to quickly feel seen and heard. It helps build students' confidence for sharing in the group. And, if you do random pairing, it breaks up the natural tendency for students to sit with their friends. If you make a routine of asking students to sit with their partner when they return to the circle, you will have naturally broken up some of the groups of students who encourage each other to distract themselves and the group from the focus of the class.

Closure Activities

Closure activities at the end of the day or the end of each class can offer students opportunities to:

1. Process and digest what has happened, consolidating their learning

2. Reflect on what was meaningful, surprising, confusing, and so on

3. Appreciate oneself as a learner or contributor

4. Appreciate the community and what others have offered

5. Transition between classes

Examples of closure activities include:

- Taking a minute or two (or more) of silence

- Listening in silence to music

- Using crayons, markers, clay, or some other medium in silence or with music to express what students are feeling as the class or day ends

- Journaling or providing loose reflections in writing to questions such as the following:

  ○ What surprised you?

  ○ What made you think?

  ○ What did you learn?

  ○ What questions do you have from today?

  ○ What would you like to learn more about?

- Writing a response to any of the following:

  ○ What's one thing you would change for next time in any of the following—

    ⊙ In your behavior?

    ⊙ In the contributions of fellow students?

    ⊙ In the contribution of your teacher?

    ⊙ What could have made this class work better?

  ○ I need . . .

  ○ I am concerned about . . .

The 5 Dimensions of Engaged Teaching © 2013 Solution Tree Press • solution-tree.com
Visit **go.solution-tree.com/instruction** to download this page.

This writing can be private or handed in to the teacher, who may write comments on sticky notes in response to students with the collected sheets then returned to students in the last month of class during the review of the year.

- Having a pair-share discussion on feelings about the class or day, or to set an intention for the evening or next day
  - Conducting a check-out circle in which students stand in a circle and speak out—
    - A word or phrase that describes one thing they are feeling right now, thinking about right now, or a question they have
    - An affirmation of something someone else did in class that day which they really appreciated or admired
- Doing a telegramming activity where you distribute index cards and then ask students to write on the cards one thing they would like to remember about today's lesson if they forget everything else. Collect the cards and redistribute them to be read in turn or, if time is short, select and read a few.
- Reading a poem or inspirational text together as a group; each student reads a phrase or a few sentences
- Reading aloud to students a brief story, parable, biography, or poem that speaks to the themes raised in the class

The 5 Dimensions of Engaged Teaching © 2013 Solution Tree Press • solution-tree.com
Visit **go.solution-tree.com/instruction** to download this page.

Success Analysis Protocol: An Exercise for Teachers

40 minutes

Roles: Rotate facilitator and timekeeper roles (one person per round).

The facilitator's role is to help the group stay focused on exploring what made the presenter's experience so successful. The timekeeper will let the group know when it needs to move on to the next step of the protocol.

- Divide the group into triads. Take a moment to reflect on a time within the last year when you felt truly successful as a teacher. Note what it was about that experience that made it so successful. Be specific about the context of the situation and your goals and objectives, and explain the challenge and how you met it in a way that satisfied you. Write down a description or some notes as you reflect on your experience (2 minutes).

- In your group of three, the first person shares his or her experience of success, the situation or context of this success, and why the practice was so successful (2 minutes).

- The rest of the group asks clarifying (informational) questions about the details of the "experience of success" (2 minutes).

- The group does an analysis of what it heard about the presenter's success and offers additional insights about why it thinks the presenter was successful in this situation (2 minutes).

- The presenter responds to the group's analysis of what made this experience so successful, reflecting back the new insights it has after listening to the group (2 minutes).

- Take a moment to celebrate the success of the presenter before moving on to the next presenter (1 minute).

- Continue the process just outlined with each subsequent presenter.

Adapted with thanks to School Reform Initiative (National School Reform Faculty, n.d.; see www.schoolreform initiative.org/protocol) and Daniel Baron.

Family Extensions

This is an example of a family member or guardian interview students complete as homework. Adapt this for your community and needs.

Note to family members and guardians: One central goal of our school is to support students to make a healthy transition from adolescence into adulthood. One aspect of achieving that goal is to encourage students to learn about and honor their roots and their own past.

1. Tell me what you would like me to know about your life just before I was born.

2. Tell me a story about one of my grandparents that you think is important for me to know.

3. Tell me about a time when you were very happy.

4. Tell me about something in your life that has turned out differently than you thought it would have when you were younger.

5. Describe the major world events that took place when you were my age. What was the world like in terms of media, technology, politics, fashion, and peers?

6. Tell me something that you would have liked to have known at my age that you know now (a story, a bit of wisdom, a truth or value, and so on).

Assessment Examples

Teacher Self-Assessment and Feedback

Marzano, R. J. (2012). *Becoming a reflective teacher.* Bloomington, IN: Marzano Research Laboratory.

Using Video in Classroom Observation

Curry School of Education, Center for Advanced Study of Teaching and Learning. (2013). *Classroom Assessment Scoring System.* Accessed at http://curry.virginia.edu/research /centers/castl/class on March 1, 2013.

Hamre, B. K., & Pianta, R. C. (2009). Classroom environments and developmental processes. In J. L. Meece & J. S. Eccles (Eds.), *Handbook of research on schools, schooling and human development* (pp. 25–41). New York: Routledge.

Hamre, B. K., Pianta, R. C., Burchinal, M., Field, S., LoCasale-Crouch, J., Downer, J. T., et al. (2012). A course on effective teacher-child interactions: Effects on teacher beliefs, knowledge, and observed practice. *American Educational Research Journal, 49*(1), 88–123.

Stuhlman, M. W., Hamre, B. K., Downer, J. T., & Pianta, R. C. (2010). *A practitioner's guide to conducting classroom observations: What the research tells us about choosing and using observational systems.* Accessed at www.wtgrantfdn.org/File Library/Resources/Practitioners Guide.pdf on March 1, 2013.

Willingham, D. T. (2009). *Why don't students like school? A cognitive scientist answers questions about how the mind works and what it means for the classroom.* San Francisco: Jossey-Bass.

Obtaining Classroom Artifacts

Borko, H., Stecher, B., & Kuffner, K. (2007). *Using artifacts to characterize reform-oriented instruction: The scoop notebook and rating guide.* Los Angeles: National Center for Research on Evaluation, Standards, and Student Testing. Accessed at www.cse.ucla .edu/products/reports/r707.pdf on October 22, 2012.

References and Resources

Abbott, R. D., O'Donnell, J., Hawkins, J. D., Hill, K. G., Kosterman, R., & Catalano, R. F. (1998). Changing teaching practices to promote achievement and bonding to school. *American Journal of Orthopsychiatry, 68*(4), 542–552.

Aber, L., Brown, J. L., Jones, S. M., Berg, J., & Torrente, C. (2011). School-based strategies to prevent violence, trauma, and psychopathology: The challenges of going to scale. *Development and Psychopathology, 23*(2), 411–421.

Azzam, A. M. (2009). Why creativity now? A conversation with Sir Ken Robinson. *Educational Leadership, 67*(1), 22–26.

Battistich, V., Schaps, E., Watson, M., Solomon, D., & Lewis, C. (2000). Effects of the Child Development Project on students' drug use and other problem behaviors. *Journal of Primary Prevention, 21*(1), 75–99.

Battistich, V., Solomon, D., Watson, S., & Schaps, E. (1997). *Caring school communities. Educational Psychologist, 32*, 137–151.

Bear, G. (2010). *School discipline and self-discipline: A practical guide to promoting prosocial student behavior.* New York: Guilford Press.

Benitez, M., Davidson, J., Flaxman, L., Sizer, T., & Sizer, N. (2009). *Small schools, big ideas: The essential guide to successful school transformation.* San Francisco: Wiley.

Benson, T., Fullan, M., Kegan, R., Madrazo, C., Quinn, J., & Senge, P. (2012). *Developmental stories: Lessons of systemic change for success in implementing the new Common Core standards—A report for the Hewlett Foundation Program on Deep Learning.* Accessed at www.academyfor change.org/wp-content/uploads/2012/08/CC7.4.12r1.pdf on March 5, 2013.

Bernard, S. (2010, December 1). *Science shows making lessons relevant really matters* [Web log post]. Accessed at www.edutopia.org/neuroscience-brain-based-learning-relevance-improves -engagement on June 18, 2012.

Bierman, K. L., Domitrovich, C. E., Nix, R. L., Gest, S. D., Welsh, J. A., Greenberg, M. T., et al. (2008). Promoting academic and social-emotional school readiness: The Head Start REDI program. *Child Development, 79*(6), 1802–1817.

Borko, H., Stecher, B., & Kuffner, K. (2007). *Using artifacts to characterize reform-oriented instruction: The scoop notebook and rating guide.* Los Angeles: National Center for Research on Evaluation, Standards, and Student Testing. Accessed at www.cse.ucla.edu/products /reports/r707.pdf on October 22, 2012.

Brackett, M. A., & Kremenitzer, J. P. (2011). *Creating emotionally literate classrooms: An introduction to the RULER approach to social and emotional learning.* Port Chester, NY: National Professional Resources.

Breines, J. G., & Chen, S. (2012). Self-compassion increases self-improvement motivation. *Personality & Social Psychology Bulletin, 38*(9), 1133–1143.

Broderick, P. C. (n.d.). *Learning to BREATHE: A mindfulness curriculum for adolescents.* Accessed at http://learning2breathe.org on June 27, 2012.

Bronson, P., & Merryman, A. (2010, July 19). The creativity crisis. *Newsweek,* pp. 44–50.

Brown, A. L. (1997). Transforming schools into communities of thinking and learning about serious matters. *American Psychologist, 52*(4), 399–413. Accessed at http://psycnet.apa.org /journals/amp/52/4/399 on October 12, 2012.

Brown, B. (2010, December 23). *Brené Brown: The power of vulnerability* [Video file]. Accessed at www.ted.com/talks/brene_brown_on_vulnerability.html on June 16, 2012.

Brown, B. (2012). *Daring greatly: How the courage to be vulnerable transforms the way we live, love, parent, and lead.* New York: Penguin.

Brown, J., & Isaacs, D. (2005). *The World Café: Shaping our futures through conversations that matter.* San Francisco: Berrett-Koehler.

Brown, K. W., & Ryan, R. N. (2003). The benefits of being present: Mindfulness and its role in psychological well-being. *Journal of Personality and Social Psychology, 84*(4), 822–848.

Brown, K. W., Ryan, R. M., & Creswell, J. D. (2007). Mindfulness: Theoretical foundations and evidence for its salutary effects. *Psychological Inquiry, 18*(4), 211–237.

Brown, P. L. (2007, June 16). In the classroom, a new focus on quieting the mind. *The New York Times,* pp. 10–13. Accessed at www.nytimes.com/2007/06/16/us/16mindful.html?sq=in the classroom a new focus&st=cse&scp=1&pagewanted=print on October 12, 2012.

Brown, R. (1999). The teacher as contemplative observer. *Educational Leadership, 56*(4), 70–73.

Bryk, A. S., & Schneider, B. L. (2004). *Trust in schools: A core resource for improvement.* New York: Sage Foundation.

Bryk, A. S., Sebring, P. B., & Allensworth, E. (2010). *Organizing schools for improvement: Lessons from Chicago.* Chicago: University of Chicago Press.

Chetty, R., Friedman, J. N., & Rockoff, J. E. (2011). *The long-term impacts of teachers: Teacher value-added and student outcomes in adulthood* (NBER Working Paper No. 17699). Cambridge, MA: National Bureau of Economic Research. Accessed at www.nber.org/papers/w17699 on October 12, 2012.

Collaborative for Academic, Social, and Emotional Learning. (n.d.a). *How evidence-based SEL programs work to produce greater student success in school and life.* Accessed at http://casel .org/publications/how-evidence-based-social-and-emotional-learning-programs-work-to-produce-greater-student-success-in-school-and-life on October 12, 2012.

Collaborative for Academic, Social, and Emotional Learning. (n.d.b). *What is SEL?* Accessed at http://casel.org/why-it-matters/what-is-sel on March 5, 2013.

Collins English dictionary: Complete and unabridged (10th ed.). (2013). New York: HarperCollins.

Committee on Psychosocial Aspects of Child and Family Health. (1998). Guidance for effective discipline. *Pediatrics, 101*(4), 723–728.

Connolly, M. (2009). *What they never told me in principal's school: The value of experience cannot be overestimated.* Lanham, MD: R&L Education.

Covey, S. R. (2004). *Seven habits of highly effective people.* New York: Free Press.

Covey, S. R. (2009). *The leader in me: How schools and parents around the world are inspiring greatness, one child at a time.* New York: Simon & Schuster.

Cox, M., Alm, R., & Holmes, N. (2004, May 13). Op-chart where the jobs are. *The New York Times,* p. A27.

Crew, R. (2007). *Only connect: The way to save our schools.* New York: Farrar, Straus & Giroux.

Cullen, M., Wallace, L., & Hedberg, B. (2009). *SMART-in-Education Teachers' Program: Instructor's manual.* Boulder, CO: Impact Foundation.

Curry School of Education, Center for Advanced Study of Teaching and Learning. (2013). *Classroom Assessment Scoring System.* Accessed at http://curry.virginia.edu/research /centers/castl/class on March 1, 2013.

Danielson, L. M. (2009). How teachers learn: Fostering reflection. *Educational Leadership, 66*(5), 5–9.

Darling-Hammond, L. (2012). *Creating a comprehensive system for evaluating and supporting effective teaching.* Stanford, CA: Stanford Center for Opportunity Policy in Education.

Darling-Hammond, L., Ancess, J., & Ort, S. W. (2002). Reinventing high school: Outcomes of the Coalition Campus Schools Project. *American Educational Research Journal, 39*(3), 639–673.

Darling-Hammond, L., Austin, K., Orcutt, S., & Rosso, J. (2001). *How people learn: Introduction to learning theories.* Stanford, CA: Stanford University.

Darling-Hammond, L., & Bransford, J. (Eds.). (2005). *Preparing teachers for a changing world: What teachers should learn and be able to do.* San Francisco: Jossey-Bass.

Darling-Hammond, L., & Richardson, N. (2009). Teacher learning: What matters? *Educational Leadership, 66*(5), 46–53.

Denton, P. (2008). The positive classroom: The power of our words. *Educational Leadership, 66*(1), 28–31.

Diamond, A. (2010). The evidence base for improving school outcomes by addressing the whole child and by addressing skills and attitudes, not just content. *Early Education and Development, 21*(5), 780–793.

Diamond, A., & Lee, K. (2011). Interventions shown to aid executive function development in children 4 to 12 years old. *Science, 333*(6045), 959–964.

Dictionary.com. (2013). *Creativity.* Accessed at http://dictionary.reference.com/browse /creativity?s=t on June 18, 2012.

Duckworth, A. L., & Quinn, P. D. (2009). Development and validation of the Short Grit Scale (GRIT–S). *Journal of Personality Assessment, 91*(2), 166–174.

Durlak, J. A., & DuPre, E. P. (2008). Implementation matters: A review of research on the influence of implementation on program outcomes and the factors affecting implementation. *American Journal of Community Psychology, 41*(3–4), 327–350.

Durlak, J. A., Weissberg, R. P., Dymnicki, A. B., Taylor, R. D., & Schellinger, K. B. (2011). The impact of enhancing students' social and emotional learning: A meta-analysis of school-based universal interventions. *Child Development, 82*(1), 405–432.

Dweck, C. S. (2006). *Mindset: The new psychology of success.* New York: Random House.

Eccles, J. S., & Roeser, R. W. (2011). School and community influences on human development. In M. H. Bornstein & M. E. Lamb (Eds.), *Developmental science: An advanced textbook* (6th ed., pp. 571–643). New York: Taylor & Francis.

Elbot, C. F., & Fulton, D. (2008). *Building an intentional school culture: Excellence in academics and character.* Thousand Oaks, CA: Corwin Press.

Elias, M. J. (1997). *Promoting social and emotional learning: Guidelines for educators.* Alexandria, VA: Association for Supervision and Curriculum Development.

Elias, M. J., & Arnold, H. (2006). *The educator's guide to emotional intelligence and academic achievement: Social-emotional learning in the classroom.* Thousand Oaks, CA: Corwin Press.

Elias, M. J., Arnold, H., & Hussey, C. S. (Eds.) (2003). *EQ + IQ = Best leadership practices for caring and successful schools.* Thousand Oaks, CA: Corwin Press.

Elias, M. J., Parker, S. J., Kash, V. M., & Dunkeblau, E. (2007). Social-emotional learning and character and moral education: Synergy or fundamental divergence in our schools? *Information Age, 5*(2), 167–181.

Elias, M. J., & Zins, J. E. (2003). Implementation, sustainability, and scaling up of social-emotional and academic innovations in public schools. *School Psychology Review, 32*(3), 303–319.

Ellinor, L., & Gerard, G. (1998). *Dialogue: Rediscover the transforming power of conversation.* New York: Wiley.

Emmons, R. A., & McCullough, M. E. (2003a). Counting blessings versus burdens: An experimental investigation of gratitude and subjective well-being in daily life. *Journal of Personality and Social Psychology, 84*(2), 377–389.

Emmons, R. A., & McCullough, M. E. (2003b). *Highlights from the research project on gratitude and thankfulness: Dimensions and perspectives of gratitude.* Accessed at www.psy.miami.edu /faculty/mmccullough/Gratitude-Related%20Stuff/highlights_fall_2003.pdf on March 5, 2013.

Fixsen, D. L., Naoom, S. F., Blase, K. A., Friedman, R. M., & Wallace, F. (2005). *Implementation research: A synthesis of the literature.* Tampa: University of South Florida.

Flaspohler, P., Duffy, J., Wandersman, A., Stillman, L., & Maras, M. A. (2008). Unpacking prevention capacity: An intersection of research-to-practice models and community-centered models. *American Journal of Community Psychology, 41*(3–4), 182–196.

Flicker, J. (2012, March 23). Mindfulness in education [Web log post]. Accessed at http://life workslearningcenter.com/2012/mindfulness-in-education on June 12, 2012.

Frey, N., Fisher, D., & Everlove, S. (2009). *Productive group work: How to engage students, build teamwork, and promote understanding.* Alexandria, VA: Association for Supervision and Curriculum Development.

Fried, R. (2001). *The passionate teacher: A practical guide.* Boston: Beacon Press.

Fritz, R. (1984). *The path of least resistance: Principles for creating what you want to create*. Salem, MA: DMA.

Fritz, R. (1994). *The path of least resistance: Learning to become the creative force in your own life*. Burlington, MA: Butterworth Heinemann. Accessed at http://books.google.com/books ?id=JHtRAAAAYAAJ&pgis=1 on October 12, 2012.

Fullan, M. (Ed.) (1997). *The challenge of school change: A collection of articles*. Arlington Heights, IL: IRI/Skylight Training.

Gambone, M. A., Klem, A. M., & Connell, J. P. (2002). *Finding out what matters for youth: Testing key links in a community action framework for youth development*. Philadelphia: Youth Development Strategies, Institute for Research and Reform in Education.

Garmston, R. J. (1998). Becoming expert teachers (Pt. 1). *Journal of Staff Development, 19*(1). Accessed at www.learningforward.org/news/jsd/garmston191.cfm on October 12, 2012.

Garrison Institute. (n.d.). *CARE for teachers*. Accessed at www.garrisoninstitute.org/index .php?option=com_content&view=article&id=77&Itemid=79 on June 27, 2012.

Gay, G. (2000). *Culturally responsive teaching: Theory, research, and practice* (Multicultural Education Series). New York: Teachers College Press.

Gerzon, M. (1997). Teaching democracy by doing it! *Educational Leadership, 54*(5), 6–11.

Gerzon, M. (2010). *American citizen, global citizen*. Boulder, CO: Spirit Scope.

Ginott, H. G. (1975). *Teacher and child: A book for parents and teachers*. New York: Avon Books.

Goddard, R. D., Hoy, W. K., & Hoy, A. W. (2000). Collective teacher efficacy: Its meaning, measure, and impact on student achievement. *American Educational Research Journal, 37*(2), 479–507. Accessed at http://aer.sagepub.com/content/37/2/479short on October 12, 2012.

Goddard, R. D, Hoy, W. K., & Hoy, A. W. (2004). Collective efficacy beliefs: Theoretical developments, empirical evidence, and future directions. *Educational Researcher, 33*(3), 3–13.

Goleman, D. (1995). *Emotional intelligence*. New York: Bantam Books.

Goleman, D. (1998). What makes a leader? *Harvard Business Review, 76*(6), 93–102.

Goleman, D. (2006). *Social intelligence: The new science of human relationships*. New York: Random House Large Print.

Goleman, D., Boyatzis, R., & McKee, A. (2001). Primal leadership: The hidden driver of great performance. *Harvard Business Review, 79*(11), 42–53.

Goodenow, C. (1993). Classroom belonging among early adolescent students: Relationships to motivation and achievement. *The Journal of Early Adolescence, 13*(1), 21–43.

Greenberg, M. T., Weissberg, R. P., O'Brien, M. U., Zins, J. E., Fredericks, L., Resnik, H., et al. (2003). Enhancing school-based prevention and youth development through coordinated social, emotional, and academic learning. *American Psychologist, 58*(6–7), 466–474.

Greenland, S. K. (2010). *The mindful child: How to help your kid manage stress and become happier, kinder, and more compassionate*. New York: Simon & Schuster.

Guhn, M., Schonert-Reichl, K. A., Gadermann, A. M., Marriott, D., Pedrini, L., Hymel, S., et al. (2012). Well-being in middle childhood: An assets-based population-level research-to-action project. *Child Indicators Research, 5*(2), 393–418.

Halgunseth, L. C., Carmack, C., Childs, S. S., Caldwell, L., Craig, A., & Smith, E. P. (2012). Using the Interactive Systems Framework in understanding the relation between general program capacity and implementation in afterschool settings. *American Journal of Community Psychology, 50*(3–4), 311–320.

Hamre, B. K., & Pianta, R. C. (2001). Early teacher-child relationships and the trajectory of children's school outcomes through eighth grade. *Child Development, 72*(2), 625–638.

Hamre, B. K., & Pianta, R. C. (2009). Classroom environments and developmental processes. In J. L. Meece & J. S. Eccles (Eds.), *Handbook of research on schools, schooling and human development* (pp. 25–41). New York: Routledge.

Hamre, B. K., Pianta, R. C., Burchinal, M., Field, S., LoCasale-Crouch, J., Downer, J. T., et al. (2012). A course on effective teacher-child interactions: Effects on teacher beliefs, knowledge, and observed practice. *American Educational Research Journal, 49*(1), 88–123.

Han, S. S., & Weiss, B. (2005). Sustainability of teacher implementation of school-based mental health programs. *Journal of Abnormal Child Psychology, 33*(6), 665–679.

Hargreaves, A. (2001). *Learning to change: Teaching beyond subjects and standards.* San Francisco: Wiley.

Hargreaves, A., & Fullan, M. (2012). *Professional capital: Transforming teaching in every school.* New York: Teachers College Press.

Hart, T. (2009). *From information to transformation: Education for the evolution of consciousness* (3rd ed.). New York: Peter Lang.

Hattie, J. (2009). *Visible learning: A synthesis of over 800 meta-analyses relating to achievement.* New York: Taylor & Francis.

Heckman, J. J., & Kautz, T. (2012). Hard evidence on soft skills. *Labour Economics, 19*(4), 451–464.

Heifetz, R. A., & Linsky, M. (2002). *Leadership on the line: Staying alive through the dangers of leading.* Watertown, MA: Harvard Business School Press.

Holzel, B. K., Lazar, S. W., Gard, T., Schuman-Olivier, Z., Vago, D. R., & Ott, U. (2011). How does mindfulness meditation work? Proposing mechanisms of action from a conceptual and neural perspective. *Perspectives on Psychological Science, 6*(6), 537–559.

Hughes, J. N., Cavell, T. A., & Willson, V. (2001). Further support for the developmental significance of the quality of the teacher–student relationship. *Journal of School Psychology, 39*(4), 289–301.

Hymel, S., Schonert-Reichl, K. A., & Miller, L. D. (2006). Reading, 'riting, 'rithmetic and relationships: Considering the social side of education. *Exceptionality Education Canada, 16*(3), 1–44.

Intrator, S. M. (2002). *Stories of the courage to teach: Honoring the teacher's heart.* San Francisco: Jossey-Bass.

James, W., Burkhardt, F., Bowers, F., & Skrupskelis, I. K. (1981). *The principles of psychology* (Vols. 1–2). Cambridge, MA: Harvard University Press.

Jennings, P. (2011). *Teachers tuning in.* Accessed at www.mindful.org/the-mindful-society/education /teachers-tuning-in on October 12, 2012.

Jennings, P. A., & Greenberg, M. T. (2009). The prosocial classroom: Teacher social and emotional competence in relation to student and classroom outcomes. *Review of Educational Research, 79*(1), 491–525.

Jennings, P. A., Snowberg, K. E., Coccia, M. A., & Greenberg, M. T. (2012). *Refinement and evaluation of the CARE for Teachers program.* In M.Greenberg (Chair), Promoting empathy, awareness, and compassion with parents, teachers, and youth. Symposium presented at the International Symposia for Contemplative Studies, Denver, CO, April 2012.

Joyce, B. R., & Showers, B. (2002). *Student achievement through staff development* (3rd ed.). Alexandria, VA: Association for Supervision and Curriculum Development.

Kabat-Zinn, J. (1994). *Wherever you go, there you are: Mindfulness meditation in everyday life.* New York: Hyperion.

Kahn, W. A. (1992). To be fully there: Psychological presence at work. *Human Relations, 45*(4), 321–349.

Kegan, R., & Lahey, L. L. (2009). *Immunity to change: How to overcome it and unlock the potential in yourself and your organization.* Cambridge, MA: Harvard Business School Press.

Kessler, R. (1999). Nourishing students in secular schools. *Educational Leadership, 56*(4), 49–52.

Kessler, R. (2000a). *The soul of education: Helping students find connection, compassion, and character at school.* Alexandria, VA: Association for Supervision and Curriculum Development.

Kessler, R. (2000b). The teaching presence. *Virginia Journal of Education, 94*(2), 4.

Kessler, R. (2002a). Adversity as ally. In S. M. Intrator (Ed.), *Stories of the courage to teach: Honoring the teacher's heart* (pp. 141–151). San Francisco: Jossey-Bass.

Kessler, R. (2002b). Nurturing deep connections: Five principles for welcoming soul into school leadership. *School Administrator, 59*(8), 22–26.

Kessler, R. (2002c). *Teaching presence extended.* Unpublished manuscript.

Kessler, R. (2004). Grief as a gateway to love in teaching. In D. P. Liston & J. W. Garrison (Eds.), *Teaching, caring, loving and learning: Reclaiming passion in educational practice* (pp. 133–148). New York: RoutledgeFalmer.

Kessler, R., & Fink, C. (2008). Education for integrity: Connection, compassion and character. In L. Nucci & D. Narváez (Eds.), *Handbook of moral and character education* (pp. 431–455). New York: Taylor & Francis.

Kitayama, S., & Uskul, A. K. (2011). Culture, mind, and the brain: Current evidence and future directions. *Annual Review of Psychology, 62,* 419–449.

Kline, K. K. (2003). *Hardwired to connect: The new scientific case for authoritative communities.* New York: Springer-Verlag, Institute for American Values.

Kouzes, J. M., & Posner, B. Z. (2010). *The leadership challenge.* Hoboken, NJ: Wiley.

Langer, E. J. (1989). *Mindfulness.* Indianapolis, IN: Addison-Wesley.

Langer, E. J. (1997). *The power of mindful learning.* Reading, MA: Addison-Wesley.

Lantieri, L. (2003). Waging peace in our schools. In M. J. Elias, H. Arnold, & C. S. Hussey (Eds.), *EQ + IQ = Best leadership practices for caring and successful schools* (pp. 76–87). Thousand Oaks, CA: Corwin Press.

Lantieri, L., & Goleman, D. (2008). *Building emotional intelligence: Techniques to cultivate inner strength in children*. Boulder, CO: Sounds True.

Lawlor, M. S., & Schonert-Reichl, K. A. (2009). *Resiliency and transitions: Early adolescents and the transition to high school*. Toronto, Ontario: Canadian Association for School Health.

Loehr, J., & Schwartz, T. (2003). *The power of full engagement: Managing energy, not time, is the key to high performance and personal renewal*. New York: Free Press.

Lorde, A. (1994). *Our dead behind us: Poems*. New York: Norton. Accessed at www.amazon.com /Our-Dead-Behind-Us-Poems/dp/0393312380 on October 15, 2012.

Lynch, M., & Cicchetti, D. (1992). Maltreated children's reports of relatedness to their teachers. In R. C. Pianta (Ed.), *Beyond the parent: The role of other adults in children's lives—New directions for child development* (pp. 81–108). San Francisco: Jossey-Bass.

MacDonald, E., & Shirley, D. (2009). *The mindful teacher*. New York: Teachers College Press.

Mandela, N. (1994). *Long walk to freedom: The autobiography of Nelson Mandela*. New York: Little, Brown.

Marzano, R. J. (2007). *The art and science of teaching: A comprehensive framework for effective instruction*. Alexandria, VA: Association for Supervision and Curriculum Development.

Marzano, R. J. (2009). *Classroom management that works: Research-based strategies for every teacher*. Upper Saddle River, NJ: Merrill. Accessed at http://books.google.com /books?id=iPOLJwAACAAJ&pgis=1 on October 15, 2012.

Marzano, R. J. (2011). The inner world of teaching. *Educational Leadership, 68*(7), 90–91.

Marzano, R. J., (2012a). *Becoming a reflective teacher*. Bloomington, IN: Marzano Research Laboratory.

Marzano, R. J. (2012b). Relating to students: It's what you do that counts. *Educational Leadership, 68*(6), 82–83.

Marzano, R. J., Marzano, J. S., & Pickering, D. (2003). *Classroom management that works: Research-based strategies for every teacher*. Alexandria, VA: Association for Supervision and Curriculum Development. Accessed at http://books.google.com/books?id=BVM2ml2Q -QgC&pgis=1 on October 12, 2012.

McCormick, K. M., & Brennan, S. (2001). Mentoring the new professional in interdisciplinary early childhood education: The Kentucky Teacher Internship Program. *Topics in Early Childhood Special Education, 21*(3): 131–149.

McCullough, M. E., Pargament, K. I., & Thoresen, C. E. (2001). *Forgiveness: Theory, research, and practice*. New York: Guilford Press. Accessed at http://books.google.com/books?hl=en&lr =&id=bXZbpTaorg4C&pgis=1 on October 12, 2012.

McIntosh, P. (2003a). White privilege: Unpacking the invisible knapsack. In P. S. Rothenberg (Ed.), *Race, class, and gender in the United States: An integrated study* (pp. 188–192). New York: Worth.

McIntosh, P. (2003b). White privilege and male privilege. In M. S. Kimmel & A. L. Ferber (Eds.), *Privilege: A reader* (pp. 147–160). Boulder, CO: Westview Press.

McMillan, J. H. (2000). *Basic assessment concepts for teachers and school administrators.* College Park, MD: ERIC Clearinghouse on Assessment and Evaluation. Accessed at www.behavioralinstitute.org/FreeDownloads/Assessment/ERIC basic assessment concepts for teachers and administrators.pdf on March 5, 2013.

McNeely C. A., Nonnemaker, J. M., & Blum, R.W. (2002). Promoting school connectedness: Evidence from the National Longi-tudinal Study of Adolescent Health. *Journal of School Health, 72*(4), 138–146.

Meador, D. (n.d.). *Qualities of an effective teacher.* Accessed at http://teaching.about.com/od/pd/a/Qualities-Of-An-Effective-Teacher.htm on June 25, 2012.

Medina, J. (2008). *Brain rules: 12 principles for surviving and thriving at work, home, and school.* Seattle, WA: Pear Press.

Meece, J. L., & Eccles, J. S. (2009). Schools as a context of human development. In J. L. Meece & J. S. Eccles (Eds.), *Handbook of research on schools, schooling and human development* (pp. 3–5). New York: Routledge.

Mendes, E. (2003). What empathy can do. *Educational Leadership, 61*(1), 56–59.

MetLife. (2012). *The MetLife Survey of the American Teacher: Teachers, parents and the economy.* New York: Author. Accessed at www.eric.ed.gov/ERICWebPortal/contentdelivery/servlet/ERICServlet?accno=ED530021 on October 12, 2012.

Meyers, D. C., Durlak, J. A., & Wandersman, A. (2012). The Quality Implementation Framework: A synthesis of critical steps in the implementation process. *American Journal of Community Psychology, 50*(3–4), 462–480.

Miller, J. P. (2007). Whole teaching, whole schools, whole teachers. *Educational Leadership, 64,* 7–10. Accessed at www.ascd.org/publications/educational-leadership/summer07/vol64/num09/Whole-Teaching,-Whole-Schools,-Whole-Teachers.aspx on October 12, 2012.

Mitchell-Copeland, J., Denham, S. A., & DeMulder, E. K. (1997). Q-sort assessment of child–teacher attachment relationships and social competence in the preschool. *Early Education & Development, 8*(1), 27–39.

Moulthrop, D., Calegari, N. C., & Eggers, D. (2006). *Teachers have it easy: The big sacrifices and small salaries of America's teachers.* New York: Perseus Books Group.

Murray, C., & Greenberg, M. T. (2000). Children's relationship with teachers and bonds with school: An investigation of patterns and correlates in middle childhood. *Journal of School Psychology, 38*(5), 423–445.

Myers, S. (2008). Conversations that matter: The positive classroom. *Educational Leadership, 66*(1).

National Coalition for Equity in Education. (n.d.). *NCEE publications.* Accessed at http://ncee.education.ucsb.edu/publications.htm on March 5, 2013.

National Council for Accreditation of Teacher Education. (2008). *Professional standards for the accreditation of teacher preparation institutions.* Washington, DC: Author.

National School Reform Faculty. (n.d.). *Success analysis protocol.* Accessed at www.nsrfharmony.org/protocol/doc/success_analysis_cfg.pdf on March 5, 2013.

Newfield Network. (n.d.). *Learning with heart: A* Newfield News *article by Bob Dunham.* Accessed at www.newfieldnetwork.com/New2/News/0212/Heart/index.cfm on March 5, 2013.

Nieto, S. (2003). *What keeps teachers going?* New York: Teachers College Press.

Noddings, N. (2011). *Philosophy of education.* Boulder, CO: Westview Press.

Noë, A. (2009). *Out of our heads: Why you are not your brain, and other lessons from the biology of consciousness.* New York: Farrar, Straus and Giroux.

Noguera, P. (2011, May 21). *Morningside Center's Courageous Schools Conference.* Accessed at www.morningsidecenter.org/noguera.html on October 12, 2012.

Nucci, L. P., & Narvaéz, D. (2008). *Handbook of moral and character education.* New York: Taylor & Francis.

Odom, S. L., Hanson, M., Lieber, J., Diamond, K., Palmer, S., Butera, G., et al. (2010). Prevention, early childhood intervention, and implementation science. In B. Doll, W. Pfohl, & J. S. Yoon, *Handbook of youth prevention science* (pp. 413–432). New York: Routledge.

Olalla, J. (n.d.). *Learning with heart.* Accessed at www.newfieldnetwork.com/New2/News/0212/Heart/index.cfm on June 26, 2012.

O'Neill-Grace, C., & Thompson, M. (2002). *Best friends, worst enemies: Understanding the social lives of children.* New York: Random House.

Orfield, G., Losen, D., Wald, J., & Swanson, C. B. (2004). *Losing our future: How minority youth are being left behind by the graduation rate crisis.* Cambridge, MA: Civil Rights Project at Harvard University. Accessed at www.urban.org/UploadedPDF/410936_LosingOurFuture.pdf on March 5, 2013.

Osher, D., Sprague, J., Weissberg, R. P., Axelrod, J., Keenan, S., Kendziora, K., et al. (2008). A comprehensive approach to promoting social, emotional, and academic growth in contemporary schools. In A. Thomas & J. Grimes (Eds.), *Best practices in school psychology V* (5th ed., pp. 1263–1278). Bethesda, MD: National Association of School Psychologists.

Ottmar, E. R., Rimm-Kaufman, S. E., Larsen, R., & Merritt, E. G. (2011). *Relations between mathematical knowledge for teaching, mathematics instructional quality, and student achievement in the context of the "Responsive Classroom (RC)" approach.* Evanston, IL: Society for Research on Educational Effectiveness.

Palmer, P. J. (1993). *To know as we are known: Education as a spiritual journey.* New York: HarperCollins.

Palmer, P. J. (1997). The heart of a teacher identity and integrity in teaching. *Change: The Magazine of Higher Learning, 29*(6), 14–21.

Palmer, P. J. (1998). *The courage to teach: Exploring the inner landscape of a teacher's life.* San Francisco: Jossey-Bass.

Palmer, P. J. (2009). *A hidden wholeness: The journey toward an undivided life.* San Francisco: Wiley.

Pausch, R., & Zaslow, J. (1990). *The last lecture.* New York: Hyperion.

Payton, J., Weissberg, R. P., Durlak, J. A., Dymnicki, A. B., Taylor, R. D., Schellinger, K. B., et al. (2008). *The positive impact of social and emotional learning for kindergarten to eighth-grade students: Findings from three scientific reviews.* Chicago: Collaborative for Academic, Social, and Emotional Learning. Accessed at http://casel.org/wp-content/uploads/PackardTR.pdf on March 5, 2013.

Pollock, J. E. (2007). *Improving student learning one teacher at a time.* Alexandria, VA: Association for Supervision and Curriculum Development.

Pool, C. R. (1997). Maximizing learning: A conversation with Renate Nummela Caine. *Educational Leadership, 54*(6), 11–15.

Porter, A. C., Gamoran, A., & Board on International Comparative Studies in Education. (2002). *Methodological advances in cross-national surveys of educational achievement.* Washington, DC: National Academies Press.

Porter, C. J., & Cleland, J. (1995). *The portfolio as a learning strategy.* Portsmouth, NH: Boynton/ Cook.

Reiss, K. J. (2012). *Be a CHANGEMASTER: 12 coaching strategies for leading professional and personal change.* Thousand Oaks, CA: Corwin Press.

Rendón, L. I. (2009). *Sentipensante (sensing/thinking) pedagogy: Educating for wholeness, social justice and liberation.* Sterling, VA: Stylus.

Resnick, M. D. , Bearman, P. S., Blum, R. W., Bauman, K. E., Harris, K. M., Jones, J., Tabor, J., et al. (1997). Protecting adolescents from harm: Findings from the National Longi-tudinal Study on Adolescent Health. *Journal of the American Medical Association, 278*(10), 823.

Roeser, R. W. (2012). *Mindfulness training for public school teachers: Rationales, processes and outcomes.* Denver, CO: International Symposia for Contemplative Studies.

Roeser, R. W., Eccles, J. S., & Sameroff, A. J. (2000). School as a context of early adolescents' academic and social-emotional development: A summary of research findings. *The Elementary School Journal, 100*(5), 443–471.

Roeser, R. W., Marachi, R., & Gelhbach, H. (2002). A goal theory perspective on teachers' professional identities and the contexts of teaching. In C. Midgley (Ed.), *Goals, goal structures, and patterns of adaptive learning* (pp. 204–241). Mahwah, NJ: Erlbaum.

Roeser, R. W., Midgley, C., & Urdan, T. C. (1996). Perceptions of the school psychological environment and early adolescents' psychological and behavioral functioning in school: The mediating role of goals and belonging. *Journal of Educational Psychology, 88*(3), 408–422.

Roeser, R. W., & Peck, S. C. (2009). An education in awareness: Self, motivation, and self-regulated learning in contemplative perspective. *Educational Psychologist, 44*(2), 119–136.

Roeser, R. W., Peck, S. C., & Nasir, N. S. (2009). Self and identity processes in school motivation, learning, and achievement. In J. L. Meece & J. S. Eccles (Eds.), *Handbook of research on schools, schooling and human development* (pp. 391–424). New York: Routledge.

Roeser, R. W., Skinner, E., Beers, J., & Jennings, P. A. (2012). Mindfulness training and teachers' professional development: An emerging area of research and practice. *Child Development Perspectives, 6*(2), 167–173.

Roeser, R., & Zelazo, P. D. (2012). Contemplative science, education and child development: Introduction to the special section. *Child Development Perspectives, 6*(2), 143–145.

Ryan, T. (2012). *A mindful nation: How a simple practice can help us reduce stress, improve performance, and recapture the American spirit.* Carlsbad, CA: Hay House.

Salovey, P., & Mayer, J. D. (1990). Emotional intelligence. *Imagination, Cognition and Personality, 9,* 185–211.

Sankowski, L. (n.d.). *Teaching from the inside out: From an interview with first-grade teacher Maura McNiff.* Accessed at www.couragerenewal.org/stories/152-stories/294-teaching-from-the-inside-out on June 2, 2012.

Sarason, S. (1990). *The predictable failure of educational reform: Can we change course before it's too late?* San Francisco: Jossey-Bass.

Scharmer, C. O. (2009). *Theory U: Leading from the future as it emerges.* San Francisco: Berrett-Koehler.

Schoeberlein, D., & Sheth, S. (2009). *Mindful teaching and teaching mindfulness: A guide for anyone who teaches anything.* Somerville, MA: Wisdom.

Schonert-Reichl, K. A. (2011). Promoting empathy in school-aged children. In K. Nader (Ed.), *School rampage shootings and other youth disturbances: Early preventative interventions* (pp. 159–204). New York: Taylor & Francis.

Schonert-Reichl, K. A., & Hymel, S. (2007). Educating the heart as well as the mind: Social and emotional learning for school and life success. *Education Canada, 47*(2), 20–25. Accessed at www.eric.ed.gov/ERICWebPortal/detail?accno=EJ771005 on October 12, 2012.

Schonert-Reichl, K. A., Smith, V., Zaidman-Zait, A., & Hertzman, C. (2011). Promoting children's prosocial behaviors in school: Impact of the "Roots of Empathy" program on the social and emotional competence of school-aged children. *School Mental Health, 4*(1), 1–21.

Schön, D. A. (1983). *The reflective practitioner: How professionals think in action.* New York: Basic Books.

Senge, P. M., Cambron McCabe, N. H., Lucas, T., Kleiner, A., Dutton, J., & Smith, B. (2000). *Schools that learn: A fifth discipline fieldbook for educators, parents, and everyone who cares about education.* New York: Doubleday.

Shulman, L. S. (2009, October 8–9). *Educating world citizens: Integrations, reflections, and future directions.* Presented at the meeting of the Mind and Life Institute, Mind and Life XIX: Educating World Citizens for the 21st Century, Washington, DC.

Siegel, D. J. (2010). *Mindsight: The new science of personal transformation.* New York: Bantam Books.

Smith, R., & Lambert, M. (2008). The positive classroom: Assuming the best. *Educational Leadership, 66*(1), 16–21.

Spaulding, T. (2010). *It's not just who you know: Transform your life (and your organization) by turning colleagues and contacts into lasting, genuine relationships.* New York: Broadway Books.

Stecher, B. M., Borko, H., Kuffner, K. L., & Wood, A. C. (2005). *Using classroom artifacts to measure instructional practices in middle school mathematics: A two-state field test.* Accessed at www.cse.ucla.edu/products/reports/r662.pdf on October 22, 2012.

Stuhlman, M. W., Hamre, B. K., Downer, J. T., & Pianta, R. C. (2010). *A practitioner's guide to conducting classroom observations: What the research tells us about choosing and using observational systems.* Accessed at www.wtgrantfdn.org/File Library/Resources/Practitioners Guide .pdf on March 1, 2013.

Sylwester, R. (1994). How emotions affect learning. *Educational Leadership, 52*(2), 60–65.

Sylwester, R. (1995). *A celebration of neurons: An educator's guide to the human brain.* Alexandria, VA: Association for Supervision and Curriculum Development.

Tomlinson, C. A., & Imbeau, M. B. (2010). *Leading and managing a differentiated classroom.* Alexandria, VA: Association for Supervision and Curriculum Development.

Thompson, S. (2005). *Leading from the eye of the storm: Spirituality and public school improvement.* Lanham, MD: R&L Education.

Thompson, M., & Grace, C. O. (2001). *Best friends, worst enemies: Understanding the social lives of children.* New York: Ballantine Books.

Tschannen-Moran, M. (2004). *Trust matters: Leadership for successful schools.* San Francisco: Jossey-Bass.

Tutu, D. (2004). *Truth and reconciliation.* Accessed at http://greatergood.berkeley.edu/article /item/truth_and_reconciliation on January 25, 2013.

Vansteenkiste, M., Simons, J., Lens, W., Sheldon, K. M., & Deci, E. L. (2004). Motivating learning, performance, and persistence: The synergistic effects of intrinsic goal contents and autonomy-supportive contexts. *Journal of Personality and Social Psychology, 87*(2), 246–260.

Vitto, J. M. (2003). *Relationship-driven classroom management: Strategies that promote student motivation.* Thousand Oaks, CA: Corwin Press.

Vygotsky, L. S., & Cole, M. (1978). *Mind in society: The development of higher psychological processes.* Cambridge, MA: Harvard University Press.

Wagner, T. (2010). *The global achievement gap: Why even our best schools don't teach the new survival skills our children need—and what we can do about it.* New York: Basic Books.

Wandersman, A., Duffy, J., Flaspohler, P., Noonan, R., Lubell, K., Stillman, L., et al. (2008). Bridging the gap between prevention research and practice: The Interactive Systems Framework for Implementation and Dissemination. *American Journal of Community Psychology, 41*(3–4), 171–181.

Watson, M., & Ecken, L. (2003). *Learning to trust: Transforming difficult elementary classrooms through developmental discipline.* San Francisco: Jossey-Bass.

Weaver, L., & Kessler, R. (2011). Six passages of childhood. In A. N. Johnson & M. Neagley (Eds.), *Educating from the heart: Theoretical and practical approaches to transforming education* (pp. 49–67). Lanham, MD: R&L Education.

Weissberg, R. P., Payton, J. W., O'Brien, M. U., & Munro, S. (2007). Social and emotional learning. In F. C. Power, R. J. Nuzzi, & D. Narvaez (Eds.), *Moral education: A handbook* (pp. 417–418). Westport, CT: Greenwood Press.

Wentzel, K. R. (2009). Students' relationships with teachers. In J. L. Meece & J. S. Eccles (Eds.), *Handbook of research on schools, schooling and human development* (pp. 75–91). New York: Routledge.

White, K. K., Zion, S., & Kozleski, E. (2005). *Cultural identity and teaching.* Tempe, AZ: National Institute for Urban School Improvement. Accessed at www.niusileadscape.org/lc/Record/605?search_query=Cultural Identity and Teaching on March 5, 2013.

Wiggins, G. (1989). A true test: Toward more authentic and equitable assessment. *Phi Delta Kappan, 70*(9), 703–713.

Wiggins, G. (2011). A true test: Toward more authentic and equitable assessment. *Phi Delta Kappan, 92*(7), 81–93.

Wilensky, R. (2013, February 6). "Mindfulness" in schools to combat stress [Web log post]. Accessed at www.ednewscolorado.org/2013/02/06/55748-voices-mindfulness-in-schools-to-combat-stress on March 5, 2013.

Willingham, D. T. (2009). *Why don't students like school? A cognitive scientist answers questions about how the mind works and what it means for the classroom.* San Francisco: Jossey-Bass.

Willis, J. (2007). The neuroscience of joyful education: Supporting good teaching practices with neuroscience. *Educational Leadership, 64*(9), 1–5.

Wilson, B. L., & Corbett, H. D. (2001). *Listening to urban kids: School reform and the teachers they want.* New York: SUNY Press.

Wiseman, L., & McKeown, G. (2010). *Multipliers: How the best leaders make everyone smarter.* New York: HarperCollins.

Witvliet, C., Ludwig, T. E., & Laan, K. L. V. (2001). Granting forgiveness or harboring grudges: Implications for emotion, physiology, and health. *Psychological Science, 12*(2), 117–123.

Zajonc, A. (2005, February 11–13). *Love and knowledge: Recovering the heart of learning through contemplation.* Presented at the meeting of the Center for Contemplative Mind in Society, Contemplative Practices and Education: Making Peace in Ourselves and in the World, New York, NY. Accessed at www.contemplativemind.org/admin/wp-content/uploads/2012/09/zajonc-love-and-knowledge.pdf on March 5, 2013.

Zajonc, A. (2008). *Meditation as contemplative inquiry: When knowing becomes love.* Great Barrington, MA: Lindisfarne Books.

Zelazo, P. D., & Cunningham, W. (2007). Executive function: Mechanisms underlying emotion regulation. In R. A. Thompson & J. J. Gross (Eds.), *Handbook of emotion regulation* (pp. 135–158). New York: Guilford Press.

Zimmerman, J. M., & Coyle, V. (2009). *The way of council.* Wilton Manors, FL: Bramble Books.

Zins, J. E., & Elias, M. J. (2006). Social and emotional learning. In G. G. Bear & K. M. Minke (Eds.), *Children's needs III: Development, prevention, and intervention* (3rd ed., pp. 1–13). Bethesda, MD: National Association of School Psychologists.

Zion, S., Kozleski, E., & Fulton, M. L. (2005). *Understanding culture.* Accessed at www.niusileadscape.org/docs/FINAL_PRODUCTS/LearningCarousel/Understanding_Culture.pdf on October 12, 2012.

Index of Engaged Teaching Principles, Practices, and Activities

Index

Building a Culture of Hope
Enriching Schools With Optimism and Opportunity
Robert D. Barr and Emily L. Gibson

Discover a blueprint for turning low-performing schools into Cultures of Hope! The authors draw from their own experiences in schools across the United States to illustrate how to support students with an approach that considers social as well as emotional factors in education.

BKF503

You've Got to Reach Them to Teach Them
Mary Kim Schreck

Navigate the hot topic of student engagement with a true expert. Become empowered to demand an authentic joy for learning in your classroom. Real-life notes from the field, detailed discussions, practical strategies, and space for reflection complete this essential guide to student engagement.

BKF404

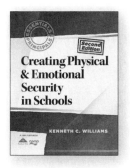

Creating Physical & Emotional Security in Schools
Kenneth C. Williams

Give your students a physically and emotionally safe learning environment. Learn how you and your teachers can nurture supportive relationships with students, develop conflict management strategies, prevent different forms of bullying, develop student initiative and resilience, and encourage celebration. 2nd Edition

BKF451

Motivating Students Who Don't Care
Successful Techniques for Educators
Allen N. Mendler

Spark enthusiasm in your classroom. Proven strategies and five effective processes (emphasizing effort, creating hope, respecting power, building relationships, and expressing enthusiasm) empower you to reawaken motivation in students who aren't prepared, don't care, and won't work.

BKF360

Solution Tree | Press

a division of
Solution Tree

Visit solution-tree.com or call 800.733.6786 to order.

Wait! Your professional development journey doesn't have to end with the last pages of this book.

We realize improving student learning doesn't happen overnight. And your school or district shouldn't be left to puzzle out all the details of this process alone.

No matter where you are on the journey, we're committed to helping you get to the next stage.

Take advantage of everything from **custom workshops** to **keynote presentations** and **interactive web and video conferencing**. We can even help you develop an action plan tailored to fit your specific needs.

Let's get the conversation started.

Call 888.763.9045 today.

solution-tree.com